The Career Fitness Program:
Exercising Your Options

SECOND EDITION

Diane Sukiennik
Lisa Raufman
William Bendat
Moorpark College

GSP
Gorsuch Scarisbrick, Publishers
Scottsdale, Arizona

Editor: John Gorsuch
Production Editor: Carol Hunter
Art Editor: Barbara Masseri
Artist: Joan Marlowe
Cover Design: Jeff George
Typesetting: Carlisle Graphics

Gorsuch Scarisbrick, Publishers
8233 Via Paseo del Norte, Suite F-400
Scottsdale, AZ 85258

10   9   8   7   6   5   4   3   2   1

ISBN 0-89787-813-2

Acknowledgments

The authors recognize that comprehensive career services are possible when a cohesive team—counselors and support staff—work together to provide quality services to students. We are indebted to our present professional staff for their valuable contributions: Frank Bianchino, Arleen Blum, Annette Burrows, Rick Cardoni, Gail Goodman, Don Henderson, John Heydenreich, Edna Ingram, Susan Izumo, Teri Lara, Bud Long, Mary Martin, Lisa Obuchon, Donna Proske-Allyn, and Jean Rule.

About the Authors

Dr. Diane Sukiennik is a national certified career counselor; licensed marriage, family and child counselor; and nationally recognized lecturer and workshop facilitator in the field of career planning. She holds advanced degrees from Columbia and Nova Universities as well as extensive post-graduate training in industrial psychology, management, and organizational development. Currently Dr. Sukiennik is a career counselor at Moorpark College, where her areas of expertise are career development, personal and professional presentation skills, and managerial effectiveness. She is also an industry consultant and has a private practice.

Dr. Bill Bendat is the Dean of Students at Moorpark College. His background includes extensive teaching and counseling in both elementary and high school settings, as well as industry consultant work. As a career counselor, Dr. Bendat has participated in numerous California Career projects and has played an important role in the award-winning efforts of the Moorpark College Counseling and Guidance Staff.

Lisa Raufman is a national certified career counselor as well as a licensed marriage, family, and child counselor. Her M.S. is in Counseling, with specilization in the community college and in vocational rehabilitation. Ms. Raufman is a counselor at Moorpark College, specializing in work with business majors. She also served as President of the Los Padres Chapter of the American Society for Training and Development (ASTD), and as an industry consultant in career and life planning. She is presently completing her doctorate degree in Higher Education, Work, and Adult Development at UCLA and is actively involved in statewide counseling associations.

Contents

v

Tables

Exhibits

Introduction

On Your Mark . . . Get Set . . .

Modern life is filled with changes and choices. An immense rainbow of possibilities makes this the most exciting time in history. Yet many of us are overwhelmed by our lack of knowledge about our choices and our place and purpose in the world. The only thing that is certain is change. It is essential to prepare ourselves to expect change, accept it, and plan for it. We can best prepare for it by learning "who we are" in terms of lifetime goals, and by taking responsibility for shaping our lives. As we gain information about ourselves and as we begin to make our own decisions, we gain self-confidence. We begin to believe in a deep, personal way that no matter how drastically the world changes, we can deal with it.

Exercising Your Options is designed to assist you in this process of self-discovery and realization. The main goal of this book is to lead you through the process of career planning, which includes self-assessment, decision making, and job search strategy; our primary objective is to assist you in making satisfactory career choices. By following our chapter to chapter program, you will learn more about yourself and how this self-knowledge relates to your emerging career plan.

The process

Let's review the contents of this book to see how it will help you achieve your career goals. The career-planning process is divided into two main parts: personal assessment, chapters 1–7; job search strategy, chapters 8–10.

1

Chapter 1   identifies reasons for planning your career and some personal and social background factors to be considered in your career planning.

Chapter 2   helps you understand the important effect your attitude has on your actions and helps you develop a positive approach to life and career planning.

Chapter 3   helps you identify your needs, wants, and values, and what they mean to you, and how they influence your career choices.

Chapter 4   helps you assess your skills and how they relate to your career decision.

Chapter 5   highlights the societal and cultural biases that subtly or blatantly affect your choice of careers and identifies trends in the workplace.

Chapter 6   explains how people make decisions, and helps you identify and improve your own decision-making skills.

Chapter 7   helps you integrate your attitudes, values, life-style preferences, cultural biases, interests, skills, and aptitudes into a tentative career plan. This includes the selection of several possible career options to begin researching. Written information sources are also highlighted.

Chapter 8   helps you systematically and assertively gather information about possible careers by learning the traditional and nontraditional approaches to job search so that you can decide whether they are viable options for you.

Chapter 9   helps you write a resumé, a cover letter, and fill out application forms.

Chapter 10   covers all aspects of the interview process, to complete the book's objective of providing you with all the strategies necessary to compete in today's job market.

Process

Meeting challenges   In many ways, the process of preparing to meet job and career challenges is much like the process by which athletes prepare to meet the challenges of competition in their particular sports. Basically, it involves establishing a fitness program in which the competitor sharpens existing skills, adds needed new skills, and most important, develops a mental attitude of success.

Theory

Any good fitness program is a combination of theory and exercise, and our career fitness program has this balance. By theory we mean that for each step of the planning process, we will explain why we are taking that step, how it relates to the previous step, how it connects to the next step, and how it moves us closer to our final goal of identifying career options.

Exercises

There will be exercises at the end of each chapter. These exercise components are designed to bring each step to life. They will serve to make you more aware of your strengths, weaknesses, attitudes, and stereotypes, and they will also help you to summarize what you think is important to remember in each chapter. Remember that just reading a chapter or a book is a passive activity. However, responding to questions makes you an active participant in the career exploration process. You may find that it helps to share your answers with at least one other person; feedback from others adds to your own awareness and perspective. It is very easy for anyone to sit back and read about career planning or fitness and agree totally with all of the text and with all of the theories and all of the exercises. But until you make the commitment to throw yourself into the process, to actually get involved, to participate, and to experience the progress and occasional discomfort along the way, you will not be able to reap the benefits of the process.

Becoming an active participant: With commitment

Discomfort

Yes, we did mention the word *discomfort*. What do we mean by that? Anytime you start out on a new physical exercise program, even if you start gingerly and sensibly in relation to your level of past activity, new muscles are being stretched. In the process of doing so, you feel them. They feel awkward. They ache. You become aware of parts of your body that you may never have noticed before. You can also expect this to happen in the process of career planning. Along the way, confusion and some discomfort may occur. We are going to be asking questions and helping you to dig deep into yourself to pull out the answers. In this process of self-awareness, you are going to discover a lot of things about yourself that you like and maybe some things that you would like to change.

The process of change and personal growth

Because of this process of self-discovery, at certain points along our fitness plan you may feel a bit confused, a bit anxious, a bit impatient. All of these feelings are normal. When you start out on a physical fitness program you idealistically hope that in a week or two you will have the body that you are imagining in your mind even though you know realistically that developing a good physique is going to take a lot longer. And so too, with your career plan, you may begin to feel impatient and want things to move along more quickly or more clearly. It is important to remember that any kind of change, any kind of growth, typically includes a bit of discomfort, uneasiness, and anxiety. Frankly, if you begin to experience some of those feelings, it is a good sign! It is a sign that you are stretching, that you are growing, and that you are moving toward a newly developed awareness of who you are and how you relate to the world of work.

Typically, when you are feeling anxious, you try to do anything and everything in your power to get rid of the discomfort. This reaction to anxiety causes many people to make career decisions prematurely, without really examining themselves and their options, and then taking care to make a considered decision about their future. Instead they simply take the first thing or the quickest thing that comes along so that they can tell themselves and other people that they have chosen a career. In many cases, this impatient, impulsive, quick decision making really does not pan out very well in the long run. People who have made quick career decisions often live to regret their haste, and making a career transition later on is much more difficult for them because of financial commitments and life-style responsibilities.

Commitment

Benefits of perseverance and belief

Those of you who are taking the time at the beginning of your adult careers to carefully and thoroughly examine your options will reap tremendous benefits in the future. The benefits you experience "at the finish line" will be directly proportional to your willingness and ability to deal with the anxiety and uncertainty you will experience at some points in the career-planning process. In essence, the more you put into any activity, the more you are likely to get out of it. Stories that we have heard and read about our cultural heroes and heroines, whether they be athletes, performers, renowned scientists, or political figures, tell us that the end results which look so easy and sound so glamorous are always the reward of tremendous sustained effort, commitment, and perseverance. A quote attributed to the famous artist Michaelangelo seems to say it all: "If people knew how hard I had to work to gain my mastery, it wouldn't seem so wonderful after all."

Your career search requires a similar commitment. It requires the willingness to go with the process; to trust your counselor's assistance; and to move through points of frustration, uncertainty, and confusion in the belief that you will come out with more awareness, and a good sense of the next steps to take along your career path. We invite you to participate in an adventure and endeavor that is every bit as exciting and every bit as rewarding as preparing for the Olympics. You are identifying your own mountain peaks and are setting out to climb them. Among your resources is the assistance of this career-planning textbook, which incorporates the wisdom and experience of the authors and of successful career planners over the past decade. Most of all, the special attributes of your own spirit, vitality, and intuition, and your desire to improve yourself will serve you well through your search. This career fitness program will help you deal with the inevitable changes that occur within yourself and in the world of work. It will help you identify options that are consistent with who you are. It will enable you to be the champion of your own career.

Part One

Personal
Assessment

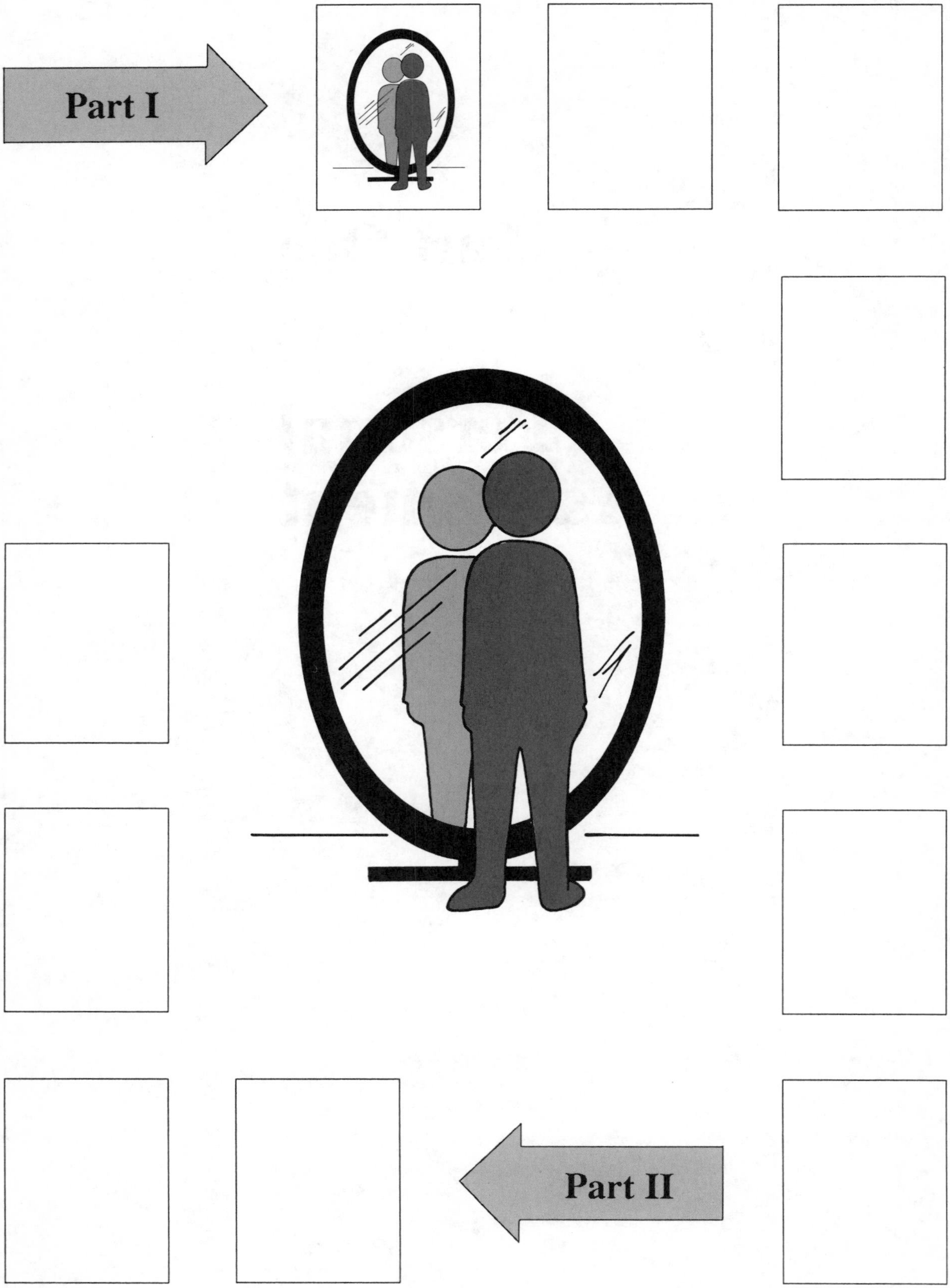
Part I
Part II

Taking Stock 1

My life is my message.
Ghandi

Learning Objectives   At the end of the chapter you will be able to:

Differentiate between a job and a career

Identify life stages as they relate to career planning

Understand that personal assessment is the key factor leading to career satisfaction

---

Do you hope to have a career that meets your needs, complements your personality, and inspires you to develop your potential? Are you someone who wants to choose the type of life you want to live? If so, you need to set goals that will take you from where you are now to where you want to be. However, such goals are products of your past experiences, your desires, your needs, interests, values, and your vision of the future.

Empowerment = Choice, not chance

Personal Assessment

This first chapter examines your past experiences, who you are right now, your stages of career and life development, and your ability to deal with new information. Once you begin to identify what energizes you about life you can then begin to incorporate those insights into a career. Self-awareness is the first stage of the career-planning process. Donald Super, a renowned psychologist from Columbia University, is credited with developing the theory that a career makes it possible for you to actualize or express your self-concept (Super 1957). Your self-concept is in essence how you see yourself. Consider the following principles of Super's theory on career development and think about how they relate to you.

9

Super's Self-Concept Theory

1. We differ in abilities, interests, and personalities.
2. Every occupation requires a characteristic pattern of abilities, interests, and personality traits. Within each occupation are workers with varying degrees of these characteristics.
3. Each of us is qualified for a number of occupations.
4. Vocational preferences and skills, the situations in which we live and work, and our self-concepts change with time and experience. These factors make choice and adjustment a continuous process based on our maturity and life style.
5. Selecting a career involves the following pattern:

   a. GROWTH: This involves your physical and emotional growth when you are forming attitudes and behaviors that relate to your self-concept. Think about what you learned about yourself from childhood games or family roles. For example, "I am a team player," "I am an individualist," "I'm a mediator," or "I'd rather read than play games." A child begins having fantasies at this period, i.e., a child's dream of becoming a doctor.

   b. EXPLORATION: This is divided into *fantasy* (i.e., a child's dream of becoming a doctor); *tentative* (i.e., high school and post–high school periods of exploration where ideas are narrowed down); and *reality testing* (i.e., in high school or early college, working part-time or volunteering in a hospital and taking math and science classes).

   c. ESTABLISHMENT: This includes initial work experience which may have started only as a job to earn a living but which offers experiences for growth such that it becomes a part of a person's self-concept. For example, "I am an assistant manager, I am responsible for the bookkeeping and look forward to becoming the manager;" rather than: "this is just a job, and I will be doing bookkeeping until I can finish my bachelor's degree and get into law school." Very often several changes in jobs will occur over a few years.

   d. MAINTENANCE: This is a time when we maintain or improve in our career area. Advancement can be to higher levels or laterally across fields. For example, "I am extremely competent," "I can compete with others," "I can cooperate and share my knowledge," or "I can train others."

   e. DECLINE: This is a stage just before retirement, or when we see no new challenges, or chances for mobility. This phase is also known as "disengagement." It actually becomes a time when there is a shift in the emphasis you place on a career. You may even seek a reduction in the hours that you work.

6. The nature of any career pattern is determined by parental socioeconomic level, mental ability, personality characteristics, and the opportunities to which the worker is exposed. Both limits and opportunities

People are motivated by self-concepts, needs, and drives

may be apparent as a result of these factors. Any limitations may be overcome only with great effort and perseverance.

7. The process of career development is essentially that of developing and implementing a self-concept. All of us try to maintain a favorable picture of ourselves.

8. Work satisfactions and life satisfactions depend on the extent to which we find adequate outlets for our abilities, interests, personality traits, and values.

What has influenced your self-concept? Do you have an accurate view of your likes and dislikes, desires, attributes, limitations, needs, wants, and values? An accurate self-assessment will enable you to make better career decisions by increasing your personal awareness and understanding. Self-awareness improves the probability of seeking and selecting jobs that fit your unique self-concept.

Job vs. Career

We will be using the words *job* and *career* throughout this book, so let's define them. There is an important difference between them. Basically, a *job* is a series of tasks or activities that are performed within the scope of what we call work. These tasks relate to a career in that a career is a series of jobs. But more than jobs, a *career* is a sequence of attitudes and behaviors that are associated with work and that relate to our total life experience. A career is really an integration of our personality with our job activities. Therefore, our career becomes a primary part of our identity or our self-concept.

A career is the integration of personality with work activities

In the past, people chose a career early in life and they tended to stay in it most of their life. Farmers worked on their farms, secretaries stayed in the office, and teachers taught in their schools until retirement. More recently the trend in America is toward multiple careers. We can now expect to have two, three, or more careers in our lives. With the rapid changes in society, new economic conditions, new jobs, and new technologies, many traditional jobs are becoming obsolete. More than ever it is important to know what you want to do so that your training and education can be relevant both to your interests and to new trends in the job market. You also need to assess your skills so that you will know which are transferable from one career to a new emerging field with a minimum amount of retraining. Knowing yourself and developing a plan of action based on *both* your needs and the needs of the job market will help you get into the career most satisfying for you rather than just following the latest trends in open fields.

Trends in the market place come and go rather rapidly. Several years ago, teachers were in demand. Then for about a decade, there was a glut of teachers on the market. Now again, there seems to be a renewed need for teachers in the work force. The same is true for engineering. Even today the demand for computer programmers, which was once thought to be inex-

Follow intuitions, not trends

haustible, may be reaching saturation. If you base your career decisions primarily on current trends, it is quite possible that by the time you obtain the training necessary to get into the "hot" field, it may well have cooled down. This strategy leaves you with slim prospects for a job that can lead to a career, and quite possibly with skills and training in a field that you weren't terribly excited about in the first place except as a quick opportunity.

Super's theory assures us that each of us is qualified for any number of occupations. Getting to know yourself better through self-assessment will help you identify careers that will be best suited to your personality. People who are not prepared for change wait until others make decisions for them. They are often frustrated and unhappy because they are forced to take whatever they can get. They were never told that they have a choice. They haven't taken the time or energy to become aware of their preferences. They settle for less than what might be best for them. Dad says get a job in business even though junior has a special talent in art. The senior high school advisor recommends engineering because scholarships are available. The employment department directs the unemployed into an electronics assembly training program because there's an opening.

Job Satisfaction

Keep your options open

No wonder that survey after survey on job satisfaction among American workers indicates that well over 50 percent of workers are dissatisfied with their *jobs*. Since people may be changing *jobs* and careers several times in their lives, there is more need than ever before to have accurate knowledge about oneself and the world of work. Chances are, in ten or fifteen years, you will face the need to reevaluate yourselves as related to your work, and quite possibly choose a very different *career*. It is useful to know about the changing world of work and to know which occupations allow you to express your highest self, your greatest talents. Analyzing your assets, we want you to ultimately think about the total job market. We want you to search for jobs that will lead you into a career. We want you to identify a variety of alternatives that allow you to express your personality. Once you have looked within yourself enough and identified what you want and need in a job, your future changes will be easier to make because you'll know when you have outgrown one job and need a new one.

What does this really mean? Well, it means that for most of us, there isn't any *one* right career. Instead, there are many careers in which we could be equally happy, equally successful, equally satisfied. We are looking, then, not for the *one* right career, but for the series of alternatives and career options that seem to make sense to us given our background, our personality, and our career and life stages. Super's theory briefly mentioned general career stages that many people have experienced. These were identified as Growth, Exploration, Maintenance and Decline. Since many of you are presently between the stages of Exploration and Maintenance, it is useful to understand that you are also experiencing transitional stages related to your age which affect your career planning.

Overview of Life Stages

The following life stage descriptions suggest that we emphasize different needs at different times of our lives. Planning a career involves thinking about your past, present, and future. The following overview summarizes what researchers know about adult life stages (Levinson, Gould, Erickson 1978). This research is based on the studies of Daniel Levinson, Gail Sheehy, Roger Gould; and Erik Erickson. Reviewing life stage information allows a career searcher or changer to gain and accept insight regarding certain personal and emotional issues that tend to influence values, future planning, and goal setting.

Ages 16–22—Late Adolescence

- Leaving parents' world, independence being established but not stable, unsure of ability to make it in the adult world, open to new ideas.

Ages 22–28—Provisional Adulthood

- Gaining independence in work, marriage, or intimate relationships, testing all of the parental shoulds and oughts, and choosing which to retain in adulthood. Still proving competence to parents; more self-reliant; building for the future; marriage and family a consideration.

Ages 28–32—The Thirties Transition

- Questioning the early commitments to marriage and relationships, family and career, reassessments and changes may take place. This is a particularly vulnerable stage for continuity, although many persons choose to continue their earlier choices.

Ages 32–39—The Time of Rooting

- Dealing with established lives, children growing and/or last chance to have children being considered, no longer proving self to parents but blaming parents for personality problems. Acceptance of the choices made and a buckling down to business, reputation established, until about age thirty-five, when questions of "Will I have time to do it all?" begin to arise. Time seems to be running out; weary of being what one is supposed to be. Asking "What do I really want to be?"

Ages 39–43—The Turning Point Years

- Experiencing a period of great upheaval and mid-life crisis when it becomes obvious that earlier dreams may not be attainable. Wondering "Why am I here, where am I going? I'm in a rut." Radical lifestyle changes may occur, often without adequate forethought. Feeling that there must be something else to life. Final thoughts about raising a family.

Ages 43–50—Restabilization/Bearing Fruit

- Feeling settled with questions of mortality, career, and lifestyle transitions, children leaving the nest, parental regrets for any errors in raising kids, careers blossoming; attending more to inner development, being a mentor for young people. Intimacy needs changing as your children become adults.

Ages 50–65—Renewal

- Enjoying a time of relative calm, boredom, or acceptance and enjoyment of life, planning for retirement. Physical energy and strength may decline, spouses and/or friends die. New life structure emerges. Risk taking seems less likely to occur. Acceptance of one's parents' role in one's life; spiritual questioning. Potential for creative growth. Disengaging from concept of "work," though some people will start new careers at this time.

Ages 65 and UP—Retirement

- As life is extended and retirement is not mandatory, this age may become the true "golden years" of continued usefulness to society and growth for oneself.

Remember that these life stages are based on social norms of the past and present. The world is changing at such a rapid pace that social norms may be different in future studies. For example, two-career families, single parents, people living alone, later marriages, alternative lifestyles, people living longer, fewer entry-level jobs, need for more people with technical skills, and need for lifelong learning, etc., may appear as trends in future studies.

Here are some examples of the kinds of career selection we've been discussing.

Sample career changers

Professor Johnson had reached his life goal or so he thought. He was one of the chosen few to be a professor of religion at a small Catholic college in the San Francisco area. One day he woke up with stomach pains and body aches and had little energy. He had to drag himself out of bed. When the pains lasted longer than three days, he visited his family physician only to find that there was no medical reason for his discomfort. He then realized he had to do some soul searching. His pains and nightmares were continuing over a period of months and only seemed to occur during the work week. On weekends when he was with his family or volunteering at a hospital, he was energetic and healthy. He soon took a leave of absence from his job and devoted more time to his hospital avocation. The physical ailments mysteriously disappeared. He spent one year examining his needs, consulting with a career counselor, and talking things over with friends. He found that his real satisfaction came from helping people in the hospital rather than in teaching religion. Shortly thereafter, a friend told him about a job opening in a hospital acting as an ombudsman. He got the job. He now lectures to local classes in career development on the hazards of keeping a job that is making you ill! Professor Johnson needed to re-examine his original goals to discover why his career as a professor wasn't meeting his needs.

Jerry was a bottled water distributor for over fifteen years. He was thirty five years old and earned over $30,000 annually. With over-time he could earn about $40,000. However, by the time he was thirty, he had become tired of lifting heavy bottles. Jerry started taking a computer course at the local college and found he enjoyed the academic environment. He continued studying and completed the necessary courses for a certificate in information systems. By the time he was thirty five, he transferred to the data processing department of his company. He is continuing his course work toward the goal of transferring into an evening bachelor's degree program. Jerry found that as he grew older mental activity was more enjoyable than physical activity no matter what the pay.

Meanwhile, Susan spent five years in college completing a bachelor's degree in teaching with an emphasis in special education. After two and a half years working in the field she decided that she needed a change; the school system was no longer challenging. She found a job as a stockbroker trainee. Within six months she was a full-fledged stockbroker. Now she's a corporate financial advisor.

Then there's Bob. He was a successful accountant for nine years. Now he's a professional comedian and is able to support himself financially in his new career.

As there is no crystal ball that will predict the one right career for you, you need to explore several options while you are in your exploration stage of career development. The previous examples illustrated people reassessing their needs and changing fields. However, it is possible to survey your needs, values, interests, skills, and aptitudes and create a broad career objective. Some careers do have career paths. In teaching one often starts out as a tutor, works up to student teacher, and then becomes an assistant teacher before becoming a full-time teacher. In the marketing profession, people often start in sales. Therefore we need to think about careers in the sense of their being both short-term and long-term. A short-term career goal is one that can be rather quickly attained. It might be, for instance, that in the process of career planning, you discover you want to be a lawyer. We would normally consider law a long-term career option because it generally takes many years of study and preparation. However, a short-term career goal that relates to law might be a job as a legal secretary or a paralegal. Either of these would give you the opportunity to be involved in an environment that excites and energizes you without having to postpone the experience until you actually achieve your final and ultimate career goal.

Preparation = Short- and long-term goals

Sandra was seventeen when she started her first secretarial job. By luck, it was in a legal office. For ten years she was happy being a secretary involved with the legal profession. This left her time to raise her family. But her employers encouraged her to continue her education. Not only did she attend evening courses, but she also became involved with the Professional Secretaries' Association. By the time her children were grown, she had completed a two-year college degree program, been president of her Association, started a training course to become a paralegal, had been promoted to legal assistant, and was teaching legal terminology at her local alma mater.

If you examine enough options during the career-planning process, hopefully you will be able to use past career experiences to move into future related career areas just as Sandra did. Future chapters will help you identify your related options.

There is a final very important reason why this effort at personal assessment is crucial as the first step in your career-planning process. Once you know who you are and what your preferences and talents are, you can better make sense of the information that continuously bombards you regarding the world of work. It's almost impossible to read a newspaper, listen to a news broadcast, or watch a television show that does not have some

Self-knowledge helps decision making

implication for you and your career. Quite frequently you may suffer from information overload. Looking at the want ads and reading about employment projections and future trends can cause confusion, frustration, and very often discouragement about what place you might have in this elusive job market. One of the best ways to achieve a sense of control and perspective on this constant stream of information is to know who you are so that when you are listening, reading, watching, and experiencing you will have a means of processing information through your consciousness, through your set of preferences, through your values and skills. Eventually, you will be able to recognize and reject information which does not apply to you, and to internalize and add to your career plan that information which does apply to you.

Summary

The best approach to the process of career planning is first to examine who you are and what you know about yourself and what you need and want, and then to mesh that information with the world of work. You then have the distinct advantage of training to do something about which you are truly excited and enthusiastic. These two qualities are probably among the most important to potential employers. Even if the job market for the field in which you have trained is extremely competitive, you will have an edge because of your sense of commitment, your passion and joy for what you

Attitudes influence action

are doing. We will elaborate further on these "attitudes for success" in chapter 2, and identify and discuss the attitudinal components that will make you a success in whatever career you choose.

?? Written Exercises

Now is the time to begin your first set of exercises to explore your personal patterns and attitudes. The following exercises serve to help you understand yourself. Begin with "First Impressions." This will help you take stock of where you are currently. The second exercise is a review of where your life focus has been. The third, fourth, and fifth exercises reflect your interests and the sixth asks for your job history. The seventh exercise asks you to identify your personal strengths. (Later when you are reading about the personality requirements of different careers, you can use this list to help you to make an appropriate decision.) The final exercise encourages you to identify job preferences by ranking occupations according to how you perceive their status.

1.1
First Impressions

Here is your first chance to think about yourself and record your responses. Fill in each blank carefully and honestly. Be true to yourself; don't try to please anyone else with your answers. Try to be spontaneous, as the longer you think before answering, the more likely you are to be censoring some of your answers.

a. I am _____

b. I need _____

c. I want _____

d. I would like to change _____
   about myself.

e. If all goes well in the next five years, I will be doing the following things: _____

   _____

f. If things go poorly in the next five years, I will be doing: _____

   _____

   _____

g. Reviewing past jobs I have had, why did I leave each one? Is there pattern? _____

   _____

   _____

   _____

1.2

Life Line

Review the Information on Life Stages. As we noted, these life stage descriptions suggest that we emphasize different needs at different times of our lives. Can you remember the highs and lows in your personal and career life, and place them on a line? It is helpful to place symbols on a line graph of your life indicating times of major decisions or changes, moves, or new jobs; times when particular mentors or other influential people entered or affected your life; and times when you had particular problems, or acquired important new skills, etc. To assist your memory, divide your age into four time periods and write five important memories (activities, people, events) in each group. For example, if you are 28 years old:

Ages 0–7 (Try remembering friends, birthday parties, or holidays, or school events to recall your earliest memories.)

1. _____
2. _____
3. _____
4. _____
5. _____

Ages 8–14

1. _____
2. _____
3. _____
4. _____
5. _____

Ages 15–21

1. _____
2. _____
3. _____
4. _____
5. _____

Ages 22–28

1. _____
2. _____
3. _____
4. _____
5. _____

Now you can transfer these memories into the life line. It may help to use symbols to save space. I.e., A = people, B = events, C = jobs, etc.

Figure 1.1
Sample Life Line

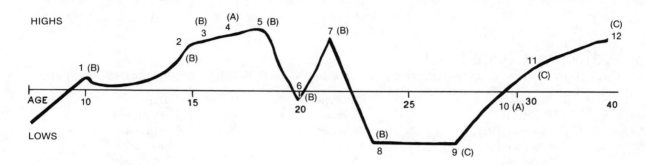

1. Leadership award in sixth grade.
2. Chosen student ambassador to France—sophomore in college.
3. Spent senior year in France.
4. Met significant man in my life.
5. Graduate school in New York City.
6. Move from New York to California (lost friends, career contacts).
7. First professional job (but not my *ideal* job).
8. Fired! (A bona-fide case of sexual harassment!)
9. After being unemployed for *nine* months, I *volunteered* at a career planning center—learned new skills.
10. Began my own serious job search, identified my ideal job (career counselor) in the ideal setting for me (a community college).
11. Success! Landed the perfect job for me!
12. Still learning on my job and beginning to explore further options and/or career enrichment opportunity.

1.3
What subjects in school do I like? _____

1.4
What books or magazines do I read? What kinds of music, art, theatre or cinema do I like? _____

_____

_____

1.5
What do I like to do for fun? In my spare time? _____

_____

_____

_____

1.6

Jobs I've had (include volunteer work): _____

_____

_____

1.7

Adjective Check List

Circle those adjectives that best describe you. Place an "X" by those adjectives that are least like you.

R *Realistic*	I *Investigative*	A *Artistic*
Practical	Careful	Emotional
Materialistic	Introverted	Expressive
Conforming	Curious	Imaginative
Persistent	Precise	Disorderly
Stable	Independent	Creative
Down-to-earth	Achieving	Impulsive
Rugged	Confident	Flexible
Athletic	Analytical	Idealistic
Frank	Intellectual	Original
Self-reliant		

S *Social*	E *Enterprising*	C *Conventional*
Helpful	Energetic	Conscientious
Insightful	Adventurous	Efficient
Kind	Ambitious	Organized
Friendly	Competitive	Obedient
Responsible	Enthusiastic	Dependable
Understanding	Driving	Moderate
Popular	Powerful	Orderly
Cooperative	Persuasive	Persistent
Tactful	Domineering	Detailed
	Flirtatious	Thorough

Next, review the adjectives you circled. In reviewing the adjective check list, you should note that it is divided into six clusters known as Realistic, Investigative, Artistic, Social, Enterprising, and Conventional (the first words of each group). Which groups of adjectives best describe you? Also note that most of the words are positive personality traits. This exercise gives you a chance to acknowledge your positive attributes. These categories are based on a theory developed by Professor John Holland and will be further discussed in chapter 7.

From which three of the six groups (RIASEC) do most of your adjectives come?

#1 _____   #2 _____   #3 _____

Each group of adjectives describes a certain kind of person. What kinds of people do you like to be around?

#1 _____   #2 _____   #3 _____

1.8
Occupational Status
Rank the following occupations in numerical order of importance. Number 1 should be the occupation which you feel is most important to you; Number 19 should be the least important.

_____ Agriculture Supervisor
_____ Auto Mechanic
_____ Barber/Beauty Operator
_____ Computer Operator
_____ Dental Hygienist
_____ Doctor
_____ Engineer
_____ Landscape Designer
_____ Laser Technician
_____ Lawyer

_____ Movie Director
_____ Musician
_____ Police Officer
_____ Public School Teacher
_____ Plumber
_____ Psychiatric Technician
_____ Robotics Technician
_____ Salesperson
_____ Secretary
_____ Waiter/Waitress

Think about what aspects of these positions really impress you. Next, think about how you define status. Is it based on probable income, amount of education required, societal standards? How individualistic do you think your rankings are? For example, was _musician_ ranked in your top five because you appreciate music? There are, in actuality, no correct or incorrect answers in this exercise. However, your ranking may reflect some of your basic preferences. If most of your top-ranked occupations were higher salaried or if your ranking was based on potential for high pay, you may be motivated by a need for security; if your highest rankings were for socially valued occupations (i.e., doctor, public school teacher), you may be oriented to the need for serving society.

Exercise Summary

Write a brief paragraph answering these questions:
What have I learned about myself? My current life stage? How does this knowledge relate to my career/life planning? How do I feel?

_____
_____
_____
_____
_____

The next class in career fitness is about to start. We hope you will join us as we begin by calling upon your spiritual and psychological resources so that you are in the mind set for success.

Part I

Part II

Programming Yourself for Success 2

If you think you are beaten, you are,
If you think you dare not, you don't
If you like to win, but you think you can't
It is almost certain you won't.

If you think you'll lose, you've lost,
For out of the world we find
Success begins with a person's will
It's all in the state of mind.

If you think you are outclassed, you are,
You've got to think high to rise
You've got to be sure of yourself before
You can even win a prize.

Life's battles don't always go
To the stronger or faster man,
But sooner or later, the person who wins
Is the person who thinks, "I can!"
Anonymous

Learning Objectives

At the end of the chapter you will be able to:

Understand the importance of a positive attitude in developing a successful career plan

Identify specific components of "the success profile"

Recognize approaches and techniques for creating success in your career planning

Attitude

During the process of career planning, you are going to learn how to take what you've got (values, skills, interests, aptitudes, qualities, limitations) and do what it takes (job search strategy) to reach your career goal. Satisfactory progress in your career is attainable if you decide you want it. We are beginning the process of career planning with an assessment of your attitudes because your mental outlook is the crucial variable that will move you toward or keep you from identifying and achieving your career goals. There is no book, set of exercises, system, or counselor that will affect your

Assessing your attitude

success as much as your own belief system, and your commitment to achieving success. Your beliefs are reflected by your actions. How many times have you told yourself, "I'm going to start on a new exercise program today"? How easy it is to find a "legitimate" excuse to postpone your efforts. Are you really ready to work on your career fitness? If so, let's examine some of the beliefs and attitudes that can assist you with your plan.

Success

Although the word means many things to many people, success in general usually means the progressive external demonstration of internalized life goals. In other words, success refers to the step-by-step movement toward the attainment of an object, quality, or state of mind that we value and wish to possess.

Develop your own definition of success

Slowly, during the last decade, the American concept of personal success has changed. Old symbols of success like money, large homes, and luxury cars have lost their prominent place. According to a 1983 Gallup Poll (*Success* 1983), good health is now the number one criteria for success, with an enjoyable job rated as number two, and a happy family, good education, peace of mind, and good friends, in that order, as the most important criteria of success. Do you have your own personal definition of success? Regardless of the particular goals you have in mind, you need to think positively to attain them.

Maintaining a Positive Outlook

Have you ever heard the saying, "It's all in your head"? People who say this believe that our minds and mental attitudes have control over our bodies and lives and can, therefore, program our success or failure. Although many of our attitudes and beliefs come from early messages we received from our parents and teachers, as adults we can choose to keep or change these messages depending on how helpful they are to us in achieving success and satisfaction in life.

Therefore, one might say "believing is seeing." To have a concept of what could be better, try examining your philosophy of life. How you see life in general is how you lead your life. A quick way to identify your philosophy is to visualize how you see the future.

Read the following scenarios and select the one that best relates to your point of view (Kauffman 1976).

1. The future is *a great roller coaster* on a moonless night. It exists, twisting ahead of us in the dark, although we can only see each part as we come to it. We can make estimates about where we are headed, and sometimes see around a bend to another section of track, but it doesn't do us any real good because the future is fixed and determined. We are locked in our seats, and nothing we may know or do will change the course that is laid out for us.
2. The future is *a mighty river.* The great force of history flows inexorably

along, carrying us with it. Most of our attempts to change its course are mere pebbles thrown into the river: they cause a momentary splash and a few ripples, but they make no difference. The river's course can be changed, but only by natural disasters like earthquakes or landslides, or by massive, concerted human efforts on a similar scale. On the other hand, we are free as individuals to adapt to the course of history either well or poorly. By looking ahead, we can avoid sandbars and whirlpools and pick the best path through any rapids.

3. The future is *a great ocean*. There are many possible destinations, and many different paths to each destination. A good navigator takes advantage of the main currents of change, adapts his course to the capricious winds of chance, keeps a sharp lookout posted, and moves carefully in fog or uncharted waters. If he does these things, he will get safely to his destination (barring a typhoon or other disaster which he can neither predict nor avoid).

4. The future is entirely random, *a colossal dice game*. Every second, millions of things happen which could have happened another way and produced a different future. A bullet is deflected by a twig and kills one man instead of another. A scientist checks a spoiled culture and throws it away, or looks more closely at it and discovers penicillin. A spy at Watergate removes the tape from a door and gets away safely, or he forgets to remove the tape and changes American political history. Since everything is chance, all we can do is play the game, pray to the gods of fortune, and enjoy what good luck comes our way.

These scenarios reflect your attitude about life. Is your life a roller coaster, out of control; a mighty river to which you must adapt; a great ocean with many directions and options; or just a game of chance? Are you a positive thinker or a negative thinker? The second and third scenarios tend to be the positive reflections. Your belief system will affect how you see life. Have you ever noticed how your most dominant thoughts reinforce what happens to you? This phenomenon is sometimes called the "self-fulfilling prophecy." Remember the times you've thought the following:

Develop the "mind set" for success

"That's just the way I am."
"I can't control what I do."
"I just can't seem to finish anything I start."
"I would like to do that differently, but it's just too hard to change."
"Yep, it happened again."
"I've never been good at that."

If you reinforce the negative, you will act negatively. If you affirm your limitations, you will be limited. Mark Twain once observed, "It ain't the things I don't know that gets me in trouble, it's the things I know for sure." Thus, your mind tends to believe what you tell it. And, yes, you can, if you *think* you can.

Cultivating a positive, assertive outlook on life is the most crucial factor that makes the difference between those people who have successful, satisfying lives/ careers and those who don't. Let's examine some of the aspects of this positive, assertive outlook so that we can put ourselves in the "mind set" for success.

The Assertive Attitude

One of the most basic choices we make on a moment-to-moment basis is whether to be assertive, aggressive, or passive in response to life situations. Basically, being assertive means being the ultimate judge of our own behavior, feelings, and actions, and being responsible for the initiation and consequence of those actions. In essence, assertive people choose for themselves and put themselves up *without* putting others down. Aggressive people choose for themselves and others; they put themselves up *by* putting others down. Passive people allow *others* to choose *for them*; they put themselves down or allow others to do so.

Maintaining control

You need to develop an assertive attitude in order to maintain some control over today's tight job market. An assertive outlook enables you to be persistent; to seek more information when you run out of leads; to weigh all alternatives equally (incorporating both your logic and your intuition); to be willing to revise your goals when necessary; and to pursue your goals with commitment and purpose. Assertiveness specifically enables you to say what you feel, think, and want. It allows you to be expressive, open, and clear in communication. You are able to say "no" under pressure, recognize and deal with manipulation, and stand up for your rights in negative, confrontational situations. You gain the ability to become a better listener. Others appreciate your directness and ability to hear them. You enjoy more positive interactions with people and feel more positive about being able to handle life situations.

Assertive personal traits include body language as well as words. Studies indicate that 93 percent of the meaning of any message is nonverbal. Look at yourself and think about your typical physical stance when you are feeling assertive in contrast to when you are feeling passive. What does your style of dress say about you? Can changing the color of your outfit change the mood you project to others? Did you ever notice your gesturing? Assertiveness is often associated with expansive gestures rather than limited ones. Finally, how do you deal with touch or physical closeness? Being assertive means feeling comfortable within your own body space.

Most importantly, positive assertive behavior suggests that you really have confidence in yourself. This behavior conveys verbally and nonverbally that you have confidence in your abilities and that you believe in your own worth. That positive, confident, and enthusiastic self will set you apart; make people take notice of you; and ultimately enable you to exercise control over your career and life.

Self-Confidence

Perhaps more than any other factor, self-confidence is the secret to success and happiness. It is the ability to recognize that even though you are imperfect, you are a unique, worthwhile, and lovable person who deserves and can attain the best things in life. You project a sense of self-confidence by your body language, your dress, your pace, your ability to take pride in your accomplishments, your ability to learn from your mistakes, and your ability to accept suggestions and praise from others. Because you believe you deserve the career of your choice, you can attain it.

You can begin to develop more self-confidence by remembering and rewarding yourself for something you did *well* each day. You may automatically seem to review, in great detail, each and every negative event that has occurred. This is indeed a common, natural understandable human reaction which can be neutralized by deliberate positive thinking. You may have to literally force yourself to think of something positive and give yourself a "pat on the back," a gold star, or better yet, make it a point to share the good news with a friend, a support person, someone who you know will delight in your small personal achievement. In fact, think about starting a support group consisting of individuals who want to share their personal victories with each other. The reinforcement and support of others is a powerful tool in our personal quest for success. Start small, remember that an Olympic gold medal, just like self-confidence, is built on hours, days, weeks, months, *and* years of small personal victories!

Personal Enthusiasm

You can always identify achievers by their consistent posture of optimism and enthusiasm. They know that life is a self-fulfilling prophecy, that people usually get what they actively imagine and expect. They choose to start the day on a positive note by listening to music, singing in the shower, or telling themselves that this will be a good day. They view problems as opportunities to be creative. They learn to stay relaxed and calm under stress. They associate with people who share their optimism about life and they support each other through praise, encouragement, and networking. When asked about their career goals, instead of saying, "I don't know," they say "I'm in the process of discovering my career goals."

When employers are asked what traits they look for in perspective employees, enthusiasm is always at the top of the list. What kind of people do you want as friends, associates, and colleagues? Chances are you want someone who is optimistic and has a zest for life. You can become more enthusiastic by getting involved in something that has meaning for you. A hobby, volunteer work, mastery of a skill, a new relationship, all provide opportunities to experience and express your enthusiasm. On the job, part of a professional attitude includes the ability to act as if things are fine even when you feel upset or depressed. At work, *acting* positive and up pays off. Not only do you come across as mature and professional, but as you begin to "act" enthusiastically you receive positive feedback from others. The smiles, nods, and positive words of others begin to make you feel enthusiastic. You discover you are no longer acting, you genuinely feel better!

Positive
Self-Talk

One of the most effective ways to improve your self-image is the deliberate use of positive self-talk. You already talk to yourself, we all do constantly! But, we usually do not consciously listen to our internal dialogue, and consequently, we often allow ourselves to listen to negative, self-defeating messages that create and reinforce a low self-image. Once you decide to take charge of your self-talk, you can begin to repeat positive messages that will reinforce a positive self-image. This technique is commonly called affirmations.

Affirmation is a statement or assertion that something is already so (Sunshine 1975). It is an existing seed or thought in the here and now that will grow as life unfolds. It is not intended to change what already exists, but to create new desired outcomes. Remember, all events begin with a thought. If you think you can, you can! Anything a person can conceive can be achieved. Good gardeners not only cultivate flowers, they cultivate soil. The thoughts you are thinking and sending out are the "soil" of your life. If you are constantly projecting thoughts of lack, you will have barren soil. If you project thoughts of prosperity, your soil will be rich. Therefore, any career you can conceive of in which you can imagine yourself being happy and successful can be achieved.

However, when writing your own affirmations, it is important to remember that you are planting a seed and the seed must carry exactly the information that you want to see grow into the result that you desire. When you become specific about what you want, you are focusing the power of your mind's energies (your thoughts) on your desires. The more specific you are about your goals, the more focused you become about what must be done to reach them. You know you are being specific enough when you can visualize details about what you want. For example, if you are a student and you want to be a college professor, you must be able to see yourself on a college campus, in a specific classroom, standing before a room of students, lecturing, interacting with other professors, and correcting papers!

Here are some hints to follow when writing your own affirmations.

1. Always write the affirmation in the present, never in the future; otherwise it may remain in the future. If you wanted a job for yourself you would write: "I now have the most appropriate, satisfying job for me."
2. Phrase your affirmation in the positive rather than the negative. In other words, avoid affirming what you don't want. Instead of writing "My present job doesn't bother me anymore," it would be much more effective to write: "My work is wonderful" or "I enjoy my job."
3. Maintain the attitude that you are creating something new and fresh. You are not trying to manipulate, re-do, or change an existing thing or condition.

Let's experience this technique in action. Think of a quality that you want to develop in yourself. Let's use enthusiasm as an example. Your first instinct might be to say or think "I'm not very enthusiastic." As soon as this thought comes to mind, replace it with the opposite thought, "I am enthusiastic." Repeat the phrase over and over, day and night, until you feel you own it, it soon will feel comfortable. At the same time, picture yourself doing something enthusiastically like explaining to your boss why you deserve a day off or starting a conversation with a stranger or honestly disagreeing with an instructor during a class. Picture yourself making your statement and being positively reinforced. Your boss says yes, you deserve it; the stranger becomes a friend; the instructor praises you for your insight.

Even before you actually do something enthusiastically you have prepared yourself mentally for a positive outcome. Your chances of experiencing the outcome improve because you are projecting a positive self-image. Try it!

Self-Image

Not only do successful people like themselves but they visualize themselves at their best and they monitor their self-talk so that they reinforce their images of success in word and action. They know that the self-image acts as a regulator, an unconscious thermostat. If you cannot picture yourself doing, being, or achieving something, you literally cannot do, be, or achieve it! Your self-image absorbs information, memorizes it, and acts accordingly. Every time you say, "I can't," you are creating a negative self-image. Every time you say, "I can and will," you are giving yourself permission to be your best self. Successful people recognize how potent their beliefs are and they take responsibility for shaping their own self-image rather than allowing others' opinions to limit them.

Self-Initiation

Successful people realize that goals activate people and fears stop people. If you dwell on your fears, whether real or imagined, you will be immobilized in the pursuit of your goals. If you concentrate on your goals, you will move toward them. People who are afraid to tell the world what they want, don't get it. The difference between those who are successful and those who are not is attitude. What side of the coin do you choose to look at, fears or goals? In what direction are you going, away from or toward your goals?

Implementing your goals

Allan had been laid off after working for a company for twenty-nine years. After the shock and disbelief of his involuntary career change had passed, he began to ask himself what he would really enjoy doing. He realized the hours spent in a library provided some of his most rewarding experiences. Because he was not a librarian, he could not imagine himself working in a library in any capacity, and could not even bring himself to volunteer his services in a library. His fears about lacking the qualifications to become a librarian (fear of inadequacy) prevented him from moving in the direction of his desire (to work in a library). After many months of fruitless job hunting, he finally mustered up the courage to become a volunteer at the library. In less than two months, the staff recognized his valuable contributions and he was offered the next paid position that became available.

Persistence

Successful people take full responsibility for the initiation and consequences of their actions. They know that life is full of choices, not chances. They realize they personally have the power to take control of their lives, both physical and mental. They know that trying to blame mother nature for a less than perfect body or calling it fate when they don't get the job is simply "copping out." Successful people really do make it happen for themselves. What might appear to be luck really is opportunity meeting preparation. As Calvin Coolidge once said:

Luck = Opportunity and preparation

> *Nothing in the world can take the place of persistence. Talent will not; nothing is more common than unsuccessful men with talent. Genius will not; unrewarded genius is almost a proverb. Education alone will not; the world is full of educated derelicts. Persistence and determination alone are omnipotent.*

Self-Discipline

Self-discipline is the conscious implanting of specific thoughts and emotions that will, through repetition, become part of our unconscious, and then our conscious mind, resulting in the creation of new habits and a new self-concept. While it is easy to marvel at the mastery of an expert, we often assume that the person was born with superhuman talents or skills. We forget that every champion athlete, every great performer, every skilled surgeon, every professional developed their expertise by endless hours of physical and mental practice. They visualize their performance, they engage in positive self-talk ("I can," "I'll do better next time") and through repetition, they become more and more of what they desire. This self-talk is also known as practicing *mental imagery,* and *mental rehearsal.* Jack Nicklaus, for example, attributes 10 percent of his success to his set up, 40 percent to his stance and swing, and 50 percent to the mental imagery he uses before he takes each stroke (quoted in *The Psychic Side of Sports* by Michael Murphy, Addison Wesley Publishing Co. 1978). The gold and silver medalists in the slalom at the 1984 Olympics were seen on television visualizing their runs as they waited in the starting line (quoted from *The C Zone* by Robert and Marilyn Kriegel, Anchor Press Double Day 1984, pp. 100–101). Equally dramatic are the results of a study using three groups of students chosen at random shooting basketball foul shots. One group visualized themselves shooting foul shots for thirty minutes a day. At the end of twenty days the first group which had practiced every day improved 24 percent. The second group which had done nothing showed no improvement. The third group which had only visualized themselves shooting fouls im-

Use mental rehearsal

proved 23 percent (quoted from *Seeing With the Mind's Eye* by Mike and Nancy Samuels, Random House 1975, pp. 166–167).

All of the people in the cited examples used visualization regularly over a period of time. This is the key to the success of mental rehearsal. Some experts say you must visualize a goal thirty minutes a day for at least a month to experience results. This discipline distinguishes visualization from random daydreaming, an effortless activity we all engage in periodically.

Goal Identification

Successful people have clearly defined plans and objectives that they refer to daily to keep in mind their lifetime goals and to order their daily priorities. Clearly defined, written goals help to move us to completion. The reason most people don't reach their goals is that they don't identify them (Waitley 1984). They don't know what they want.

If you don't know where you are going, you probably won't get there. Even though you are just embarking on your career fitness plan and you probably don't have a specific career in mind as yet, you can still begin the process of goal setting. Your first goal might be to read this workbook with purpose, one chapter a week, and complete all the exercises after each chapter with attention and the intent of learning more about yourself so you can make appropriate career choices when the time is right. Ideally, you should set aside a specific time and place each week so that you will get into the habit of working on your career fitness plan in the same way that you would work on a physical fitness plan—with consistency and commitment.

Knowing what you want is Step #1

What makes workers succeed
Executives say these personality traits are most important:

Enthusiasm	80.6%
"Can Do" Attitude	65.1%
Loyalty	62.6%
High Energy	40.3%
Assertiveness	30.5%

Source: Management Dimensions Inc.; survey of 241 executives from all types of companies

By Elys McLean-Ibrahim, USA TODAY

Summary

Programming yourself, "psyching yourself up," for success is the first step of your personal assessment program. Getting into a positive frame of mind on a daily basis is just as important as a regular round of calisthenics to "rev up" your internal engine and start the day off right! Once you begin to develop a positive outlook, you are ready for step two of the personal assessment program, values clarification.

?? Written Exercises

This section of exercises is designed to review your attitude and assertion skills. Try to answer the first set of questions as quickly and spontaneously as possible. Do not censor your answers. These are called open-ended questions. These questions sometimes make people think about different responses each time they see them. Therefore it's all right to have more than one answer as well as to change an answer whenever you review the questions. These questions will also cause you to review your past actions so that you can better identify how your past actions reflect who you are today. Answer the rest of the exercises to reflect your ideal environment and how you see yourself.

2.1
Past Actions and Influences

Fill in each blank carefully and honestly. Be true to yourself; don't try to please anyone else with your answers.

a. I am proud that _____

_____

b. One thing I can do which I couldn't do a few years ago is: _____

_____

c. Name the person you most admire. This person can be living, historical, or fictional. Write down the specific characteristics of this person that you admire (i.e., famous, rich, loving, generous, etc.).

_____

_____

_____

d. Write the name of the person you least admire and why?

_____

_____

e. Name a person who is like you and describe him or her.

_____

_____

f. What activities or people in the last two weeks gave you a feeling of being energized?

_____

_____

_____

g. What have you always wanted to do in your life? What's keeping you from doing it? What action could you take in the next year to get closer to this goal?

_____

_____

_____

h. What habit have you successfully attempted to change?

_____

i. What three words would you like others to use in describing you?

_____

2.2
Two Perfect Days

a. Written Description.

In order to be clear about what you want in your life, write a one-page description about two ideal days in your future. One day should be related to leisure and one day should be related to work. Think about where you would be, what you'd be doing, who, if anyone, would be with you, if your major activity would be work or leisure, etc. Try to be as detailed as possible.

Use this space for notes: _____

_____

_____

_____

b. Summarize in two or three words.

Try to think of two or three words that would capture the *essence of the quality of these two days,* e.g., peaceful, challenging, fun, harmonious, exciting, restful, productive. You may summarize each day separately if you wish.

2.3
Assertiveness and Attitude Checklist

Answering the following questions will give you a better idea about how your attitude is reflected by your actions. Consider asking several important people in your life to respond to these questions about you. Compare their answers with yours. Choose two or three areas to work on to improve your attitude and assertiveness skills.

	Satisfied	Need to Improve
a. Do I always do my best?		
b. Do I tend to look at the bright side of things?		
c. Am I friendly and cooperative?		
d. Am I prompt and dependable?		
e. Do I do more than my share?		
f. Do I appear to be confident?		
g. Am I believable?		
h. Do people ask my opinion of things?		
i. Do I appear to be trustworthy, intelligent?		
j. Am I poised, well-mannered, tactful, considerate of others?		
k. Do I dress appropriately?		
l. Do I put others before myself? To what extent?		

	Satisfied	Need to Improve

m. Can I accept compliments?
n. Do I give compliments?
o. Do I make suggestions?
p. Can I say no?
q. Do I wait for others to decide for me?

2.4
Affirmations

a. Write ten affirmations related to being successful in your career and life planning: Put them on 3 x 5 cards (one per card).

1. _____   6. _____
2. _____   7. _____
3. _____   8. _____
4. _____   9. _____
5. _____   10. _____

b. Read your affirmations to yourself two times during the day, once in the morning as you awake and once just before going to sleep.
c. To accelerate their effectiveness try the following suggestions:
   1. *Write your affirmations in longhand while speaking them aloud to yourself ten, twenty, or more times.*
   2. *When writing affirmations try writing in different persons, such as "I, Marilyn, am highly employable." "You, Marilyn, are highly employable." "She, Marilyn, is highly employable."*
   3. *Record your affirmations on a cassette tape recorder and listen to them as you drive, or while doing chores around the house.*
   4. *Before going to sleep at night or upon arising in the morning, visualize yourself as you are becoming. For example see yourself as more assertive, loving, social, enthusiastic.*
   5. *Chant or sing your affirmations aloud while driving or during any appropriate activity.*
   6. *Meditate on your affirmations.*
   7. *Tape them up around the house; on the telephone; on the mirrors; on the refrigerator; on the ceiling above your bed; on the dash of your car; in your dresser drawers.*
   8. *Use affirmations as book markers.*
d. It has been said that three conditions must be present to create change. First, there must be real dissatisfaction with what is, then there must be a concept of what would be better, and last, there must be a belief that there is a way to get there. This whole process must additionally generate the idea that the benefits of the change outweigh the costs of making the change. Affirmations help you believe that there is a way.

   The following questions relate to *obstacles* that may be interfering with the achievement of your desires:
   1. How much intention do you really have?
   2. What identity would be threatened by achieving your goal? For example, would a better job make you too independent or allow you to earn more than your mate?
   3. Do you secretly feel you don't deserve to obtain your desires?
   4. Are you proving to anyone else that you can't change?
   5. Is it worth it to you? (The work, concentration, time.)
   6. Are you following all the steps suggested?

7. Is it what you really want? George Bernard Shaw once commented that "The only thing worse than not getting what you want, is getting what you want!" In other words, "Many men go fishing all their lives, only to realize later that it wasn't the fish they wanted."

Exercise Summary

What have I learned about myself? _____

_____

I want to improve _____

_____

I admire the following qualities in people: _____

_____

My affirmations are: _____

_____

What can I do in the next two weeks to improve my self-confidence? _____

_____

What lies behind us and what
lies before us are tiny matters
compared to what lies within us.
Ralph Waldo Emerson

Part I

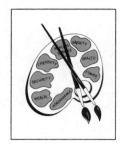

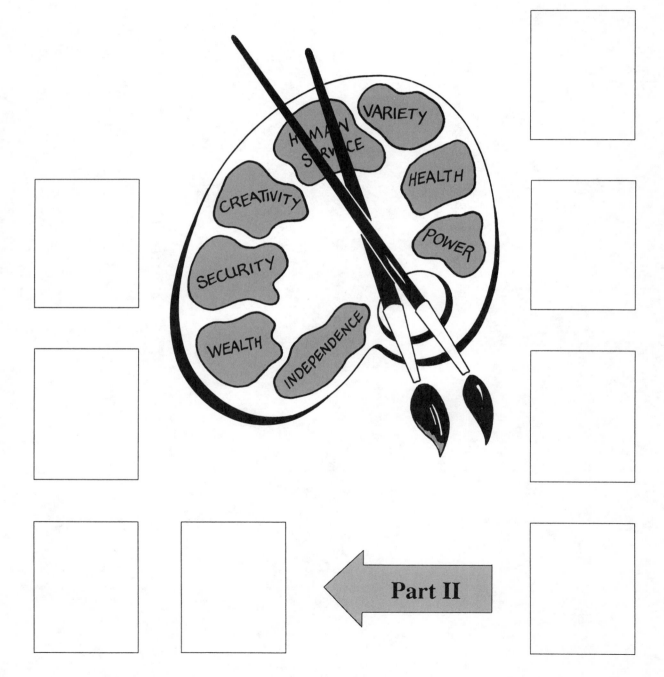

Part II

Values Clarification

3

He who has a why to live can bear with almost any how.
Nietzsche

Learning Objectives

At the end of the chapter you will be able to:

Define and clarify your values

Understand how your values motivate you

Demonstrate how your values affect your career decisions

Importance of Values

What causes someone to study for years before entering a career like medicine or law while others are looking for the quickest, easiest way to make a buck? What causes someone to switch careers midstream after spending years developing mastery and a reputation in a field? The answer to these questions is *values.* Your values are the often unidentified, but nevertheless all-pervasive, forces that guide and influence your decisions throughout your life. If you value fitness and good health, you make time for daily exercise, positive self-talk, and proper nutrition. If you value career satisfaction, you will take the time to examine your values and begin to make choices consistent with your values.

The basis for decisions

Definitions

Values are the self-motivators that indicate what is important in your life. Values are reflected in what you actually do with your time. They indicate what you consider most important in your life. This chapter will help you identify what is needed in your work environment to make you feel satisfied with your job. You may discover that the reason you are dissatisfied with your present job is that it contains few of your values. People often

Self-motivators

39

settle for a job just to bring in money. Once you become aware of your values, you can make more personally meaningful decisions about satisfying jobs. In other words, your decisions can be based on what's really important to you.

Clarification

Now that you have begun to take charge of your mental attitude, identifying your values becomes the next step in your personal assessment program. By age ten, most of you unconsciously adopt the values of your parents, teachers, and friends. By adolescence, you begin to sort out which of these adopted values you want to freely choose as your own. This process is often generalized as "teenage rebellion." Parents, in particular, often take offense when you question or reject a value that they hold dear. In fact, this process of values clarification is an essential part of growing up. Mature, independent, successful individuals typically act upon their own values rather than those of others. This frees them from unnecessary guilt ("What would my mother say if . . . . ?") and indecision ("What would Dad do in this situation?") and fosters satisfaction and self-confidence ("Regardless of the outcome, I'm in control of my life."). Many adults fail to reassess *Acting on your* their values as life goes on. Research about life stages indicates that adults *values* can and do make dramatic changes in their personal and career lives based on changes in values. This process of change can be less traumatic for all of the individuals involved if, as adults, we periodically review and reassess what is important to us.

> Mary was one such individual who benefited from reviewing her values. A secretary, she was delighted that her company, an air freight carrier, had contracted for the services of a career counselor. She couldn't wait to get some help in choosing a new job. She felt bored and stagnant where she was. As the counselor helped Mary to identify her values, she realized that she liked security and didn't mind routine, structure, or taking orders. As she further explored her feelings of boredom, she remembered that the main reason she chose to work with an airline was for the travel privileges. Yet it had been years since she actually took advantage of the travel opportunity. Once she remembered and reevaluated her desire for travel, she began to utilize this benefit and she was quite content to continue working with her current employer.

Evaluating Yourself

By this time, you are probably wondering how you can recognize your values. The more intense your favorable feelings are about some activity or *Recognizing* social condition, the more you value it. Is there anything in the current *your values* news that excites you or makes you angry? Are there certain activities that energize you? Are there circumstances in your life that lead you to certain activities? All of these indicators reflect your values.

More specifically, the following criteria will help you determine your values. Values which are alive and an active part of you have the following qualities (Raths, Simon, & Harmin 1966):

1. *Prized and Cherished.* When you cherish something, you exude enthusiasm and enjoyment about it. You are proud to display it and use it.
2. *Publicly Affirmed.* This involves being willing to and even wanting to state your values in public.
3. *Chosen Freely.* No one else is pressuring you to act in a certain way. You own these values. They feel like a part of you.
4. *Chosen from Alternatives.* When given a choice whether to play a leading role in a Hollywood film or to be provided with a full scholarship to study at Harvard Business School, which would you choose? Acting in Hollywood would highlight such values as creativity, prestige, glamour, possible monetary returns, and high risk taking, while acquiring a Harvard MBA would suggest such values as prestige, monetary returns, education, intellectual stimulation, and security.
5. *Chosen after Consideration of Consequences.* You tend to consider the consequences when you have to make a decision that is very important. Consider the immediate impressions that come with the idea of relocating to a job that is 2,000 miles from where you've lived all your life, or marrying someone who is thirty years older than you, or buying a car from a used car salesman. What values come into play?
6. *Acted Upon.* Again, values are reflected by what you do with your time and your life; they are more than wishful thinking or romantic ideals about how you should lead your life.
7. *Acted Upon Repeatedly and Consistently to Form a Definite Pattern.* The main idea is that you repeatedly do activities which relate to your highest values. For example, complete the "Values Grid" in the exercise section that follows. List five to ten aspirations or goals you have achieved in your lifetime; e.g., finished high school, member of debate team, planned surprise party, found a job. Check the values that you use repeatedly.

As you begin to think about it, you will come to realize how much you rely on your values to make decisions. People involved in career planning often wonder how they will ever choose any one career when they have so many possibilities in mind. This is precisely the time when knowing your values is important. Let's say you've discovered that economic return, helping others, and security are your three top values. You are thinking about becoming an artist, an actor, or a speech teacher. You might well be able to do all three, even simultaneously! However, in order to choose one career direction, try deciding which career would best satisfy your top three values. You are likely to experience the most success and happiness from this kind of choice. In this case, speech teacher most closely incorporates the values mentioned.

Needs and Motivators

So far we have discussed self-motivation based on successful attitudes and values. In addition, inner drives or needs also influence how you choose your career. People experience psychological discomfort when their needs are unmet. We best meet our needs by identifying them and then setting goals to meet our needs. Once our needs are met the tension and discomfort is reduced. There are five primary needs as identified by Maslow, a famous psychologist (Maslow 1970). They are: (1) physiological (basic survival, food, water, etc.); (2) safety (both physical, i.e., security, shelter, protection, law and order, health insurance, pension plans, secure job; and psychological, i.e., freedom from fear, anxiety, etc.); (3) belongingness and love (friends, affiliation, affection, relationships, love, etc.); (4) self-esteem/ego-status (prestige, self-respect, competency, self-confidence, sense of self-worth); and (5) self-actualization (achieving one's potential, being creative, serving a cause, contributing to society, etc.). As you can see, these needs progress from the most basic and biologically oriented (survival needs) to the more complex and socially oriented level of needs. When people are preoccupied with finding ways to put food on the table (physiological needs), they have little time or desire to work on developing relationships or to search for jobs which utilize their talents. Rather, they work at any job that will bring in immediate money. A person becomes aware of a higher-order need only when a lower need has been met. Although these needs seem to move from "lower to higher," in actuality people address their various needs at all levels throughout their lives. These needs are such primary, intense, self-motivators that your values may be eclipsed while you are being influenced to meet primary needs.

Job Satisfaction: Internal vs. external motivators

Once you have stabilized your ability to meet your physiological and safety needs you may find that you demand more feedback (satisfaction of social needs) in your work environment. A researcher, Frederick Herzberg, has examined what creates job satisfaction for most workers (Herzberg 1966). We have already explained that being in a job that reflects your top values brings you job satisfaction. However, Herzberg has also found that we have external motivators and internal motivators. The external motivators include salary, working conditions, company policy, and possibility for advancement. These just happen to fulfill physiological and safety needs. Meanwhile, internal motivators involving the amount of responsibility, the type of work accomplished, recognition, and achievement all contribute to job satisfaction. These motivators have proven to be most important for people who value and need status and self-actualization. Each person does not necessarily respond to each need with the same intensity of desire. For your own benefit, it would be useful for you to examine what brings satisfaction to you on the job. Figure 3.1 illustrates how Herzberg's research on job satisfaction overlaps with Maslow's needs.

Figure 3.1

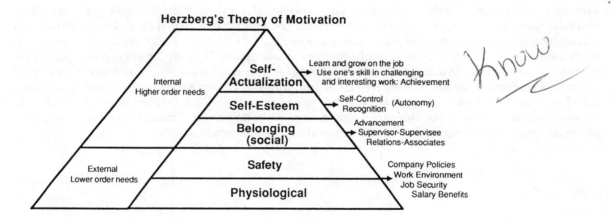

Summary

In the last two chapters, we have discussed forces that propel you to act on your goals, attitudes, values, and needs. In the next chapter, we will focus on the skills you possess and the skills you need to get you where you want to go. Once you know what skills you have, which ones you need to develop, and what skills you most want to use in the future, you will be well on your way to making some intelligent career plans.

?? Written Exercises

The following written exercises will help to identify your specific values. As you complete the exercises, look for the values that occur repeatedly in your answers. By the end of the exercises you will identify the five values that come up most often. These are your primary work values. Note them in the exercise summary at the end of the chapter.

The exercises are divided into six parts. Exercise 3.1 is called the Values Grid. It will demonstrate how activities that you consider accomplishments or aspirations contain your values. It also shows how your highest values recur and are implemented repeatedly in a variety of activities. Exercise 3.2 seeks to clarify what is important to you in all aspects of your life, from hobbies to work environments. The "job descriptions" are actually general descriptions of both jobs and values. Try guessing the name of the value and jobs described. The answers can be found at the end of this chapter. Exercise 3.3 asks you to prioritize your values by ranking what is most important in four different situations. Often, in our career decisions and life in general, we do not get all we want and must give up something desirable to get something more desirable. Exercise 3.4 asks you to examine what you say you want to do in your life. If you haven't taken any actions to get what you want, your goals need to be reevaluated. The premise is that what is really valued serves as a driving force motivating you to take action. Exercise 3.5 asks you to identify the types of careers that would utilize the values you hold dear. Exercise 3.6 asks you to identify some of your fantasy careers and what about them appeals to you. You will be introduced to the research technique called *practice interviewing* and you will be asked to gather information on one of your fantasy careers. As you continue to identify possible career options you will be doing more practice interviewing to gather firsthand, real-life information so that your career decisions are based on facts.

_____ 3. A professional position. Position of responsibility. Secretarial assistance provided. Pay dependent upon experience and initiative. Position requires a high level of education and training. Job benefits are high pay and public recognition.

_____ 4. A job with a guaranteed annual salary in a permanent position with a secure, stable company. Supervisory assistance is available. Minimum educational requirement is high school. Slightly better pay with one or two years of college or vocational training. Position guarantees cost-of-living pay increases annually. Retirement benefits.

_____ 5. Looking for an interesting job? One that requires research, thinking, and problem solving? Do you like to deal with theoretical concepts? This job demands constant updating of information and ability to deal with new ideas. An opportunity to work with creative and intellectually stimulating people.

_____ 6. This job requires an extraordinary person. The job demands risk and daring. Ability to deal with exciting tasks. Excellent physical health a necessity. You must be willing to travel.

_____ 7. An ideal place to work. An opportunity to work with people you really like, and just as important, who really like you. A friendly congenial atmosphere. Get to know your co-workers as friends. Pay and benefits dependent on training and/or experience.

_____ 8. Work in a young fast-growing company. Great opportunities for advancement. Starting pay is low, but rapid promotion to mid-management. From this position, there are many opportunities and directions for further advancement. Your only limitation is your own energy and initiative. Pay and benefits related to level of responsibility.

_____ 9. Set your own pace! Set your own working conditions. Flexible hours. Choose your own team or work alone. Salary based on your own initiative and time on the job.

_____10. Start at the bottom and work your way up. You can become president of the firm. You should have the ability to learn while you work. Quality and productivity will be rewarded by rapid advancement and recognition for a job well done. Salary contingent on rate of advancement.

_____11. Ability to direct work task of others in a variety of activities. Leadership qualities in controlling work force and maintaining production schedules. Ability to maintain a stable work force. Coordinate work of large management team. Instruct work force. Evaluate work completed. Hiring and firing responsibilities.

_____12. Great opportunity for money! High salary, elaborate expense accounts, stock options, extra pay for extra work. Christmas bonus. All fringe benefits paid by company. High pay for the work you do.

_____13. Are you tired of a dull routine job? Try your hand at many tasks, meet new people, work in different situations and settings. Be a jack-of-all-trades.

_____14. Does the thought of a desk job turn you off? This job is for the active person who enjoys using his/her energy and physical abilities, since it requires brisk and lively movement.

_____15. Opportunity to express your personal convictions in all phases of your job. Devote your life style to your work.

From the above list, identify the five jobs that best express your values, then least express your values. Use the list of values at the end of the chapter.

Best Express Values	Least Express Values
1. _____	1. _____
2. _____	2. _____
3. _____	3. _____
4. _____	4. _____
5. _____	5. _____

3.3

Your Values—Some Hard Choices

In this exercise you are asked to choose the best and worst among sets of options all of which are more or less unpleasant. Rank the situations and individuals which, however unpleasant, you could best and most easily accept as number one, and the "worst bad case," the situations you would find hardest to accept, as number five or six, with the intervening cases ranked accordingly.

a. Job situations:

_____ To work for a boss who knows less than you do about your work and over whom you have no influence.

_____ To be the key person in a job, while someone else gets all the credit for what you do, and is paid much more than you.

_____ To work with a group where trust is very low.

_____ To work in an organization whose job is to serve the poor but which instead wastes huge amounts of its resources on red tape.

_____ To work day-to-day with someone who is always putting in really second-rate work.

b. People:

_____ The industrialist who in public gives lip service to anti-pollution concerns but orders his factory to emit heavy pollutants at night to avoid detection.

_____ The man who dislikes swimming with Blacks so much that he forms a swimming club with the unwritten but clear understanding that no Blacks will be admitted.

_____ The mother who, when she finds her two-year-old son playing with his genitals, slaps him across the face and says, "Don't you know that will make you go crazy?"

_____ The college student who sells pot to high-school students at cost, because he sincerely thinks they should have a chance to experience it.

_____ The man who works at a neutron bomb manufacturing company who, when confronted by his college-age daughter about how he can take part in such an industry, snaps back: "Shut up! The money I make there is putting you through college!"

c. Environment:

_____ In the Arabian desert (120 degrees F.) with a well-paying job.

_____ On a small subsistence-level farm in Appalachia.

_____ In an efficiency apartment in New York City on a tight budget.

_____ In an urban commune where all resources are shared.

_____ In a middle income suburban housing development, with a fifty-five-minute commute (one way), totally dependent on a car.

d. Risks:

_____ Bet $10,000 in a gamble.

_____ Put $10,000 into a new business venture.

_____ Go into business for yourself.

_____ Without an assured job, move to a remote place where you always wanted to live.

_____ Have an affair with a married person.

_____ Risk arrest in a public demonstration for or against something about which you feel strongly.

3.4
Top Five

List five things you want in life. Examine each of these to see what each has to do with what is most important to you. What have you done to support or express these values? What actions have you taken that have moved you closer towards what you most want in life? The answer to this question compares what you say is important with what you are actually willing to do.

1. _____
2. _____
3. _____
4. _____
5. _____

3.5
Values Related to Careers

List (A) your top five values and (B) careers that would allow you to actualize many of those values. For example, creativity, prestige, variety, money, and independence might all be associated with a career as a lawyer.

A. Values

1. _____
2. _____
3. _____
4. _____
5. _____

B. Careers

1. _____
2. _____
3. _____
4. _____
5. _____

3.6
Your Fantasy Careers

List your current fantasy careers on a sheet of paper. Then think back chronologically from the ages of 1–5, 5–10, 10–15, and try to recall what were some of your past fantasy careers and list them as well. We develop fantasy careers at a very young age. Most children see cartoons, books, and television dramas about doctors, nurses, police officers, firefighters, astronauts, teachers, and scientists, to name a few popular careers. Books about children solving mysteries (Hardy Boys, Nancy Drew) and TV series (such as Charlies Angels or Magnum P.I.) created an image of excitement about being a detective. James Bond movies influenced many to secretly dream of being a political secret agent. What did you read about or see in the movies that seemed like an exciting career?

A. For each career on your list ask yourself this question: "What about that career is or was appealing to me?" Many of us might have the same fantasy career for different reasons.

Fantasy Careers . . . "wouldn't it be great to be . . . .

Current	*What about this career appeals(ed) to me?*
1. _____	_____
2. _____	_____
3. _____	_____
4. _____	_____

Chronological Past (*In 5-year increments*)	What appealed most to me about this fantasy career?
1–5 _____	_____
_____	_____
_____	_____
5–10 _____	_____
_____	_____
_____	_____
10–15 _____	_____
_____	_____
_____	_____
15–20 _____	_____
_____	_____
_____	_____

B. Now, choose the one fantasy career that is most appealing. Try to locate someone who is doing that for a living. If you are part of a class, ask your instructor and classmates if they can refer you to someone. Otherwise, try to make a connection by asking people you know at school, work, and social gatherings. Read the information in chapter 8 on informational interviewing. Arrange an interview, preferably in person, and ask the questions in the sample list of typical questions under "Information Interviewing Outline."

Exercise Summary

1. List the values that are reflected from your answers in this chapter.

    a. _____

    b. _____

    c. _____

    d. _____

    e. _____

2. Prioritize the values listed above into your top five:

    a. _____

    b. _____

    c. _____

    d. _____

    e. _____

3. List the top values that could most likely be satisfied by a future career.

    _____

    _____

    _____

    _____

4. What I have learned from reading and answering the exercises:

    _____

    _____

    _____

5. I feel _____ after completing this chapter (i.e., more aware, confused, satisfied, etc.).

6. I am energized by the following types of activities: (Use Values Grid, past jobs, or hobbies.)

    a. _____

    b. _____

    c. _____

JOB DESCRIPTION ANSWERS
(from page 45)

Job Number	Value
1	Altruism
2	Creativity
3	Prestige
4	Security
5	Intellectual
6	Adventure
7	Associates
8	Advancement
9	Independence
10	Productivity
11	Power
12	Money
13	Variety
14	Physical Activity
15	Life Style

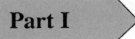 **Part I**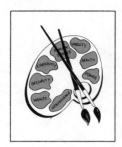

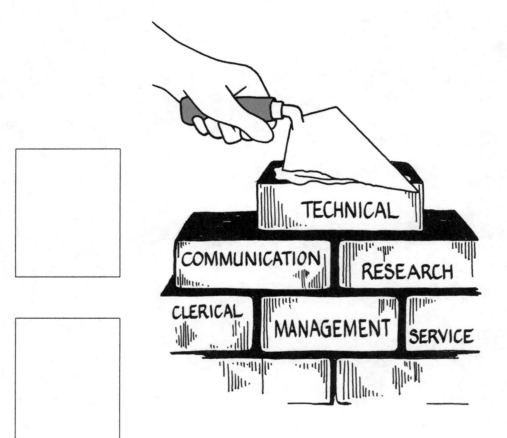

 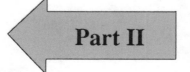 **Part II**

Skills Assessment 4

To find out what one is fitted to do and to secure an opportunity to do it is the key to happiness.
John Dewey

Learning Objectives	At the end of the chapter you will be able to:

At the end of the chapter you will be able to:

Understand the importance of skills in your career search

Define and identify your skills

Recognize the power of the transferability of your skills

Skills

The next step in the career-planning process is identifying your skills. Skills are the building blocks for your future career just as muscles are the building blocks for your future body shape. A career fitness program helps you identify your current skills and the new skills you want to develop. A thorough skills analysis is a critical component of the career-planning process.

Definitions of Skills

Skills include the specific attributes, talents, and personal qualities that we bring to a job as well as the learned procedures that a job teaches us. Every job requires some skills. We also develop skills in the process of living, interacting with others, and going through our daily routines. Your personal preferences often affect your skills and abilities. You tend to be motivated to repeatedly use skills that are a part of enjoyable activities. Your repeated use of and success with certain preferred skills identifies them as your *self-motivators* (also known as your *motivated skills*). Self-motivators are skills you enjoy and do well.

Motivated skills: Those you enjoy and do best

55

By learning the vocabulary of skills you can recognize the hundreds of skills that may be within your grasp. Skills are generally divided into three types: functional, work-content, and adaptive. *Functional skills* are those that may or may not be associated with a specific job, such as answering a telephone, maintaining schedules, collecting data, diagnosing and responding to problems, measuring productivity, etc. These are called functional skills because they are tasks or functions of a job. *Work-content skills* are specific and specialized to one job, e.g., bookkeeping is done by bookkeepers, assigning grades is done by teachers, interpreting an EKG is done by specific medical practitioners. *Adaptive skills* are personal attributes; they might also be described as personality traits. The ability to learn quickly, the ability to pay close attention to detail, task orientation, self-direction, congeniality, and cooperativeness are some examples of adaptive skills.

Importance of Skills

Basically, the job market pays for skills; the more skills you have the more valuable you are, and the more you are paid. Individuals who can describe themselves to a potential employer in terms of their skills are the people most likely to enjoy such careers. People who enjoy their work tend to be more productive and healthy. After completing this chapter, you will be able to analyze a potential job on the basis of how the skills the job requires compare with the skills you possess and enjoy using (your motivated skills), and the skills you want to develop. Furthermore, you will have an improved vocabulary to use in describing your strengths in future job interviews.

Assessing Skills

Can you list your skills?

If you were asked right now to enumerate your skills, what would your list look like? It might be a pretty short list, not because you do not have skills, but simply because you are not accustomed to thinking and talking about your skills. Reflecting on your own skills is difficult because most of us have been taught to be modest and not to brag. It is difficult to recognize that we possess hundreds of skills just by virtue of our life experiences. This chapter seeks to help you learn the vocabulary of skills and to acknowledge the skills you possess.

Implications

Once you have begun to recognize your skills, you will become aware that your own identity extends beyond the narrow limits you tend to apply to yourself. We all tend unconsciously to categorize ourselves too narrowly. For instance, you might typically answer the question "Who are You?" with statements like "I am a student," "I am a history major," "I am a teacher," or "I am a conservative." The problem with these labels is that they tend to stereotype you. This is especially true when you are interviewing for a job. If you say you are a student, the interviewer might stereotype you as not having enough experience. If you say you are a secretary, the interviewer may consider you only for a secretarial job, or insist that you start as a secretary. But suppose you say your experience has involved public speaking, organizational work, coordinating schedules, managing budgets, researching needs, problem solving, following through with details, motivating others, resolving problems caused by low morale and lack of cooperation, and establishing priorities for allocation of available time, resources, and funds. Sounds impressive! (See the chapter on resumes for the "Creative Resume" that incorporates these skills into the resume.)

Employers look for employees who are task oriented, who think and talk in terms of what they as employees can do for the employer to make the employer's operation easier, better, and more efficient. The best way to describe what you can do for an employer is to develop the ability to talk about your skills.

Can you talk about your skills?

Unfortunately not only have most of us been raised to be modest ("It's impolite to brag or boast"), but also once we accomplish a task we tend to discount the worth of our skill development. Most people tend to deny that they have done much of anything. They say, "I haven't climbed the highest mountain," or "I can't run a four-minute mile," or "I haven't been president of the student body," or "I haven't been elected to public office." Yes, those are accomplishments, but so are the following:

babysitting	getting into college
delivering on a paper route	using a word-processing machine
riding a bicycle	repairing a car
designing a costume	completing a computer course
planning a surprise party	raising money
giving a speech	writing a term paper
getting a first job	consoling a child
graduating from high school	planning a trip and traveling

Sample accomplishments

In reviewing this list, you probably are thinking that some of these activities are simple, "no big deal." These tend to be activities that you can do without much thought or preparation. Just because they don't take much preparation does not mean they aren't accomplishments. Start thinking of goals that you have set and then later met as accomplishments!

Identifying Skills

You can begin to recognize your skills by identifying and examining your most satisfying accomplishments. Your skills lead you to achieve these accomplishments. The analysis of these accomplishments is likely to reveal a pattern of skills (your self-motivators) that you repeatedly utilize and enjoy using. Again, accomplishments are simply completed activities, goals, projects or actual jobs held.

There are several ways to analyze accomplishments. *The first way* is to describe to someone something that you are proud of having completed and then to describe the skills that seemed to be required to complete it. Let's look at John as an example.

> John, an eighteen-year-old freshman, had planned a surprise party for his girlfriend. He persuaded several friends to contribute decorations and to assist in decorating her house. He had a few other friends divert her from arriving home until everything was in place. Additionally, he arranged for entertainment and party food. In discussing his completed goal (to surprise his girlfriend) he discounted his efforts and said, "Anyone could do it." However, in analyzing this accomplishment he identified the following skills: organization, persuasiveness, thoroughness, leadership, creativity, communication skills, determination, drive, persistence, dependability, courage, attentiveness to details, and supervisory ability.

Can you think of any that he missed? We have many more skills than we ever credit to ourselves.

Another method used to identify skills is to write a story about one of your accomplishments and then to identify the skills used. Richard Bolles has popularized this approach in his *Quick Job Hunting Map*, a booklet that lists hundreds of skills (Bolles 1979).

The following is an example of one student's story and how a group of classmates helped her to list her skills. Her classmates listened to her read her story and were able to identify twenty skills. The list follows the story.

> "Typing My Husband's Masters Thesis on a Word Processor"
> My husband's typist at work could not complete his thesis, but had done most of the graphs. It was necessary for me to learn how to use the word processor at a simple level to assist my husband in his final project.
>
> I knew the traditional keyboard and could type. At night when the children were ready for bed, we went to his company and used the office equipment.
>
> After instruction on how to use all the additional keys, I wrote down on paper all the key functions I had to use in order to give the correct commands to the machine. My husband and co-workers gave me a mini- operations course. I learned the following:
>
> 1. Find any page.
> 2. Enter the file.
> 3. Transfer material to different pages.
> 4. Type simple graphs.
> 5. How to print out on printer.
> 6. Make corrections.
> 7. Delete and insert characters.
>
> Together we proofread, corrected, and typed 150 pages in one month.

The paper received an "A" and has since been put in the library. My husband has a degree and new job title. Since the experience, I am taking a class in word processing.

List of Skills

1. learns quickly	11. works in a team
2. displays flexibility	12. displays patience
3. meets challenges	13. attends to detail
4. helps others	14. overcomes obstacles
5. follow through	15. communicates clearly
6. faces new situations	16. works under stress
7. proofs and edits	17. displays persistence
8. translates concepts	18. asks questions
9. types	19. gets the job done
10. organizes	20. directs self

Note that the list includes a combination of all three kinds of skills—adaptive, functional, and work-content.

A final method can be used if you have had several jobs. You can research the skills associated with these jobs by reading job descriptions usually located in the personnel office of any company or by researching the job in the Dictionary of Occupational Titles (D.O.T.). The D.O.T. is an excellent reference for identifying skills required in over 20,000 different occupations. Below are two examples.

Research skills in the D.O.T.

> *131.067.014 COPY WRITER (Profess. & Kin.)*
> *Writes advertising copy for use by publication or broadcast media to promote sale of goods and services: Consults with sales media, and marketing representatives to obtain information on product or service and discuss style and length of advertising copy. Obtains additional background and current development information through research and interview. Reviews advertising trends, consumer surveys, and other data regarding marketing of specific and related goods and services to formulate presentation approach. Writes preliminary draft of copy and sends to supervisor for approval. Corrects and revises copy as necessary. May write articles, bulletins, sales letters, speeches, and other related informative and promotional material.*

> *241.267.030 INVESTIGATOR (clerical)*
> *Investigates persons or business establishments applying for credit, employment, insurance, loans, or settlement of claims: Contacts former employers, neighbors, trade associations, and others by telephone, to verify employment record and to obtain health history and history of moral and social behavior. Examines city directories and public records to verify residence history, convictions and arrests, property ownership, bankruptcies, liens, and unpaid taxes of applicant. Obtains credit rating from banks and credit concerns.*

Analyzes information gathered by investigation and prepares reports of findings and recommendations. May interview applicant on telephone or in person to obtain other financial and personal data for completeness of report. When specializing in certain types of investigations, may be designated CREDIT REPORTER (bus. ser.); INSURANCE-APPLICATION INVESTIGATOR (insurance).

In addition to defining specific skills for each job, the D.O.T. divides all jobs into skills relating to the three broad categories of DATA (instructions and information), PEOPLE (dealing with supervisors, co-workers, or the public), and THINGS (dealing with materials, equipment, or products) as shown in table 4.1.

Table 4.1
Skills Relationships of Jobs to Data, People, and Things as Identified in the (D.O.T.) Dictionary of Occupational Titles

DATA (4th Digit)	PEOPLE (5th Digit)	THINGS (6th Digit)
0 Synthesizing	0 Mentoring	0 Setting-Up
1 Coordinating	1 Negotiating	1 Precision Working
2 Analyzing	2 Instructing	2 Operating-Controlling
3 Compiling	3 Supervising	3 Driving-Operating
4 Computing	4 Diverting	4 Manipulating
5 Copying	5 Persuading	5 Tending
6 Comparing	6 Speaking-Signaling	6 Feeding-Offbearing
7 No significant relationship	7 Serving	7 Handling
	8 No significant relationship	8 No significant relationship

Skills clusters

In addition to analyzing your skills by examining your completed projects and goals, a list such as the one in table 4.2 can help you become aware of some of the skills that you possess. In table 4.2 we have listed almost two hundred skills in twelve different categories. The categories mentioned are useful because they're familiar to employment counselors and often show up in job announcements. Read the items in table 4.2, considering carefully how each applies to you as a unique person.

Table 4.3 demonstrates how the tasks or functions of one occupation, teaching, can be translated into skills that apply to many other occupations. This awareness opens up options and expands individuals choices (Elliot 1982).

For each item in table 4.2, mark an "X" next to each activity that you enjoy doing. Then go over the list again and mark a check next to each activity that you do well. Underline any skills that you have ever used. Note that these categories contain work-content, functional, and adaptive skills.

Table 4.2
Skills

MANAGEMENT SKILLS

Planning
Organizing
Scheduling
Assigning/Delegating
Directing
Hiring
Measuring production
Setting standards
Work under stress
Work with people
Travel frequently
Work as a team member
Personnel practices
Time Management
Negotiating strategies

COMMUNICATION SKILLS

Reasoning
Organizing
Defining
Writing
Listening
Explaining
Interpreting ideas
Reading
Handle precise work
Work with committees
Public speaking
Correct English usage
Subject knowledge
Operate communication
  systems
Good sense of timing

RESEARCH SKILLS

Recognizing problems
Interviewing
Developing questions
Synthesizing
Writing
Diagnosing
Collecting data
Extrapolating
Reviewing
Work without direction
Work very long hours
Work on long-term projects
Statistics
Algebra
Research design

FINANCIAL SKILLS

Calculating
Projecting
Budgeting
Recognize problems
Solve problems
Finger dexterity
Able to concentrate
Handle detail work
Work under stress
Orderly thinking
Accounting procedures
Data processing
Operate business machines
Financial concepts
Investment principles

MANUAL SKILLS

Operating
Monitoring
Controlling
Setting-up
Driving
Cutting
Do precise machine work
Do heavy work
Work on assembly line
Work independently
Knowledge of tools
Safety rules
Basic mechanics
Basic plumbing
Electronic principles

SERVICE SKILLS

Counseling
Guiding
Leading
Listening
Coordinating
Work under stress
Respond to emergencies
Work under hazardous
  conditions
Work on weekends
Work nightshifts
Knowledge of a subject
Human behavior principles
Community resources
Agencies' policies

Table 4.2 (continued)
Skills

CLERICAL SKILLS	TECHNICAL SKILLS	PUBLIC RELATIONS SKILLS
Examining	Financing	Planning
Evaluating	Evaluating data	Conducting
Filing	Calculating	Maintaining favorable image
Developing methods	Adjusting controls	
Improving methods	Aligning fixture	Informing the public
Recording	Following specifications	Consulting
Computing	Observing indicators	Write news releases
Recommending	Verifying	Researching
Work as team member	Drafting	Representing
Work in office	Designing	Work with people
Follow directions	Work in an office/outdoors	Work under stress
Do routine office work	Work in small studios	Work very long hours
Basic clerical skills	Odd hours	Work odd hours
Bookkeeping	Economics	Negotiating principles
Data-entry operations	Investigations principles	Media process
Telephone protocol	Balancing principles	Human relations

AGRICULTURAL SKILLS	SELLING SKILLS	MAINTENANCE SKILLS
Diagnosing malfunctions	Contacting	Repairing equipment
Repairing engines	Persuading	Maintaining equipment
Maintaining machinery	Reviewing products	Operating tools
Packing	Inspecting products	Dismantling
Replacing defective parts	Determining value	Removing parts
Wood working	Informing buyers	Adjusting functional parts
Constructing buildings	Promoting sales	Lubricating/cleaning parts
Hitching	Work outdoors/indoors	Purchasing/ordering parts
Work outdoors	Work with people	Climbing
Work in varied climate	Work under stress	Work indoors/outdoors
Manual work	Work long hours	Lift heavy equipment
Do heavy work	Knowledge of products	Work as a team member
Operating basic machinery	Human relations	Basic mechanics
Safety rules	Financing	Electrical principles
Welding	Budgeting	Plumbing principles
Horticultural procedures		

Summary

Past accomplishments reveal skills

We each have our own special excellence. This excellence is most likely to be demonstrated in experiences that you consider to be achievements or life satisfactions. Your most memorable achievements usually indicate where your greatest concentration of motivated skills exists. Analyzing several such achievements is likely to reveal a pattern of skills used repeatedly in making such accomplishments occur. The more you know about your motivated skills, the better you will be able to choose careers that require the use of these skills. Using these skills gives you a sense of satisfaction. You will be happier, more productive, and more successful if you can incorporate your motivated skills into your life work. You may also find that your skills transfer to many different jobs.

Table 4.3
Identifying Transferable Skills for Teachers

Tasks	Functional Skills
Teaching	Training, coordinating, communicating, arbitrating, coaching, group facilitating.
Making lesson plans	Designing curricula, incorporating learning strategies, problem solving, developing rapport.
Assigning grades	Evaluating, examining, assessing performance, interpreting test results, determining potential of individuals, monitoring progress.
Writing proposals	Assessing needs, identifying targets, setting priorities, designing evaluation models, identifying relevant information, making hypotheses about unknown phenomena, designing a process, judging likely costs of a project, researching funding sources.
Advising the yearbook	Planning, promoting, fund-raising, group facilitating, handling detail work, meeting deadlines, assembling items of information into a coherent whole, classifying information, coordinating, creating, dealing with pressure, delegating tasks, displaying ideas in artistic form, editing, making layouts.
Supervising teacher interns	Training, evaluating, mentoring, monitoring progress, diagnosing problem areas, inspiring, counseling, guiding.
Interpreting diagnostic tests	Screening, placing, identifying needs, diagnosing.
Interacting with students, parents, and administration	Confronting, resolving conflicts, establishing rapport, conveying warmth and caring, drawing out people, offering support, motivating, negotiating, persuading, handling complaints, mediating, organizing, questioning, trouble shooting.
Chairing a department	Administering, anticipating needs or issues, arranging meetings, creating and implementing committee structures, coordinating, delegating tasks, guiding activities of a team, having responsibility for meeting objectives of a department, negotiating, organizing, promoting.

?? Written Exercises

The following exercises will assist you in identifying your personal constellation of skills. Exercise 4.1 asks you to write about several major experiences in your life with enough detail so that you will be able to analyze each experience for particular skills utilized. Exercises 4.2 and 4.3 ask you to list ten accomplishments and then to describe them in detail. Exercise 4.4 asks that you identify the skills used in the accomplishments described in exercises 4.2, 4.3. Exercise 4.5 helps you to distinguish between the work-content, adaptive, and functional skills that you possess. Exercise 4.6 identifies your favorite cluster of skills. Exercise 4.7 helps you to identify whether or not you've developed experiences related to job responsibilities in your ideal job. Exercise 4.8 serves to review and summarize your most often used and most preferred skills.

4.1
Experiography

In order for you to explore your past experiences and relate them to your career plan, we'd like you to write an account of the significant experiences in your life up to this time; in other words, write an *experiography*. The best way to go about this task is to think of three or four major experiences in each of the following categories and then describe each of them in writing in as much detail as you can. It is important to describe not only what happened but also your feelings (good or bad) about the experience or person, and what you learned from the experience. The categories to include are:

a. work experience
b. activity experience—school, clubs, etc.
c. important life events
d. leisure time
e. important persons in your life
f. life's frustrations
g. life's rewards

Remember, neither the chronology nor the order of significance is important. What is important is that you describe people or events that have had an impact on who you are right now. Keep in mind that we need enough specifics to be able to analyze these experiences for particular skills you have demonstrated.

4.2
Accomplishments

Write a list of ten accomplishments. You may find that you have already listed some in the Value Grid in chapter 3.

1. _____

2. _____

3. _____

4. _____

5. _____

6. _____

7. _____

8. _____

9. _____

10. _____

4.3
Description of Accomplishments

Select one or two of your accomplishments listed and describe each of them. Use one sheet of paper for each. In order to be as detailed as possible in your description of the event, try to elaborate on *who* influenced you, *what* you did, *where* it happened, *when* it occurred, *why* you did it, and *how* you did it. Think of the word-processing accomplishment as a sample of how your essay should look.

4.4
The Skills

List the skills you used in your story (You may refer to table 4.2 in this chapter).

4.5

As a starting point for analyzing your skills, let's look at you and your work experience. You may choose to look at present employment, either full- or part-time, or volunteer experience, past or present. With that experience in mind, review the definitions and examples of work-content, adaptive, and functional skills at the beginning of this chapter, and then complete this exercise.

Name three specific *work-content* skills you used in that experience; list three *adaptive* skills; and list three *functional* skills.

Work-Content	Adaptive	Functional
_____	_____	_____
_____	_____	_____
_____	_____	_____

4.6
Your Favorite Skills

Rank order the following skills categories as you feel they reflect your best skills:

a. Help people, be of service, be kind.
b. Write, read, talk, speak, teach.
c. Analyze, systemize, research.
d. Invent, create, develop, imagine.
e. Persuade, sell, influence, negotiate.
f. Build, plant crops, use hand-eye coordination, operate machinery.

4.7
Ideal Job

Write five ideal job responsibilities. Next to each one write two or more experiences that illustrate your background in each of these areas (i.e., "writing"—I wrote a twenty-page report that was used to justify a grant application). In areas where you have not developed numerous experiences, you may want to create additional learning experiences for yourself to make yourself eligible for your ideal jobs. You may create learning experiences or gain experience by taking classes, volunteering for extra work in your present job or by finding another job more closely related to your ideal jobs.

4.8
Review

Identify the skills that you most often use and enjoy. _____

_____

_____

4.9

Review your responses to Table 4.2, Skills Identification. What skills would you most like to use in your future career?

Which of the above skills do you need to develop?

How will you develop these?

    You have now identified your foundation, where you have been most effective and successful in your life. By examining these successes or achievements, you now know what you can handle and what motivates you. It is especially important that you focus on skills you use and enjoy.

Summary—Write a Brief Paragraph Answering These Questions

What did you learn about yourself? How does this knowledge relate to your career/life planning? How do you feel?

_____

_____

_____

_____

_____

Part I →

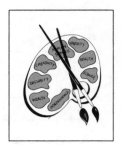

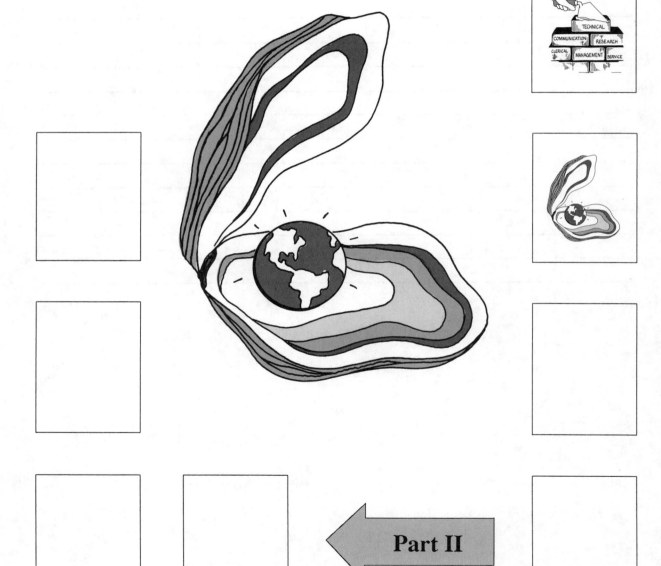

← Part II

The World and You   5

People are lonely because they build walls
instead of bridges.
John Newton

Learning Objectives   At the end of the chapter you will be able to:

Recognize how social and cultural conditioning influences your career choice

Identify trends that will affect your career planning through the 1990s

Understand that options are available for the nontechnical, liberal arts graduate

Your assumptions, limitations, aspirations, dreams, and fantasies are all shaped by the spoken and unspoken rules and norms of the society in which you live. Career choice does not exist in some countries because in those societies, the government tells you what your career will be. It is common to see women in construction work and the medical profession in the Soviet Union even though many Americans still believe this is "men's work." These facts may seem strange if you take for granted all of the physical, social, and cultural dictates of our society.

The next step in the career-planning process is to examine the societal and cultural factors that subtly or blatantly affect your career choice. The goal is to heighten your awareness of the biases, beliefs, and assumptions that influence your choice of possible occupations. It is important to analyze these cultural norms because they are often limiting. It is in your best interest to examine your own belief system as it relates to gender inequities and future trends in the work force, the two main topics of this chapter. As you come to terms with your own feelings about these issues, you can decide whether you basically want to go with the norms, or to buck them and be a maverick in a nontraditional profession. Every person in a nontradi-

Society's norms influence your career choice

69

tional occupation, such as female weight lifters and male nurses, has had to resolve this same issue before embarking upon their chosen path.

Influences

Career planning does not happen in a vacuum. Your life situation influences what decisions you make and how you make them. The society in which you grow up, your background, your present family, your peers, and the way you feel about yourself are all influences on the decisions that you make. Sometimes these factors make satisfying decision making easier. For instance, a friend who encourages you may help build your confidence and, therefore, make a final decision less difficult.

However, your society, family, peers, and feelings about yourself can also act as obstacles to making satisfying decisions. For example, many women are eager to return to school or to work. But, they may avoid con-

Common obstacles

fronting this decision, due to family and peer pressure and feelings about themselves, such as lack of self-confidence, fear of failure, age, race, and sex role stereotyping.

"Sure, I'd like to go back to school, but how could I get all the cooking, laundry, and shopping done, and who would look after the kids?"

"I don't really know what I want to do. Besides, I'm too old to start anything now."

"What I would really like to be is a lawyer, but I've given up on that because I know it's so hard for women to succeed in law."

"I don't know whether I'm going to apply for that job or not. Besides, they're not going to hire a black."

"I'm not really qualified to do that kind of job, and I'm too old to get more training."

Do any of the preceding statements describe something you have heard people say or maybe even something you have said or felt? It is possible that you identify with a number of these statements. They represent some of the most common obstacles that people face when making decisions. An obstacle to a satisfying decision is anything or anyone that prevents you from adequately considering all the possible alternatives. For example, someone said, "I'm too old to start something new." When looking for a job, such people might not even consider some positions for which they are well qualified. Age stereotyping prevents these people from considering all the possible alternatives.

Social and cultural conditioning

This chapter will focus on some of the social and cultural conditioning that has affected the roles people play in the job market. This will be typified by examples related to women's changing roles in our society. Next, we will discuss occupational trends, in order to inform you about predictable changes in society. The section after future trends will include a discussion about the current job market and how nontechnical and liberal arts oriented people are finding employment.

Finally, we will provide some written exercises for you to identify your own barriers, attitudes, and biases, and to predict your own future.

Social Conditioning—Sexism as One Example

Compare three different advisors' career advice to a woman student with your own experiences.

1. Your scores in math and science are excellent. Why don't you get your degree in math education? That would only take four years, whereas medicine would take many more—probably longer than you want to wait before marrying. Furthermore, teaching, unlike other jobs, will let you be home at three o'clock when your children return home from school.
2. Your scores in math and science are excellent. Perhaps you want to consider a career in medicine. You might be almost a pioneer. There aren't too many brain surgeons who are women. And brain surgeons, of course, can pretty much set their own schedule so you could plan to be home at three o'clock when your children return home from school.
3. Your scores in math and science are excellent. Perhaps you want to consider a career in medicine. You might be almost a pioneer. There aren't too many brain surgeons who are women. It could be an immensely rewarding profession not only financially but in the great intangibles of power, prestige, and honor.

Sex role stereotyping

As recent as twenty-five years ago, most women typically heard advice similar to the first example. About fifteen years ago, counselors started appreciating the fact that female roles in society were expanding and yes, women could even be surgeons. Yet there was still a basic belief that women should be home when the children came home. Now more school counselors are trying to be *sex fair* (see definitions, table 5.5 at the end of this chapter). That is, they are treating both males and females similarly. In the context of this chapter the term *sex roles* relates to social behavior that is prescribed and defined *only* by tradition. Unfortunately past practices have suggested that there are "men's jobs" and "women's jobs." For example, table 5.1 reflects the percentages of occupational roles that have been assigned to women in the past, and tables 5.2, 5.3, and 5.4 reflect the pay inequity in occupations traditionally filled by women or men.

Sex equity in employment standards

In an ideally unbiased society that has 50 percent men and 50 percent women, it would be assumed that there would be 50 percent women and 50 percent men in most occupations. Yet these statistics illustrate an unequal distribution of jobs. Many of our past biases have been based on the social custom that the man in a typical four-member family was the principal wage earner and the wife was primarily responsible for raising the children. Since society was principally composed of families, women were socially restricted to the role of homemaker. Sexism is only one form of stereotype.

Table 5.1
Percentage of Women in Selected Occupations in the United States

Occupation	Percentage of Women
Law	
Lawyers	26.8
Supreme Court Justices	0.11
Education	
Teachers, college and university	26.1
Elementary School Teachers	82.9
Secondary School Teachers	51.1
School Administrators, college	43.4
Health	
Physicians, Medical and Osteopathic	24.4
Dentists	4.6
Pharmacists	30
Registered Nurses	93.6
Health Administrators	60.6
Social Scientists	
Economists	37.8
Psychologists	47.7
Engineering and Science	
Electrical and Electronic Engineers	8.3
Civil Engineers	5
Industrial Engineers	9.8
Mechanical Engineers	5.1
Architects	16
Arts	
Writers, Artists, Entertainers, and Athletes	41.2
Designers	44.7
Musicians and Composers	24.8
Photographers	21.4
Religion	
Clergy	4.3
Protective Service Workers	
Firefighters	1.4
Police and Detectives	10
Sheriffs and Bailiffs	8
"Traditional" Occupations:	
Bank Tellers	94.1
Billing Clerks	86.5
Bookkeepers	89.9
File Clerks	80.7
Secretaries	98.2
"Non-Traditional" Occupations:	
Airplane Pilots	1.8
Electricians	1.5
Auto Mechanics	0.6
Truck Drivers	3

Source: EMPLOYMENT AND EARNINGS, U.S. Department of Labor, Bureau of Labor Statistics (1985).

Table 5.2
Pay Inequity

Occupations	% Women	Income	Occupations	% Men	Income
Secretaries	99.2%	$12,636	RR Switch operators	100 %	$22,828
Receptionists	97.5%	$10,764	Firefighters	99.5%	$20,438
Typists	96.6%	$11,804	Plumbers, pipefitters	99.2%	$21,944
Registered nurses	95.6%	$18,980	Auto mechanics	99.1%	$15,964
Sewers, stitchers	95.5%	$ 8,632	Carpet installers	98.8%	$15,392
Keypunch operators	94.5%	$12,480	Surveyors	98.5%	$17,472
Bank tellers	92.0%	$10,348	Truck drivers	97.9%	$17,160
Telephone operators	91.9%	$13,988			

Source: *USA Today, January, 1984*

Table 5.3
Wage Gap

The median income in 1984:

All women	$14,780	All men	$23,218
White women	14,904	White men	23,962
Black women	13,720	Black men	16,940
Hispanic women	12,545	Hispanic men	16,636

Source: U.S. Dept of Labor, 1986

Social and Cultural Considerations

Statistics from the Department of Labor and Census Bureau show that society is changing radically. Consider the following major shifts:

1. *Marriage.* Twenty-five years ago, 28 percent of women aged 20–24 had not yet married; today, that figure is 48 percent. Fifteen years ago, the number of unmarried couples living together totaled half a million. Five years later there were more than a million. *Societal trends*
2. *Divorce.* The divorce rate is presently 40 percent, but of the couples getting married today, it is projected that half will get divorced.
3. *Birthrate.* In 1965, the overall birthrate per 1,000 population was 19.4. By 1976, it had fallen to 14.7, the lowest ever recorded. Since then, it has edged up over 15.0 per 1,000, with the average family size expected to remain around 2.1 children per family. Teenage mothers give birth to one out of five babies.
4. *Children.* Between 1960 and 1980, the number of children living with only one parent, usually their mothers, increased from one in nine to one in five. By now, that figure is closer to one out of every two children.

Table 5.4

The Top-paying Occupations for Women and Men—1981; 1986 Median Weekly Earnings

Occupational title* Female earnings,	1981	1986	Occupational title* Male earnings,	1981	1986
Operations and systems researchers and analysts	$422	511	Aerospace and astronautical engineers	$619	722
Computer systems analysts	420	537	Stock and bond sales agents	589	740
Lawyers	407	624	Chemical engineers	583	721
Physicians, dentists and related practitioners	401	505	Economists	580	794
Social scientists + urban planners	391	470	Lawyers	574	806
Teachers, college and university	389	479	Computer Programmers		519
Postal clerks	382	429	Physicians, medical and osteopathic	561	728
Engineers	371	580	Electrical and electronics engineers	555	715
School administrators, elementary and secondary	363	495	School administrators, college and university	552	691
Life and physical scientists	357	471	Industrial engineers	549	647
Health administrators	357	463	Computer systems analysts	546	672
Public administration officials and administrators, not elsewhere classified	337	378	Health administrators	545	543
Vocational and educational counselors	336	471	Engineers, not elsewhere classified	530	691
Registered nurses	331	458	Airplane pilots	530	760
Personnel and labor-relations workers	330	411	School administrators	520	610
Computer programmers	329	477	Operations and systems researchers and analysts	515	695
Editors and reporters	324	373	Bank officers and financial managers	514	703
Secondary-school teachers	321	443	Personnel and labor-relations workers	514	606
Librarians	318	408	Civil engineers	507	620
Securities & Financial Services Sales		423	Teacher, college and university		656

*Occupations listed are those in which male employment was 50,000 or more in 1981.

Source: Bureau of Labor Statistics

5. *Working Women.* During the 1970s more than a million women a year entered the work force. That trend has continued in the 1980s.
   a. Women have made up 60 percent of the net additions in the work force since World War II. In 1970, only one in every four women sixteen and over was in the labor force. Today, it is one in every two. By 1990, 55 percent of all women sixteen and over will be working.

b. There are 44 million women employed in the USA, compared with 26.2 million in 1970. 43.7 percent of the 120 million people working last year were women, up from 38.4 percent of a total 85 million workers a decade ago. By 1995, 80 percent of women between 25 and 44 will be in the work force. In 1970, 30 percent of all mothers with children under six years old worked. That figure has now increased to over 50 percent. Since 1970, households headed by women increased 70 percent. Women are the sole earners in more than 15 percent of families.

c. Three-fourths of all women work thirty-five hours a week or more, and two-thirds of married women work full time. In the 1950s women earned sixty-three cents for every dollar earned by a man. Today, that has dropped to sixty cents for every dollar. Of women working full time, 66 percent earn less than $10,000 annually, compared to 20 percent of men.

d. Low income is related to the fact that *two-thirds* of employed women now hold clerical, service, nursing, and education jobs; these are traditionally low paying occupations. Ninety-nine percent of secretaries, 96 percent of nurses, 91 percent of bank tellers, 89 percent of health aides, and 87 percent of librarians are women. Women managers and administrators earn 60.5 percent of what men earn; women in blue collar jobs 67.1 percent; and women professionals earn 70.8 percent of what male professionals earn.

e. While percentages of women in nontraditional jobs have increased, often the increase is in the lower paying areas. About 17 percent of women work in what the U.S. Census labels "professional and technical jobs;" however, women are employed in only 5 out of the 50 job titles that comprise that area!

f. Women make up 40.9 percent of managers and 48.1 percent of professionals, including teachers and registered nurses. In professions, women have made the following gains in the last ten years: women are 15.8 percent of doctors and dentists, up from 9.3 percent. And in traditional male jobs, women are now 2.1 percent of pilots and navigators, up from 1.5 percent and 1 percent of firefighters, up from .5 percent. Since 1976 women full-time workers have increased more than 10 percent in accounting and computer programming.

6. *The Aging Population*. Ten years ago, there were 20 million persons over age sixty-five. Today, the figure is 24 million or 12 percent of the population; by 2000, it will be 35 million or 14 percent; and by 2030, it could go as high as 55 million or 15 percent. There will be more single people over age sixty-five, particularly women, and more of them will be older. Now 38 percent of the elderly are over seventy-five but by 2000, it will be 45 percent.

If trends stay as they are today, the older generation of women will be the poorest in society. Additionally, health care of aging adults will be as common a concern as child care is today. Many women are divorced and must continue to work long after men of similar ages have retired because of no fault divorce laws and lack of retirement plans in their traditionally female jobs.

7. *College Education*. In 1900, one out of sixty was a college graduate, now it is closer to one out of six. Over half of all college-educated women work after marriage. Although a technical bachelor's degree is most marketable, a liberal arts degree plus a technically oriented master's degree could equip people for some of the new careers that call for broad general knowledge in economics, financial planning, resource management, and general business management. College graduates will continue to be less likely to be unemployed (though they may be underemployed) and more likely to hold the highest paying professional and managerial positions.

8. *"High Tech."* By 1995, no more than one out of eight jobs will be high technology. However, it will be necessary to be computer literate even if you work in a nontechnical job.

9. *Global Competition*. In 1900, the Western world accounted for 30 percent of the world population. Presently, the United States's population accounts for 15 percent. A decade ago the United States was generating 75 percent of the world's technology. Now the United States shares about 50 percent. Even China, with over 20 percent of the world population, expects to be at the leading edge of every technology by the end of the century. Perhaps half of the new scientists and engineers will be in developing countries (and many will obtain their training in the United States).

10. *Temporary Agencies*. In the last decade, more employers have turned to temporary office help for both clerical and professional workers.

11. *Two-Income Families*. In 1973, males 25 years old and over who worked full time earned $469 weekly in 1980 dollars. By 1984, a decade later, their earnings had declined 10 percent to $421 weekly. Logically, one would assume that declining income would signal a declining standard of living. This has not been the case. Rather, American families have opted to have the wife work outside the home. As male incomes dropped over the decade, more and more women joined the work force. Additionally, society has begun to accept the concept of "working women."

12. *The Changing Economy*. Global competition, two-income families, and older people remaining in the work force have already been mentioned. However, the corporate world is changing its structure. What was once a hierarchy where young professionals could look forward to "climbing the ladder" at the same company for the rest of their lives is becoming an unstable job market. Middle management is being reduced. Each year, large companies change their organizations to be-

come more competitive and more productive. Each year, several hundred thousand workers lose their jobs because of import competition. According to the United States Office of Technology Assessments, between 1979 and 1984 11.4 million workers lost jobs due to plant closings and layoffs.

Other Cultural Customs

Other economic, social, and cultural customs present possible obstacles to opportunities. Black and Hispanic women are more likely to be living without a husband, have more dependents, a shorter life span, and lower education, and are more likely to be unemployed or underemployed. Asian and Asian-Pacific women (Philippine, Japanese, Chinese, Vietnamese, Thai, Cambodian, Hawaiian, Samoan) are likely to be part of a family where tradition is very strong and women are not taught to voice their opinions. It is harder for them to learn to assert themselves in this society where some assertiveness is necessary for success.

Cultural biases

Additional conditions that limit opportunity include living in a rural area with few job options, lack of transportation, being a former prisoner, or being a former mental patient. Anyone possessing these identities needs to strengthen his or her self-confidence and skills, and focus on a specific job target.

Implications

1. How do all these social and cultural changes affect you? Basically your expectations about your future are shaped by your early socialization. You might look back at Super's theory in Chapter 3. Work and life satisfactions depend on the extent to which you have found or can find adequate opportunities to use and develop your abilities, interests, personality traits, and values. Opportunities can be found through family, childhood play, school experiences, and early work activities. But opportunity is not equally distributed throughout the society. As this chapter has illustrated, job opportunities may be limited by sex stereotyping, by educational requirements, by discrimination, or by the changing economy. With changing perceptions about sex stereotyping in occupations, there is more encouragement for men and women to train for the type of career that best suits their personalities.

2. As longevity increases, there should be more jobs related to serving senior citizens. People who remain healthy and live longer may change careers more than five times during their lifetime. Your most prosperous time may be after age 50. Colonel Sanders started Kentucky Fried Chicken after he was 50; Armand Hammer became an oil czar (Occidental Petroleum) after he was 60. At the same time, the "greying of America" will reduce the market for competitive sports-related merchandise for a while because it's always been younger people who have been involved in such sports. Walking shoes may become more popular

than running shoes. Finally, the younger people coming into the job market will find more opportunities as the older generation begins to retire.

3. High technology means that new jobs will be created for those who have the math and science background; also, jobs will be improved and enhanced for many who do not possess high tech skills. The printer of yesterday can complete many more projects using computer graphics than anyone could have imagined 20 years ago. However, technology will make some jobs obsolete. There are already computers that can listen to voices in a courtroom and print out a transcript of multiple voices immediately. Once such technology becomes less costly, fewer court reporters will be needed. There are word processors that are being designed specifically for radiologists who must review x-rays and make immediate reports. Such technology can produce a precise 150-word summary without misspelling a word (such as "lymphadenopathy") on the basis of a few trigger phrases in a few minutes. Such a system only costs $22,000 now and may reduce the number of medical transcribers in the future. Remember that high technology will only account for less than ten percent of jobs. Services related to technological jobs will involve, at most, an additional 20 percent of jobs. Meanwhile, as Table 5.7 shows, hundreds of thousands of entry level ("low tech") jobs will continue to have openings in every community. Traditionally, custodians, cashiers, and sales clerks have high turnover.

   Because you are reading this book, you are preparing for the career that best fits your personality. Thus, you won't get stuck in just any job that happens to be available. Hopefully you will look at the jobs that are most available that will allow you to maximize your values, interests, and skills and review present careers with the future in mind.

4. Global competition can mean possibilities for you with an American firm in Japan, China, or Indonesia. These locations are called the Pacific Rim. Now is the time to learn a foreign language and think about working in the Pacific Rim for a while. As the newspaper article below suggests, global competition may also mean that you will work for a foreign employer in the United States.

> The British are coming. And so are the Swedes, the Japanese, the Italians and retailers from dozens of other countries.
>
> Foreign specialty stores are invading America's malls and fashion avenues in record numbers. At least 89 international retailers have set up shop in the United States—most during the past five years—and 32 have opened or announced store openings in the past 12 months.
>
> Most of the largest chains appear to be flourishing in this country. Laura Ashley, which carries fine lace clothing and home fashions, in April reported annual sales of $279.6 million. At the time, company officials announced plans to operate a store in every U.S. city with a population of 1 million or more.
>
> Benetton, with 4,000 licensed stores in 50 countries—including 700 in the Unit-

ed States—is the most ubiquitous international retailer. Known as the McDonald's of retailing, it racked up more than $1 billion in sales last year. (1986–7)

By Denise L. Smith
Orlando Sentinel

5. Temporary Employment Agencies. In addition to the secretarial and clerical professionals that traditionally have been available on a contract basis, today's "temps" work in such areas as accounting, health care, telemarketing, paralegal, and computers. There are also technical service contracting firms, often known as job shops, that place a range of engineering and computer professionals as well as technicians and draftsmen. With the new trend in temporary employment, many people will find themselves working for an employee leasing firm. The firm sets wages, offers benefits, incentives, and raises even though the employee may work at one or several other companies.

6. In an attempt to attain and maintain a high standard of living, many Americans are marrying later, having fewer or no children, and both husband and wife are working outside the home.

In choosing college majors students put top priority on a major that will lead to a good paying job, often disregarding their feelings or aptitude for the work itself.

Trends—Moving into the Twenty-First Century

It helps to have a picture of tomorrow's opportunities when defining a reasonable job target. For example, experts are suggesting that now is not the time to prepare for a lifelong job in a factory assembling auto parts. Such positions are predicted to be phased out in the next twenty years, with computerized robots taking over such tasks in the future; as a matter of fact, 70 percent of General Motors employees today work at jobs other than assembly.

Tomorrow's opportunities

The so-called Third Wave or Information Society, will accelerate faster than other ages. Some observers say that within a decade or two, the sum of all human knowledge will have doubled. In fact, approximately 90 percent of all scientific knowledge has been generated in the last 30 years AND 90 percent of all scientists who have ever lived are alive today! The development of the computer is the greatest indicator of the arrival of the new age. Computers are used for everything from data processing to product design and manufacturing. In an increasingly white-collar work world, computer-based record-keeping, report-writing, decision-analysis, and communication networks have emerged. Most of the largest corporations have begun to adopt these systems. Furthermore, automated telecommunications (as in telemarketing, teleconferencing, telepolling, instant tellers) are becoming commonplace.

The Information Society

Getting the right skills and education now will give you an advantage tomorrow. There is a great fear among employers that jobs will be impossible to fill until enough workers learn the needed skills. There appears to be no shortage of jobs being created. Twenty-one million new jobs were created in the last decade. Currently, there are an additional 4 million jobs advertised but unfilled. Over 80 percent of jobs need some post-secondary education. Computer literacy along with strong reading and writing skills will open up job possibilities for people. Meanwhile, the Bureau of Labor Statistics has made some predictions for 1990 based on projected demands for products and services, advances in technology, and changes in business practices. Service occupations are expected to grow the fastest, between 23 percent and 30 percent during the 1980s. These include jobs in food, health, maintenance, personal, and protective services.

Growth Areas

Eighty percent of new managerial positions will be in service industries. In actuality, 70 percent of the United States workforce is employed in the service sector. The following list of occupations are a cross-section of some of the growth areas in the United States:

Health services. Demand will be especially great for primary-care workers such as nurse practitioners, nutrition counselors, and gerontological social workers.

Hotel management and recreation. This category includes restaurants, resorts and travel, as well as opportunities in conference planning.

Food service. Managers and chefs will be in demand for all those restaurants and hotel kitchens, as well as for food processing plants and labs.

Engineering. In-demand specialties will be as diverse as robotics, aviation and aerospace, and waste management.

Basic science. Look at molecular biology, chemistry, and optics.

Computers. Opportunities will continue strong in design, engineering, programming, and maintenance.

Business services. Accounting, statistical analysis, and payroll management.

Human resources or personnel. This includes job evaluation, hiring and firing, benefit planning, and training.

Financial services. Financial planning and portfolio management.

Teaching. Demand is growing in primary and elementary grades to serve the children of the baby-boom generation, and in certain specialties: math, sciences, engineering, computer operations, and foreign languages, such as Russian and Japanese.

Maintenance and repair. Somebody's got to take care of all the equipment that will keep tomorrow's world running.

Artistic: writers, entertainers, party planners, painters, and advertisers will have good prospects but must be entrepreneurial types.

Furthermore, demand for computer service technicians should expand 93–112 percent, systems analysts 68–80 percent, and legal assistants 109–139 percent. Other expanding areas not even reported by the Bureau include laser technicians and jobs related to medical technology, biochemistry, biogenetics, energy storage, resource exploration, the space shuttle, and artificial intelligence. For specific predictions, see tables 5.6, 5.7, 5.10, 5.12, 5.13, 5.14, 5.15, and 5.16 at the end of this chapter. The best locations for jobs are listed on table 5.12.

Flexibility

More important than knowing what jobs will be open is having the ability to adapt to this changing world of work. Sixty percent of the jobs available by the year 2000 are yet to be created. Furthermore it is estimated that people will have three to five careers during their lifetime. Thus they will need to seek out new training opportunities a number of times. It has been estimated that up to 80 percent of a worker's development occurs on the job, and only 10 percent comes through formal continuing education courses. A general education is important to provide flexibility, as is computer literacy, competency in mathematics, science, and oral and written communication skills. Since information is accumulating at such a fast pace, it is also useful to be able to know how to retrieve and manage information and see the common threads and patterns in the information.

"On-going educational requirements"

As many avenues for promotion will involve managerial-level openings, information management and interpersonal communication skills will be especially important abilities to possess. However, there will be stiff competition for these positions from the "baby boom" population, which will equal one-third of the entire population by 1990. This is the generation that increased the percentages of college-educated in the general population. They are finding that in order to compete for the "best" jobs, they need to commit to lifelong continuing education to bolster job skills or prepare for a change in careers. Engineers, computer scientists, and others in fast-changing technical fields are constantly pressured to update their knowledge. According to one estimate, an engineer's knowledge either becomes obsolete or is incorporated into computers every ten years. Remember, 90 percent of all scientific knowledge has been generated in the last 30 years. This knowledge will again double in the next 10–15 years!

"Life-long Learning"

Twenty-three million Americans—ten million more than in 1970—are involved in continuing education programs and more than two-thirds of them take job related courses (*US News & World Report,* March 19, 1984, p. 51).

Although the job market may seem as if it's becoming totally technical and computerized, businesses still need clerical support services, public relations, technical and advertising copywriters, personnel experts, and sales and marketing staff. Some fields have always been difficult to enter, yet some people have managed to get jobs in them. Thus, it isn't absolutely necessary to prepare only for those areas most likely to have openings. In fact, as will be discussed in job search strategy considerations, the best direction to follow might rather be to head towards what you really want to do. The key is *desire*. Desire plus talent and perseverance get people jobs in even the tightest job markets.

The Nontechnical Person

Career opportunities for the Liberal Arts graduate

One might ask what kind of jobs are available to people who don't train for the technical job market. The Department of Labor indicates that already more than 60 percent of the work force is composed of computer programmers, teachers, accountants, stock brokers, secretaries, and technicians. The majority of people who graduate with a liberal arts degree do not find employment in fields related to their majors (i.e., history majors do not necessarily become historians). For example: In a survey of 1,072 humanities majors (with a 51 percent return) over 11 percent became attorneys, 10 percent sales representatives and buyers, 9.8 percent administrators or managers, 5.1 percent clerks and tellers, and 4.2 percent retail clerks and waiters, and the remaining replies represented a variety of miscellaneous occupations (Trzyna 1980). In addition, teachers with liberal arts degrees have moved into a variety of alternate careers. Such occupations include: administrative assistants, association executives, building managers, cable TV program coordinators, communication experts, computer sales reps, employment agency staffers, educational brokers, financial planners, fitness program coordinators, insurance agents, parenting workshop leaders, personnel and training coordinators, public relations experts, purchasing agents, relocations managers, researchers (for city planning, developers, government proposals, stock brokers), technical writers, wastewater managers, as well as business owners. By and large, liberal arts graduates obtain management training or other entry-level positions in industry and work their way up.

On-the-job training

Furthermore, college is no longer a four-year-degree process. More and more people are working full-time and attending college part-time. Many companies are paying tuition costs for their employees and encouraging them to attend college to learn technical skills. Additionally, many companies have in-house educational programs to help employees master new skills and upgrade old skills. As mentioned previously, most continuing education occurs on the job.

Careers that do not require a degree

Opportunities in small business

In case you aren't interested in a job that requires a degree, there will always be a need in society for people selling merchandise, running businesses, maintaining homes, doing the laundry, caring for children, working in restaurants, attending to health and fitness needs, and working in a variety of trades which may or may not require further training beyond high school. In fact, many of these jobs will increase due to a sociological change mentioned previously in this chapter: the increase in the number of two-income households. People don't often regard the above mentioned jobs as careers. But consider the fact that more jobs are created by small businesses than by large corporations. During the 1970s, 9.6 million jobs were generated by firms with fewer than 20 employees; in contrast, the largest 1000 firms created only 75,000 jobs. Between 1981 and 1985, small firms created 14.2 million new jobs. If you want variety, responsibility and are results-oriented, a small business might be the place you'll want to work. All of the above jobs can be considered careers if you are using your best talents in them and if you feel energized by the work that you do.

Summary

This chapter has explored social and cultural considerations, highlighted future trends, indicated where the general population is employed, and discussed the value of a liberal arts degree, as well as indicated that many companies have comprehensive training programs to supplement formal education. In addition, job trends and salary information are in the tables at the end of this chapter.

THE UNKNOWN FUTURE—BEWARE OF ACCEPTING ALL PREDICTIONS AS FACT:
   More than two decades ago—on Feb. 16, 1964, to be exact—we ran the following item, titled "No Housework": "Twenty years from now, claims the American Home Economics Association, the average U.S. housewife will lead a life without housework. Plastic crockery will be disposed of after each meal. Clothing will be made of disposable paper. Homes will be electronically dusted and deodorized. Madame will do little or no cleaning, will have more time for children, leisure, study and husband.

THE FUTURE IS ONLY PARTIALLY PREDICTABLE
But It's a Good Idea to be Prepared!!

?? Written Exercises

It is our hope that you will develop your own personal objective, believe in yourself, acknowledge stereotypes in occupations, and develop a strategy to enter the career of your choice. Whether or not you have consciously or directly experienced stereotype barriers to employment, we would like you to use the following written exercises to reflect upon your personal, social, and cultural opinions and biases. Exercise 5.1 helps you to become aware of how you could react to events and people that may be different from those to which you are accustomed. Exercise 5.2 lists fifteen questions about things that tend to be common knowledge to people of different ethnic and age groups. Lack of knowledge about these questions suggests a lack of exposure to a variety of ethnic groups. Exercise 5.3 asks you to list your own ideas about stereotypes. Be spontaneous with your answers; do not censor because you may suspect that your answers are only partially true. Exercise 5.4 asks you to list the advantages and disadvantages of belonging to several distinct groups. Exercise 5.5 helps you to become aware of your amount of association with different groups of people. The more difficult for you to identify names of people the less likely that you have associated with such people. Stereotypes tend to develop when there is a lack of interaction between groups. Exercise 5.6 asks you to think about how stereotypes about you would affect your ability to get a job.

5.1
First Impressions

What are your first impressions about each of the following situations?

1. You are applying for a job. A male receptionist ushers you into an office where you are greeted by a female vice-president who will conduct the interview.
2. You are flying to Chicago. A male flight attendant welcomes you aboard the plane and later a female voice says, "This is your captain speaking."
3. You go to enroll your four-year-old in a nearby nursery school and discover that all three teachers at the school are males.
4. You are introduced to a new couple in the neighborhood and discover that the man stays home all day with two small children while the wife is out working.
5. You live in a neighborhood which is multi-ethnic.
6. You have a conference with your child's teacher who grew up in Vietnam.
7. You are in a class with other students whose native language is different from yours.
8. You move into an apartment and your neighbors are homosexual.
9. You are temporarily disabled and must use a wheel chair.
10. You arrive at your new dentist's office and find she has green and orange spiked hair.
11. You are referred to a hospital known for excellence in surgery and your team of doctors are all Hispanic.
12. You go to court and find you have an all Black jury.
13. You go to a job interview and find yourself faced with a panel of older Caucasian men.
14. You find yourself in a statistics class where all the other students are Asian-Americans.

5.2
Ethnic Intelligence Test

How many answers do you know? (answers on page 87)

1. "Nochebuena" refers to (a) dark, sweet sugar (b) Christmas Eve (c) a clear, starry night (d) "Goodbye"?

2. "Mariachi" refers to (a) a musical instrument (b) a hopping beetle (c) the first president of Mexico (d) a musical group?
3. A "koto" is (a) an article of clothing (b) one of the movements in karate (c) an endearing term for "grandfather" (d) a musical instrument?
4. The principal ingredient of menudo is (a) tripe (b) chorizo (c) corn (d) chicken?
5. "Juneteenth" is (a) a mint julip mixed with scotch (b) a Black term for Flag Day (c) the day slaves were freed in the U.S.A. (d) ghetto slang for the tenth day of June?
6. A "canton" or "chante" refers to (a) a song (b) a home (c) a kind of food (d) a dance?
7. Joseph was the head of which tribe (a) Hoopa (b) Hopi (c) Clatsop (d) Nez Perce?
8. Which name is out of place (a) Muhamed Ali (b) Ali Akbar Khan (c) Kareem Abdul-Jabbar (d) Malcolm X?
9. Chop suey originated in (a) Formosa (b) Hong Kong (c) California (d) Tokyo?
10. "Mano" is a slang term for (a) a pickpocket (b) a close friend (c) "all man" or masculine (d) tomorrow?
11. Sashimi refers to (a) a traditional dance (b) a kind of fish (c) the ink used in scroll painting (d) a major religious holiday?
12. A "mensche" is (a) a real human being (b) an exotic fruit (c) a tool (d) a place of residence?
13. A "Homeboy is (a) one of us (b) comfortable at home (c) Mamma's Boy (d) Couch Potatoe's Cousin?
14. Yom Kipper is (a) a fish (b) a young boy (c) a game (d) a holiday?

5.3
Sex Roles Questionnaire
Complete these sentences:

a. Women are happiest in careers when _____.

b. Men are happiest in careers when _____.

c. The most difficult emotion for a man to display is _____.

d. The most difficult emotion for a woman to display is _____.

e. Women tend to be better than men at _____.

f. Men tend to be better at _____.

g. Men get depressed about _____.

h. Women get depressed about _____.

i. Men are most likely to compete over _____.

j. Women are most likely to compete over _____.

k. Men tend to get angry about _____.

l. Women tend to get angry about _____.

m. As a man/woman I was always taught to _____.

n. Men feel pressured on the job when _____.

o. Women feel pressured on the job when _____.

5.4
Pros and Cons
List advantages and disadvantages of being any of the following:

a. Female
   Advantage:
   Disadvantage:
b. Male
   Advantage:
   Disadvantage:
c. Caucausian
   Advantage:
   Disadvantage:
d. Black American
   Advantage:
   Disadvantage:

e. Hispanic American
   Advantage:
   Disadvantage:
f. Asian American
   Advantage:
   Disadvantage:
g. Native American
   Advantage:
   Disadvantage:

5.5
Famous People
For each of the groups listed above, name five famous people (may be currently living or an historical character).

5.6
What About You
How do you think sex, race, or physical disability could affect your ability to get a job? Did you discover anything about your stereotypes of people? Please summarize.

Summary—Write a Brief Paragraph
Answering These Questions:

What did you learn about yourself? How does this knowledge relate to your career/life planning? How do you feel?

_____
_____
_____
_____
_____
_____
_____
_____
_____
_____

Answers to Exercise 5.2

1. b	6. b	11. b
2. d	7. d	12. a
3. d	8. b	13. a
4. a	9. c	14. d
5. c	10. b	

Table 5.5
Gender Equity Definitions

Sex role: Social behavior that is prescribed and defined by tradition, as contrasted with actual biological differences.

Sexism: Any attitude, action, or institution that subordinates, or assigns roles to, a person or group because of their sex. Sexism may be individual, cultural, or institutional; intentional or unintentional; effected by omission or commission.

Sex discrimination: Sexist practices, policies, or procedures that are specifically prohibited by law; any action which limits or denies a person or group of persons opportunities, privileges, roles, or rewards on the basis of their sex.

Sex bias: An attitude or behavior which reflects adversely upon a person or group because of sex, but which may not be covered under present legislation; behavior resulting from the assumption that one sex is superior to the other.

Sex stereotyping: Attributing behaviors, abilities, interests, values, and roles to a person or group of persons on the basis of their sex.

Sex fair: Practices and behaviors that treat males and females similarly; may imply separate but equal.

Sex affirmative: Refers to programs, policies, or procedures that attempt to overcome the effects of past sex discrimination, bias, and/or stereotyping.

Feminist: Any person (male or female) who believes that women should have political, economic, and social rights equal to those of men.

Nontraditional job: A man in an area of work that has typically 80 percent or more female population or a woman in an area of work that has typically 80 percent or more males employed; e.g., nursing has only 5 percent males employed, while construction work has only 1 percent women employed.

Pay inequity: Occupations employing a majority of male workers paying more than occupations employing a majority of female workers.

Table 5.6
Fastest Growing Occupations, 1986–2000, Moderate Alternative
(Numbers in thousands)

Occupation	Employment		Change in Employment, 1986–2000		Percent of Total Job Growth, 1986–2000
	1986	Projected, 2000	Number	Percent	
Paralegal personnel	61	125	64	103.7	.3
Medical assistants	132	251	119	90.4	.6
Physical therapists	61	115	53	87.5	.2
Physical and corrective therapy assistants and aides	36	65	29	81.6	.1
Data processing equipment repairers	69	125	56	80.4	.3
Home health aides	138	249	111	80.1	.5
Podiatrists	13	23	10	77.2	0
Computer systems analysts, electronic data processing	331	582	251	75.6	1.2
Medical records technicians	40	70	30	75.0	.1
Employment interviewers, private or public employment service	75	129	54	71.2	.3
Computer programmers	479	813	335	69.9	1.6
Radiologic technologists and technicians	115	190	75	64.7	.3
Dental hygienists	87	141	54	62.6	.3
Dental assistants	155	244	88	57.0	.4
Physician assistants	26	41	15	56.7	.1
Operations and systems researchers	38	59	21	54.1	.1
Occupational therapists	29	45	15	52.2	.1
Peripheral electronic data processing equipment operators	46	70	24	50.8	.1
Data entry keyers, composing	29	43	15	50.8	.1
Optometrists	37	55	18	49.2	.1

The Bureau of Labor Statistics predicts the labor force will grow at only half the rate experienced in the mid-1970s, while job opportunities will grow by more than a million a year, topping 122 million by 1995. There are now 106.5 million jobs.

Out of the fastest growing occupations, only six will require a baccalaureate degree for job entry, while most of the other jobs will require some form of post-secondary education. The associate degree is becoming the preferred entry ticket for a whole host of midrange occupations.

Table 5.7
Occupations with the Largest Job Growth, 1986–2000, Moderate Alternative
(Numbers in thousands)

Occupation	Employment		Change in Employment, 1986–2000		Percent of Total Job Growth, 1986–2000
	1986	Projected, 2000	Number	Percent	
Salespersons, retail	3,579	4,780	1,201	33.5	5.6
Waiters and waitresses	1,702	2,454	752	44.2	3.5
Registered nurses	1,406	2,018	612	43.6	2.9
Janitors and cleaners, including maids and housekeeping cleaners	2,676	3,280	604	22.6	2.8
General managers and top executives	2,383	2,965	582	24.4	2.7
Cashiers	2,165	2,740	575	26.5	2.7
Truck drivers, light and heavy	2,211	2,736	525	23.8	2.5
General office clerks	2,361	2,824	462	19.6	2.2
Food counter, fountain, and related workers	1,500	1,949	449	29.9	2.1
Nursing aides, orderlies, and attendants	1,224	1,658	433	35.4	2.0
Secretaries	3,234	3,658	424	13.1	2.0
Guards	794	1,777	383	48.3	1.8
Accountants and auditors	945	1,322	376	39.8	1.8
Computer programmers	479	813	335	69.9	1.6
Food preparation workers	949	1,273	324	34.2	1.5
Teachers, kindergarten and elementary	1,527	1,826	299	19.6	1.4
Receptionists and information clerks	682	964	282	41.4	1.3
Computer systems analysts, electronic data processing	331	582	251	75.6	1.2
Cooks, restaurant	520	759	240	46.2	1.1
Licensed practical nurses	631	869	238	37.7	1.1
Gardeners and groundskeepers, except farm	767	1,005	238	31.1	1.1
Maintenance repairers, general utility	1,039	1,270	232	22.3	1.1
Stock clerks, sales floor	1,087	1,312	225	20.7	1.0
First-line supervisors and managers	956	1,161	205	21.4	1.0
Dining room, cafeteria attendants, and barroom helpers	433	631	197	45.6	.9
Electrical and electronics engineers	401	592	192	47.8	.9
Lawyers	527	718	191	36.3	.9

Source: Silvestri and Lukasiewicz (1987); Bureau of Labor Statistics, 1986.

Table 5.8
Median weekly earnings of wage and salary workers who usually work full time by detailed (3-digit census code) in selected occupation and sex, annual averages
1986
Numbers in thousands

Occupation	Both sexes		Men		Women	
	Number of workers	Median weekly earnings	Number of workers	Median weekly earnings	Number of workers	Median weekly earnings
TOTAL	78,727	$358	46,233	419	32,494	$290
Managerial and Professional Specialty Occupations	20,095	505	11,333	608	8,762	414
1. Executive, administrative, and managerial occupations	9,777	511	5,980	620	5,797	395
Administrators and officials, public administration	434	513	259	617	176	414
Financial managers	396	584	245	703	150	458
Personnel and labor relations managers	109	621	57	759	52	474
Managers, marketing, advertising, and public relations	421	680	320	751	101	470
Manager, properties and real estate ...	233	375	109	407	124	343
Management-related occupations	3,004	474	1,592	565	1,412	390
Accountants and auditors	1,083	478	589	554	493	398
Underwriters, and Other financial officers	600	500	321	617	279	394
Management analysts	102	567	63	673	40	(1)
Personnel, training, and labor relations specialists	327	485	148	606	179	411
Purchasing agents and buyers, farm products	11	(1)	11	(1)	-	-
Buyers, wholesale and retail trade, except farm products	177	397	79	501	98	314
2. Professional Specialty Occupations	10,317	500	5,353	599	4,965	428
Engineers, architects, and surveyors ..	1,751	676	1,636	685	115	551
Architects	87	577	77	592	10	(1)
Engineers	1,644	682	1,540	691	104	580
Mathematical and computer scientists .	588	628	375	696	213	521
Computer systems analysts and scientists	337	631	219	687	118	537
Operations and systems researchers and analysts	203	617	127	695	77	511
Natural scientists	339	570	265	603	74	471
Chemists, except biochemists	116	601	92	624	24	(1)
Biological and life scientists	59	503	37	(1)	22	(1)
Health diagnosing occupations	254	653	188	722	66	499
Physicians	219	653	160	728	59	505
Dentists	13	(1)	11	(1)	2	(1)
Veterinarians	14	(1)	11	(1)	3	(1)
Health assessment and treating occupations	1,464	456	243	497	1,220	449
Registered nurses	1,068	460	84	490	984	458
Pharmacists	109	607	71	613	38	(1)

NOTE: Please notice the ratio of men to women in each occupation and the difference between their salaries.

Table 5.8 (continued)
1986
Numbers in thousands

Occupation	Both sexes		Men		Women	
	Number of workers	Median weekly earnings	Number of workers	Median weekly earnings	Number of workers	Median weekly earnings
Dietitians	53	336	3	(1)	50	342
Therapists	195	404	58	415	136	400
Inhalation therapists	64	386	28	(1)	36	(1)
Occupational therapists	19	(1)	1	(1)	18	(1)
Physical therapists	44	(1)	13	(1)	30	(1)
Physicians' assistants	39	(1)	27	(1)	12	(1)
Teachers, college and university	443	600	322	656	122	479
Counselors, educational and vocational	146	494	72	535	74	471
Librarians, archivists, and curators . . .	150	425	27	(1)	123	410
Social scientists and urban planners . . .	229	569	131	683	98	470
Economists	96	704	59	794	37	(1)
Psychologists	100	491	51	581	49	(1)
Social, recreation, and religious workers	750	389	413	420	337	350
Lawyers and judges	342	767	256	812	85	609
Writers, artists, entertainers, and athletes	979	455	589	504	390	374
Designers	292	490	182	574	110	350
Photographers	59	392	42	(1)	17	(1)
Editors	199	425	107	480	92	373
Public relations specialists	130	518	67	698	63	440
Technical, Sales, and Administrative Support Occupations	24,060	320	8,977	437	15,083	282
1. Technicians and related support occupations	2,821	416	1,597	490	1,224	343
Health technologists and technicians . .	852	328	167	405	685	317
Clinical laboratory technologists and technicians	239	388	68	436	170	371
Licensed practical nurses	281	300	9	(1)	272	299
Engineering and related technologists and technicians	843	447	699	471	144	356
Electrical and electronic technicians .	303	477	265	493	38	(1)
Industrial engineering technicians . . .	4	(1)	4	(1)	0	(1)
Mechanical engineering technicians . .	9	(1)	9	(1)	-	-
Engineering technicians, n.e.c.	205	458	157	486	49	(1)
Drafting occupations	248	412	198	431	50	351
2. Sales occupations	7,395	351	4,373	447	3,021	239
Supervisors and proprietors	2,103	392	1,436	460	667	282
Sales representatives, finance and business services	1,388	453	789	519	599	360
Insurance sales	358	418	225	500	133	352
Real estate sales	326	457	145	518	181	389
Securities and financial services sales .	215	608	164	740	52	423
Sales workers, retail and personal services	2,660	215	1,122	301	1,538	183
3. Administrative support occupations, including clerical	13,844	300	3,006	403	10,838	284
Supervisors, administrative support . . .	709	424	296	521	413	385

Table 5.8 (continued)
1986
Numbers in thousands

Occupation	Both sexes		Men		Women	
	Number of workers	Median weekly earnings	Number of workers	Median weekly earnings	Number of workers	Median weekly earnings
Computer operators	716	318	234	396	482	296
Secretaries, stenographers, and typists .	3,893	287	65	322	3,828	286
Transportation ticket and reservation agents	99	420	29	(1)	70	366
Receptionists	459	242	9	(1)	450	242
Mail carriers, postal service	280	477	229	482	51	429
Service Occupations	8,061	223	3,987	284	4,074	191
1. Private household occupations	334	121	14	(1)	320	119
2. Protective service occupations	1,589	392	1,433	402	156	292
Supervisors, protective service occupations	165	516	158	528	8	(1)
Supervisors, firefighting and fire prevention	39	(1)	39	(1)	0	(1)
Supervisors, police and detectives	89	558	83	575	5	(1)
Supervisors, guards	37	(1)	36	(1)	2	(1)
Firefighting and fire prevention occupations	222	455	217	461	4	(1)
Police and detectives	648	431	579	443	69	350
3. Service occupations, except protective and household	6,138	209	2,540	39	3,598	195
4. Health, service occupations	1,277	216	145	252	1,132	213
Dental assistants	112	243	-	-	112	243
Health aides, except nursing	254	242	43	(1)	212	241
Nursing aides, orderlies, and attendants	910	206	102	253	808	202
5. Cleaning and building service occupations, except household	1,883	238	1,236	266	647	197
6. Personal service occupations	691	212	187	255	504	203
Precision Production, Craft, and Repair Occupations	10,851	408	9,973	418	878	277
1. Mechanics and repairers	3,723	414	3,588	413	136	431
Supervisors, mechanics, and repairers .	219	524	199	523	20	(1)
Mechanics and repairers, except supervisors	3,504	408	3,388	408	116	420
Vehicle and mobile equipment mechanics and repairers	1,444	375	1,426	375	19	(1)
Automobile mechanics	658	324	647	326	10	(1)
Bus truck, and stationary engine mechanics	310	402	307	402	3	(1)
Aircraft engine mechanics	96	505	94	508	3	(1)
2. Construction trades	3,469	401	3,413	401	56	333
Supervisors, construction occupations .	420	500	413	300	6	(1)

Data not shown where base is less than 50,000.
Salary levels are somewhat misleading because they may have fewer workers earning at higher levels. For example, if 11 people earn under $10,000 and 9 people earn over $100,000, the median salary is $10,000.

Table 5.9
1987 Salary Estimates
(Most of these salaries are averages, not entry level unless otherwise stated.)

ACCOUNTANT/AUDITOR

	Public	*Corporate* (Financial)
Manager, large firm	$38,000–$59,000*	$35,000–$51,000*
Entry, large firm	20,500–23,000*	18,500–21,000*

*Subtract .5% if not a CPA; add 10% for a graduate degree.
Source: Robert Half International, Inc.

ADVERTISING
Agencies

Account Dept Head/Sup	$45,000
Account Rep	32,300
Copywriter	27,800

Source: Corporate Marketing/Advertising

	Male	*Female*
Advertising Manager	45,900	32,000
Sales Promotion Manager	50,000	40,000

Source: Adweek Magazine, May 18, 1987

ARCHITECT

Entry level with BA	$18,500
Level IV: 2 yrs at Level III (Licensed)	28,590
Chief Architect	52,500

Source: Detrich Associates, Phoenixville, PA

ATTORNEY
Corporate

Chief Legal Officer	$141,457
Non-Supervisory	60,850
Legal Administrator	45,268
Paralegal Assistant	29,225

Legal Assistant starts at $15,000; federal government average: $27,700
1986 Career Resources Digest
Source: Altman & Well, Inc., Haverford, PA

BANKER/FINANCIAL OFFICER

By Bank Assets:	*Up to $300 Million*	*Over $300 Million*
Senior Loan Officer	$34,500–46,000	$38,000–57,000
Commercial Lender	26,000–39,000	31,000–42,000
Branch Manager	22,000–34,000	28,500–36,500
Trust Officer	25,000–35,000	32,000–42,000

Source: Robert Half International, Inc.

BROADCASTING (TV & RADIO)

	Male	*Female*
News Anchor	$35,180	$14,000
Reporter	19,300	14,000
Operations Manager	35,000	N/A
Program Director	33,000	19,200
News Director	43,500	16,450
Sales Account Executive	36,939	20,000

(Median salaries for stations nationwide; salaries at network affiliate and in major markets are much higher.)
Source: Robert Half International, Inc.

Table 5.9 (continued)

CHEMIST

(9 years after BS)	BS	MS	PhD
Male	31,009	32,980	41,550
Female	29,690	31,450	40,755

Source: American Chemical Society *Copyright* 1987

COMPUTER SPECIALIST

	Years of Experience		
Non-Management	2+	5+	7+
Systems (Software) Programmer	33,000	38,000	42,000
Senior Analyst/Project Leader	33,000	37,700	42,000
Management (By size of system or staff)	*Small*	*Medium*	*Large*
Technical Services Manager	37,800	46,000	52,500
Sales			
Representative	48,000		
Manager	70,000		

Source: 1987 Souce Edp.

DENTIST

(Net after Expenses)	*Incorporated*	*Unincorporated*
General	$ 96,770	$ 62,663
Orthodontist	131,111	90,769

Source: Dental Management Magazine

EDUCATOR

	Public		*Private*	
College and University	*Male*	*Female*	*Male*	*Female*
Professor	45,610	41,020	51,200	43,330
Instructor	22,730	21,040	21,200	19,530

ENGINEER

Junior	28,040
Engineer or Assistant	30,900
Senior Engineer	49,520

Source: National Society of Professional Engineers

HOTEL MANAGEMENT By Size:

	1-99	*200-399*	*600-799*
General Manager (w/o Maintenance)	35,341	64,850	77,903
Front Office Manager	17,624	21,554	27,960
Controller	20,350	37,969	49,087
Executive Housekeeper	17,554	21,664	27,560
Sales/Marketing Director	22,375	43,576	53,012

Source: American Hotel & Motel Association

INSURANCE

Female Life Insurance Agent

Less than 3 Years	21,000
3-5 Years	30,000
6-10 Years	44,000

Source: NALU-LIMRA Survey of Producer Opinion

NURSE

Head Nurse	36,444
Staff Nurse	29,088
Average	25,000

Table 5.9 (continued)

NURSE *(continued)*

LVN	20,052
Surgical Tech	19,164

Source: U of Texas Medical Branch of Galveston

PERSONNEL (HRD) - LABOR RELATIONS

Top Corp HRD Management Executive	101,100
Employment and Recruiting Manager	41,900
Compensation Manager	48,200
Benefits Administrator	28,500
Labor Relations Supervisor	54,100

Source: ASPA/Jarsen, 1987

PHYSICIAN

General Practice/Family Medicine	77,900
Internal Medicine	101,000
Surgery	155,400
Pediatrics	77,100
Ob/Gyn	122,700
Psychiatry	88,600

Source: AMA

PUBLIC RELATIONS

	Male	*Female*
Executive or Sr. VP (Corp) (Top Pay)	85,000	60,000
Account Executive	35,500	30,500

Source: PR Reporter, Sept 14, 1987

SALES MANAGER

Manufacturing	50,400
Banking/Financial	42,000
Retail, Wholesale Sales	42,000
Utilities	44,100

Source: Administrative Management Society, Trevose, PA

SECURITY SALES

(Subject to fluctuation in stock market - upper range)

Institutional Broker	227,412
Retail Broker	97,100

Source: Securities Industry Association, 1986

TEACHER

Elementary	25,960
Secondary	27,283

Source: National Education Association

All sources were contacted by *Working Woman Magazine* for their Annual Salary Survey published January, 1988. Compiled by Richard S. Hollander.

Table 5.10
Estimated Average Starting Salaries
Class of 1985 & 1986

Bachelor's Degrees	1985 Starting Salary	1986 Starting Salary
Electrical engineering	$ 28,086	29,680
Metallurgy/material science	28,012	28,309
Mechanical engineering	28,004	29,636
Chemical engineering	27,827	29,254
Computer engineering	26,690	28,087
Physics	25,411	21,269
Packaging engineering	23,358	
Civil engineering	22,789	25,399
Mathematics	20,630	20,804
Financial administration	19,506	20,517
Accounting	19,262	21,037
Marketing/sales	19,157	20,809
General business administration	17,782	19,643
Social science	17,640	
Personnel administration	17,181	19,267
Education	17,082	17,074
Hotel, restaurant and institutional management	16,871	17,099
Agriculture natural resources	16,658	19,293/17,077
Communications	16,299	17,953
Arts & letters	15,124	16,975
Human ecology	14,827	16,499

Source: John D. Shingleton and L. Patrick Scheetz, *Recruiting Trends, 1984-86* Michigan State University, Placement Services, East Lansing, Mich. 48824.

Table 5.11
20 Best Bets

Job Title	Training Needed	Total Employed	Growth by 1995	Salary
Accountants/auditors	4 yrs. college	882,000	34.8%	$ 35,000
Computer operators	1-2 yrs. technical training	241,000	50.0	16,000
Computer programmers	varies: 1-2 yrs. technical training; 4 yrs. college	341,000	71.7	24,000+
Computer service technicians	1-2 yrs. technical training	55,000	56.0	22,350
Computer systems analysts	4 yrs college	254,000	68.7	28,500+
Cosmetologists	6 mos.-1 yr. cosmetology school	524,000	29.0	16,800
Dietitians	4 yrs. college	48,000	26.0	24,800
Electrical & electronics technicians	2 yrs. technical training	404,000	50.0	23,000
Engineers	4-8 yrs. college	1,331,000	36.0	30,000+
Flight attendants	Airline training school (some college preferred)	64,000	20.0	21,000
Food service & lodging managers	varies: on the job; technical training; 4 yrs. college	657,000	13.6	27,000
Lawyers	7 yrs. college	490,000	35.5	50,000
Medical assistants	1-2 yrs. technical training preferred	100,000	62.0	15,000
Paralegals	2-4 yrs. college	53,000	98.0	23,750
Physical therapists	4 yrs. college	58,000	42.0	23,000+
Physicians & surgeons	8-10 yrs. college	476,000	23.0	100,000
Registered nurses	2-4 yrs. college or hospital-based program	1,377,000	32.8	20,000+
Secretaries	varies: career or business school; jr. college; 4 yrs. college	2,797,000	9.6	19,500
Teachers, kindergarten & elementary	4 yrs. college	1,381,000	20.3	21,000
Travel agents	varies: travel school; jr. college; 4 yrs. college	72,000	43.9	17,000

Table 5.12
Best Locations to Find Jobs

THE FASTEST-GROWING JOB MARKETS	
METRO AREA	ANNUAL JOB GROWTH 1985–2010
1. NAPLES, FLA.	2.81%
2. FORT MYERS, FLA.	2.75
3. FORT PIERCE, FLA.	2.61
4. ORLANDO, FLA.	2.42
5. ATLANTIC CITY, N.J.	2.40
6. ANAHEIM-SANTA ANA, CAL.	2.37
7. LAS VEGAS, NEV.	2.36
8. WEST PALM BEACH-BOCA RATON—DELRAY BEACH, FLA.	2.33
9. FORT LAUDERDALE-HOLLYWOOD—POMPANO BEACH, FLA.	2.31
10. BRADENTON, FLA.	2.25
11. RENO, NEV.	2.22
12. OCALA, FLA.	2.13
13. PHOENIX, ARIZ.	2.11
14. SARASOTA, FLA.	2.09
15. GAINESVILLE, FLA.	2.08
16. BRYAN—COLLEGE STATION, TEX.	2.07
17. TUCSON, ARIZ.	2.07
18. BOULDER-LONGMONT, COLO.	2.06
19. PORTSMOUTH-DOVER-ROCHESTER, N.H.	2.04
20. SANTA ROSA-PETALUMA, CAL.	2.02
21. SANTA FE, N.M.	2.01
22. MONMOUTH-OCEAN, N.J.	2.01
23. OXNARD-VENTURA, CAL.	2.01
24. TALLAHASSEE, FLA.	2.00
25. BOISE CITY, IDA.	1.99
U.S. AVERAGE	1.22%

Source: National Planning Assn.

Table 5.12 (continued)

THE BIGGEST NEW-JOB MARKETS	
METRO AREA	**INCREASE IN JOBS 1985–2010 (thousands)**
1. LOS ANGELES-LONG BEACH, CAL.	1,399.4
2. WASHINGTON, D.C.	1,145.9
3. ANAHEIM-SANTA ANA, CAL.	978.4
4. HOUSTON, TEX.	957.2
5. ATLANTA, GA.	862.5
6. PHILADELPHIA, PA.	857.2
7. DALLAS, TEX.	849.8
8. BOSTON-LAWRENCE-SALEM-LOWELL-BROCKTON, MASS.	814.0
9. CHICAGO, ILL.	787.2
10. NEW YORK CITY	719.5
11. PHOENIX, ARIZ.	880.8
12. SAN DIEGO, CAL.	850.2
13. MINNEAPOLIS-ST. PAUL, MINN.	575.8
14. DENVER, COLO.	565.9
15. NASSAU-SUFFOLK, N.Y.	552.8
16. TAMPA-ST. PETERSBURG-CLEARWATER, FLA.	522.0
17. SAN JOSE, CAL.	502.5
18. SAN FRANCISCO, CAL.	466.0
19. BALTIMORE, MD.	465.2
20. SEATTLE, WA.	464.1
21. OAKLAND, CAL.	434.6
22. DETROIT, MICH.	433.7
23. MIAMI-HIALEAH, FLA.	412.8
24. FORT LAUDERDALE-HOLLYWOOD-POMPANO BEACH, FLA.	412.3
25. ORLANDO, FLA.	408.3
TOTAL, 25 METRO AREAS	17,318.1
U.S. TOTAL	42,977.2

Source: National Planning Assn.

Table 5.13
Fastest Growing Occupations Requiring a High School Diploma or Less

	PERCENT CHANGE 1984–95
MEDICAL ASSISTANTS	62
CORRECTION OFFICERS	35
NUMERICAL CONTROL MACHINE-TOOL OPERATORS, METAL AND PLASTIC	30
PLASTIC MOLDING MACHINE OPERATORS	30
CASHIERS	30
COOKS, RESTAURANT	30
NURSING AIDES, ORDERLIES, AND ATTENDANTS	29
SOCIAL WELFARE SERVICE AIDES	29
SWITCHBOARD OPERATORS	29
COMBINATION MACHINE TOOL SETTERS, METAL AND PLASTIC	29
BARTENDERS	28
HOSTS AND HOSTESSES, RESTAURANTS, LOUNGES, AND COFFEE SHOPS	28
PHOTOGRAPHIC PROCESS WORKERS, PRECISION	27
PHOTOGRAPHIC PROCESSING MACHINE OPERATORS	27
AMUSEMENT AND RECREATION ATTENDANTS	26

Source: Bureau of Labor Statistics, 1986

Table 5.14
Fastest Growing Occupations Requiring a Bachelor's Degree

	PERCENT CHANGE 1984–95
COMPUTER PROGRAMMERS	72
COMPUTER SYSTEMS ANALYSTS	69
ELECTRICAL AND ELECTRONICS ENGINEERS	53
PHYSICAL THERAPISTS	42
SECURITIES AND FINANCIAL SERVICES SALES WORKERS	39
LAWYERS	36
ACCOUNTANTS AND AUDITORS	35
MECHANICAL ENGINEERS	34
PUBLIC RELATIONS SPECIALISTS	32
OCCUPATIONAL THERAPISTS	31
AERONAUTICAL AND ASTRONAUTICAL ENGINEERS	30
INDUSTRIAL ENGINEERS	29
CHIROPRACTORS	29
ARCHITECTS	27
OPTOMETRISTS	27

Each of these top three will generate less than 100,000 new jobs between 1984–95—adding in replacement openings will raise total openings to 500,000–700,000.

Source: Bureau of Labor Statistics, 1986

Table 5.15
Service Workers Are Projected to Have Larger Job Gains Than Other Major Occupational Groups

	EMPLOYMENT GROWTH, 1984–95	
	THOU-SANDS	PERCENT DISTRI-BUTION
ALL OCCUPATIONS	15,919	100.0
SERVICE, EXCEPT PRIVATE HOUSEHOLD	3,328	20.9
PROFESSIONAL	2,773	17.4
EXECUTIVE, ADMINISTRATIVE, AND MANAGERIAL	2,488	15.6
SALES	2,220	13.9
ADMINISTRATIVE SUPPORT, INCLUDING CLERICAL	1,783	11.2
PRECISION PRODUCTION, CRAFT, AND REPAIR	1,425	9.0
OPERATORS, FABRICATORS, AND LABORERS	1,277	8.0
TECHNICIANS AND RELATED SUPPORT	913	5.7
FARMING, FORESTRY, AND FISHING	− 107	− .7
PRIVATE HOUSEHOLD	− 182	− 1.1

Source: Bureau of Labor Statistics, 1986

Table 5.16
Predicted New Jobs for the Year 2000

<hr>

What Jobs Should We Be Training Students For?

The *Monthly Labor Review** projects strong growth in health care, business services, and professional services. Occupations expected to grow at the fastest rate are computer service technician, legal assistant, computer systems analyst, computer programmer, and computer operator. A very different list emerges in terms of NUMBERS of jobs. Just forty occupations are expected to account for about half of all job openings between now and 1995. Leading this list are building custodian, cashier, secretary, general office clerk and sales clerk. Kindergarten and elementary school teachers appear on the most-growth list for the first time in many years.

In an article entitled "Getting Ready for the Jobs of the Future" in *The Futurist,* June 1983, Melvin Cetron projects the following new technician jobs will be opening up in the 1990s.

Energy Technician (650,000 jobs)

Housing Rehabilitation Technician (500,000 jobs)

Hazardous Waste Management Technician (300,000 jobs)

Industrial Laser Process Technician (600,000 jobs)

Industrial Robot Production Technician (800,000 jobs)

Materials Utilization Technician (400,000 jobs)

Genetic Engineering Technician (250,000 jobs)

Holographic Inspection Specialist (200,000 jobs)

Bionic-Medical Technician (200,000 jobs)

Automotive Fuel Cell (Battery) Technician (250,000 jobs)

On-Line Emergency Medical Technician (400,000 jobs)

Geriatric Social Worker (700,000 jobs)

Energy Auditor (180,000 jobs)

Nuclear Medicine Technologist (75,000 jobs)

Dialysis Technologist (30,000 jobs)

Computer Axial Tomography (CAT) Technologist/Technician (45,000 jobs)

Position Tomography (PET) Technologist (165,000 jobs)

Computer-Assisted Design (CAD) Technician (300,000 jobs)

Computer-Assisted Graphics (CAG) Technician (15,000 jobs)

Computer-Assisted Manufacturing (CAM) Specialist (300,000 jobs)

Computerized Vocational Training (CVT) Technician (300,000 jobs)

<hr>

**Monthly Labor Review* of the Bureau of Labor Statistics. It is available from the Bureau of Labor Statistics regional offices and the Government Printing Office.

Part I

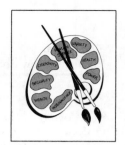

Part II

Sizing Up Your Options

6

TOMORROW

She was going to be all she wanted to
be . . . . tomorrow.
None would be smarter or more successful than
she . . . . tomorrow.
There were friends who could help her—she knew,
Who'd be only too happy to see what they could do.
On them she would call and pay a visit or
two . . . . . . tomorrow.

Each morning she stacked up the letters she'd
write . . . . tomorrow,
And thought of the things that would give her
delight . . . tomorrow.
But she hadn't one minute to stop on her way,
"More thought I must give to my future," she'd
say . . . . tomorrow.

The greatest of workers this gal would have
been . . . . . tomorrow.
The world would have hailed her—had ever she
seen . . . . tomorrow.
But, in fact, she passed on, and she faded from view,
And all that was left here when living was through
Was a mountain of things she intended to
do . . . . . . tomorrow!

Anonymous

Learning Objectives

At the end of the chapter you will be able to:

Identify and explore the decision-making process.

Apply the principles of decision making to your career search.

Identify psychological barriers to decision making and develop alternative strategies for success.

Decision Making

Career decisions are the Olympic trials of your career fitness program. They give you an opportunity to integrate and test out all the components of your career fitness program—your attitude, values, skills, interests, and biases. For most of us it is safe to assume that whatever decisions we make are the best we can make given the information, circumstances, and feelings of the moment. However, we can all improve our decision-making performance by examining some of the assumptions and strategies that other people have used in the decision-making process.

This chapter will review decision-making strategies that are potentially limiting and those that are potentially empowering and success oriented. The primary focus of this chapter is devoted to explaining a decision-making model that involves setting realistic goals. To bring about change, you must set specific goals with specific time frames. These must be realistic for you and you must maintain an attitude that you are deserving and capable of reaching these goals. In past chapters, exercises have been placed at the end of the chapter. This was done to help you solidify and integrate what you had read in the entire chapter. In this chapter on decision making, you will find some of the exercises included in the text as well as at the end. This is done so that you can turn immediately to the exercise and begin to test your aptitude for utilizing various aspects of the decision-making model directly after they are presented in the chapter.

Overcoming Barriers to Decision Making

Attitude affects decisions

Because you are reading this book, you probably want to improve your life and increase your career options. Attitude has already been identified as an important internal factor in making decisions. Essentially, your ability to use your skills and potential is controlled by your attitude. Our attitudes are "gut level" feelings which indicate what we expect of ourselves. We must be aware of our attitudes and habits to enhance our daily effectiveness. A decision is accepted only if it is compatible with our current attitudes and self-concepts. Again, if we believe we can, we can!

Much of human behavior is based on attitudes that are limiting. People often make decisions that involve limited conscious involvement or personal responsibility, sometimes in an effort to simplify or accelerate the decision-making process. The following list suggests some of the ways people go about making decisions.

Decision-Making Strategies

- Planning: "Weighing the facts." Consideration of values, objectives, necessary information, alternatives, and consequences. A rational approach with a balance between thinking and feeling.
- Impulse: "Don't look before you leap." Little thought or examination; taking the first alternative.

- Intuitive: "It feels right." Automatic, preconscious choice based on "inner harmony."
- Compliant: "Anything you say, Sir." Nonassertive; let someone else decide; follow someone else's plans.
- Delaying: "Cross that bridge later." Procrastination, avoidance, hoping someone or something will happen so that you won't have to make a decision. Taking a moratorium; postponing thought and action.
- Fatalistic: "It's all in the cards." What will be, will be. Letting the environment decide; leaving it up to fate.
- Agonizing: "What if? I don't know what to do." Worrying that a decision will be the wrong one. Getting lost in all the data; getting overwhelmed with analyzing alternatives.
- Paralytic: "Can't face up to it." One step further from "what if"—complete indecision and fear. Accepting responsibility, but being unable to approach it.

Read the following story to determine what decision-making strategies Art used.

At the age of 21, Art decided to leave Southern California and go to Alaska to work on the pipeline. He left his friends and his easy-going sun and surf life-style behind to make his fortune. After two years in the fields, Art was promoted to lead supervisor and was earning close to $100,000 a year. He met and married a young woman who was earning $60,000 as an apprentice heavy-equipment operator. Although the climate was severe and the life-style pressures (intense work, intense alcohol, and drug parties) were not to their liking, they adjusted well, saved, invested, and made the best of the circumstances. After two successful years together, Art, along with many others, was laid off. The couple decided that he would go back to California to pursue his educational goals and she would stay on to finish her apprenticeship. Initially they were able to maintain their relationship through letters, phone calls, and frequent visits. After several months, she began to succumb to the "heavy party scene" that was part of the life-style in the labor camps, which were hundreds of miles from civilization. Despite all of Art's attempts to support and reinforce his wife to maintain her values and her commitment to him, Art felt his wife slipping away. They are currently involved in divorce proceedings.

An example of decision making

Were Art's decisions appropriate to his circumstances? What would you have decided given similar circumstances? (Answer exercise 6.1 at the end of this chapter.)

Choosing a career is a life development process. At different points of the process different issues must be decided. Thus, planning (the first of the strategies listed above) is the key to reaching your goals. It implies gaining control of your life. You might glance back at the life line you completed several chapters earlier. Analyze which strategy you used most often. Then note the other strategies used. Planning and intuitive strategies are the only two positive strategies listed. The others contain a hint of fear . . . fear of failure, fear of imperfection, fear of rejection, fear of ridicule.

Getting unstuck, gaining control

When you feel "stuck" or unable to make a decision, try asking the following questions:

1. What are my assumptions (attitudes)?
2. What are my feelings?
3. Why am I clinging to this behavior? (What rewards or payoffs?)

There is no one "right" decision

1. What are my assumptions? Many of us assume that if we could only make the one right decision about the matter at hand, everything else would fall into place and we'd be happy. In fact, most decisions do not have such power over our lives. Decisions are not typically black and white in terms of their consequences. Decisions simply move you in one direction rather than another. Decisions open up some options and close off others. If you assume that most decisions can be changed or altered, that most decisions are not, in fact, life or death, then you will not be as hesitant to make a decision, act on it, assess the implications as they occur, and make adjustments (or new decisions) as necessary.

Avoid "either/ or" ultimatums

2. What are my feelings? Some people create unnecessary stress about making decisions because they give themselves an "either-or" ultimatum. Neither option really feels right but they panic and impulsively choose one just to ease the anxiety, or they become paralyzed and don't make any choice, allowing circumstances to decide for them. When you are feeling impulsive or paralyzed about making a decision, stop, take several deep breaths, and begin to generate some additional alternatives. A friend, counselor, or skilled listener can often help with this process. As you gain more information about your options, you will realize which decision is best for you.

Other people cry over spilled milk; in other words, they think back over past decisions and lament not having decided differently. This psychological stance wastes time and energy and can be destructive to your self-image. When you begin to feel self-doubt or regrets over decisions, remind yourself that you made the best decision you could, given the time, circumstances, and information available.

Old habits can limit you

3. Why am I clinging to this behavior? If you acknowledge that you are causing this indecisiveness, it may generate a different point of view. For example, sometimes people cling to old nonproductive behaviors because they are the safe ways to act; you don't have to deal with the unknown or the possibility of making mistakes (also known as taking risks). Without risk there is no challenge and no growth.

Visualize yourself at your best

We find that it is difficult to change habits because such habits usually give us some form of positive payoff or reward. A person who enjoyed the status and praise of being an excellent and achieving student might find that being equally achieving in a work environment alienates others on the job. You must recognize when the old comfortable way of doing things no longer gives you the payoffs you once received.

Whether you consider yourself a risk taker or not, it is important to remember that we have all taken risks. What has been your greatest risk? What risk have you taken in the last two weeks? In its most basic sense, risk taking means moving from the safe and familiar to the unknown and scary. Most of us are fairly safe risk takers in that we want the odds to be at least 50-50 before we jump in. Yet millions of people play the lottery, start businesses, and get married even when the odds are clearly not in their favor. Why, because along with the probability of success (the odds) people take risks based on the desirability of the anticipated outcome. As with the lottery, the probability is a million to one against winning, yet, people continue to gamble because of the high desirability of the outcome—winning. You are in the best position to take a calculated risk when you assess both the probability and desirability of an outcome and weigh it against the other possible outcomes. Failure to consider outcomes in this fashion is the most common cause of unsuccessful risk taking. For example, most people are afraid to take the risk of changing careers or even changing jobs. They immediately think of the worst possible outcome, "I'll fail" or "I will never find another job if I quit this one." They don't ask themselves how probable is this to happen, how desirable is this outcome. The probability of their worries actually materializing is very low, and the likelihood of a negative outcome is very low. Many people paralyze themselves with this "worst possible consequence" thinking, they decide not to risk it and they feel trapped. What they haven't done is generate other possible outcomes that are more probable and more desirable. What are some of these? A new job that is more energizing and financially rewarding, a new career with an opportunity to grow and develop, a chance to get retraining. The probability and desirability is, in fact, much higher, and therefore the decision is less risky. Yet, many people miss opportunities because they fail to generate and assess all their outcomes. This process often takes the assistance of another person who can help you identify your negative or limiting thinking and help you identify some realistic and positive outcomes.

Decision-Making Model

Table 6.1, "Choice, Not Chance: Decisions Are in Our Power" summarizes a suggested model for making informed decisions. The five steps necessary to make an informed decision are the following: defining your goal; knowing your alternatives; gathering information; considering the consequences (both probable and desirable); and defining your plan of action or the steps needed to achieve your goal.

Goal Setting

Your goals and objectives are the vehicles that lead you to what you want to attain in your life. A goal must be distinguished from an objective. *Goals* are broad statements of purpose. They are general, and long range. They

Table 6.1
Choice, Not Chance—Decisions are in Our Power

1. Define goal or objective

Can you change part of the problem into a definite goal?

What do you want to accomplish by what date?

Can you state your objective clearly?

2. Assess alternatives

What are your alternatives or options?

Are your alternative choices consistent with your important values?

Can you summarize your important values in writing?

What is a reasonable amount of time in which to accomplish your alternatives?

3. Gather information

What do you know about your alternatives?

What more do you need to know about your alternatives?

What sources will help you gather more information about your alternatives?

What sources will help you discover further alternatives?

4. Assess outcomes or consequences

Probability:

 What is the probability of success of each alternative?

 Are your highest values part of each alternative?

Desirability:

 Can you eliminate the least desirable alternatives first?

 When you consider the best possible alternative, how much do you want it?

 What are you willing to give up in order to get what you want?

5. Establish a Plan of Action

Weighing everything you now know about your decision, what is your Plan of Action?

What dates will you start and complete your Plan of Action?

Does your Plan of Action state a clear objective?

Does your Plan of Action specify the steps necessary to achieve its objective?

Does your Plan of Action specify the conditions necessary to achieve its objective?

Until you start your Plan of Action, you haven't really made a decision. So start now. Make systematic decision making an adventure!

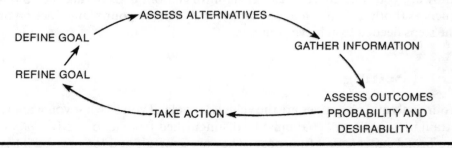

refer to an ongoing process, a challenge that's meant to stretch our limits. If you have trouble defining your goal, try listing the dissatisfactions and problems in your life that are bothering you. Now ask yourself what you can do about them. You have just defined a goal. Thus, if you have been analyzing yourself while reading each chapter, you may now recognize that your problem is that you are not working in a field that utilizes your values, interests, attitudes, and skills. The goal would be to find a career that best allows you to utilize your talents. (At this point answer exercise questions 6.2 and 6.3. Exercise 6.2 will help you identify and prioritize some long term goals that have importance for you. Exercise 6.3 will help you assess how ready you are to begin working on your goals.)

Goals

Meanwhile *objectives* are the specific and practical steps used to accomplish our goals. Objectives are short-term "baby steps." They are visible and measurable signposts that indicate where we are relative to reaching our goal.

Objectives

The more specific our objectives are, the higher is the probability that we will accomplish them. A specific objective has some indication of the action, conditions, and amount of time it will take to achieve it. Most of us have said, "I'm going to lose weight." That's an example of an unspecific objective. We know what the action is but we don't know how, when, and to what extent it will be accomplished. We rarely follow through with an unclear objective. Occasionally you will hear someone say, "I'm going to lose one pound this week by cutting out all bread, butter, and sweets from my diet." Now, that's an example of a specific objective with the action, losing weight, made specific by information on how much, when, and how it will be accomplished. If you had to put your money on someone losing weight which statement would you choose, the former or the latter? At this point complete exercise 6.17 to reinforce your ability to formulate clear, specific objectives.

Four points should be remembered in setting goals. First, *consider what you are willing to give up* to get what you want. When most people make career changes, life in general changes for them. You may need to give up free time to take special courses. You may need to take a cut in pay (temporarily or permanently) to obtain better fringe benefits, security, and a potential chance for growth in another field, or you may need to give up being the old-timer and become the new kid on the block (and need to prove to others again that you are a competent worker).

What will you give up to get what you want?

Second, *give yourself a realistic timeline* to reach your goal. If you've incorporated "baby steps" (objectives) into your timeline you are more likely to achieve your goals. A *timeline* is just a way of listing in chronological order all the objectives needed to accomplish your goal. For example:

Have a timeline

Goal: To explore alternative careers to teaching by August of this year.
Objectives:

1. By February I will start reading *Exercising Your Options* and finish it by June.

2. Each week I will complete reading and responding to one chapter.
3. I will allow myself three or four separate weeks to "goof off."
4. By May, I will have identified the strategies needed to identify three jobs that utilize my talents.
5. By June, I will have attended one workshop on job searches conducted at the college.
6. By July, I will have researched three jobs by reading about them in a career center or local library and identifying three or more local people working in those fields.
7. By August, I will have visited three people at their jobs.

Once you've written a timeline, it's a good idea to show it to a close friend or counselor and to sign and date it as if it were a contract. In actuality, this can be considered a contract with yourself! At best, you will achieve your goals; at worst you will need to revise them and change the timeline. At this point complete exercise 6.17 to reinforce your ability to formulate clear objectives.

Set your goals high

Third, *set your goals high*. You must believe you are deserving and capable. The goal still must be realistic enough to be achievable. If your baby steps are specific, clear, and small enough, you will achieve them. The example stated above seeks to illustrate that each objective must have importance in itself and must help lead to the overall (larger) goal.

Finally the fourth point about setting goals is quite simple, indeed: Be sure to *reward yourself* after completing each objective and after reaching each goal. Some say that the mere accomplishment of the goal should be reward enough. However, most of us tend to be more motivated toward success when we have both internal and external reward systems. The internal reward is the feeling of success; the external reward is something outside of ourselves, e.g., crossing off the objective on the check list, a grade on a paper, recognition from a group of friends, dinner at a special place, a new outfit. How do you reward yourself when you attain an objective or reach a goal?

Reward yourself

One way that you can reward yourself is by learning to manage your time so that you can create the best possibilities for success. Alan Lakein, a time-management expert, gives some practical tips on how to set and prioritize goals as well as how to make the best use of your time. These remarks on rational decision making incorporate his suggestions. People who are successful in reaching their goals know how to manage their time. Try using the following tips from Lakein (Lakein 1973):

Manage your time

1. *I build on successes.*
2. *I don't waste time regretting my failures.*
3. *I don't waste my time feeling guilty about what I don't do.*
4. *I remind myself that there is always enough time for the important things; if it is important, I'll make the time to do it.*
5. *I skim books quickly looking for ideas.*

6. *I've given up forever all "waiting time." If I have to wait I consider it a "gift of time" to relax, plan, or do something I would not otherwise have done.*
7. *I keep my watch three minutes fast, to get a head start on the day.*
8. *I always plan first thing in the morning and set priorities for the day.*
9. *I keep a list of specific items to be done each day, arrange them in priority order, and then do my best to get the important things done as soon as possible.*
10. *I have confidence in my judgment of priorities and I stick to them.*
11. *If I seem to procrastinate I ask myself: "What am I avoiding?"*
12. *I concentrate on one thing at a time.*
13. *I set deadlines.*
14. *I try to listen actively in every discussion.*
15. *I make use of specialists to help me with special problems.*
16. *I recognize that inevitably some of my time will be spent on activities outside my control and don't fret about it.*
17. *I'M CONTINUALLY ASKING MYSELF: "WHAT IS THE BEST USE OF MY TIME RIGHT NOW?"*

Summary

Successful career planning involves two processes related to goals: (1) defining your goals and (2) knowing how to reach them. The more completely you plan out your objectives the more likely you will be to achieve your goals. The key to the process is overcoming the hurdle of negative thinking. You must temporarily block out the tendency to be critical. You must dare to put aside your anticipation of failure, your fears and excuses, your past habits, and create goals that energize you and take you beyond your past efforts.

Define your goals and know how to reach them

The following exercises are designed to help you become aware of your decision-making process and to encourage you to set some career and life goals. For example, you will be asked to decide what you want to do by the end of the current year and then one year from now. This can mean acquiring new skills or improving current skills, moving toward career advancement or career change, or staying where you are. Don't forget, try to picture in your mind what you want in your work life (e.g., type of work, responsibility, surroundings, salary, management relationship, etc.) and then focus on the exact steps necessary to help you reach your goals. If you can't picture the necessary steps, you still need to gather more information in order to make attainable career decisions (e.g., from people who have been in similar positions or from written materials about the field). Following the outline from the decision-making model, you need to choose from alternatives, select the one that has the best possibility of success for you, create a plan of action, set specific objectives, and take action. As you attain objectives that move you toward your goal reassess your decisions. Constantly take in and process information about how you feel moving toward this goal. Be honest with yourself. If you do not feel successful enlist the help of a career guidance professional to assist you in formulating a goal that you can successfully attain.

?? Written Exercises

The written exercises that follow serve to increase your awareness about how you make decisions. Exercise 6.1 asks that you rank yourself on two dimensions of decision-making styles. There are no right or wrong answers. This is a chance to become aware of your personal style of decision making. Exercises 6.2 and 6.3 review goal setting. Exercises 6.4–6.7 assess whether you actually do what you say is important to you. Exercises 6.8–6.15 should clarify other factors that can affect your decisions. Exercise 6.16 asks you to think about some alternatives to your present life choices. Exercise 6.17 will indicate your ability to recognize and state clear objectives. (There are right and wrong answers.) Exercise 6.18 checks your ability to solve a problem creatively. Exercise 6.19 asks that you list your "time savers." Lastly, exercise 6.20 asks you to choose a long-term goal along with clear short-term activities that will start you toward the long-term goal now.

6.1
Ranking Yourself

On a scale of 1 to 10, rank yourself as a decision maker. Circle one number for each line.

cautious	1 2 3 4 5 6 7 8 9 10	risk taking
intuitive	1 2 3 4 5 6 7 8 9 10	logical
dependent	1 2 3 4 5 6 7 8 9 10	independent
influenced by others	1 2 3 4 5 6 7 8 9 10	self-motivated
feeling/emotional	1 2 3 4 5 6 7 8 9 10	rational
passive	1 2 3 4 5 6 7 8 9 10	active
quiet	1 2 3 4 5 6 7 8 9 10	assertive

6.2
Reviewing Goal Setting

In chapter 2, the What, What, What? exercise (exercise 2.1l) looked at some general life or long-term goals. Now, let's try to become much more specific. List three specific long-term goals. Use additional paper if you have more than three.

1. _____

2. _____

3. _____

Let's assume you knew that you'd die in an earthquake six months from now. Would your long-range goals now be any different? List at least three objectives that imply how you would live in the next six months.

1. _____

2. _____

3. _____

Now you have a list of long-term goals and objectives. Deciding which ones are most important to you is the next step. This is called *setting priorities.* To do this you will want to mark those goals that are of most importance or value to you, with the letter A. Those of medium importance, with a B, and those of low importance with the letter C. Let's look at the As first. Go back to your long and short-term goals list and mark the As, the Bs, and the Cs. With more than one A lifetime goal, you will want to prioritize the As. For example, A_1, A_2, A_3 with the A_1 goal being the most important to you at this time. Do the same for B and C marked goals. Now prioritize your long and short-term A, B, and C goals.

Activities are those things we do to accomplish our objectives, which in turn are getting us closer to accomplishing our long-term goals. Take a sheet of paper for each of your three long-term goals and list as many activities as you can think of to get you close to that goal. Don't question or judge those activities that come to your mind. Just list whatever they are. After you've listed these activities ask yourself this question: Am I willing to commit five minutes in the next week to working on this activity? If your answer is No, then draw a line through the activity. It's okay if you don't want to spend the time on the activity. You don't have to make excuses. Your decision to choose those activities you'll commit five minutes toward will enable you to choose the high priority tasks. Now prioritize (A_1, A_2, A_3 etc.) those activities you will do in the next week. Now your activities are organized. You're on the way toward meeting your goals. Make it an adventure!

6.3
Write a Goal Statement
Can you answer "yes" to the following questions about this goal?

a. Did I choose it personally?
b. Am I ready to make a written commitment to this goal?
c. Am I setting a deadline?
d. Is it within my control?
e. Have I thought through the consequences?
f. Is the goal based on my values?
g. Can I visualize it in considerable detail? (Is this goal specific?)
h. Will I work toward it?
i. Am I taking responsibility for this goal?
j. Is this goal measurable?

6.4
Task Identification
In five minutes, on a separate piece of paper, write all the tasks that you need to do in the next week.

6.5
One Year to Live
If you had only one year to live, which of the tasks listed above would still be important to you?

6.6
Meeting Your Needs
How much of a week's work is spent reaching your own personal goals versus meeting others' needs?

6.7
Your Energizers
What percentage of your daily activities give you energy? List your energizing activities.

6.8
Recent Decisions
What are some decisions you have made recently?

6.9
Prioritizing
Were some of these decisions more important than others? Why?

6.10
Irrevocable Decisions
Give an example of a decision you made, or might have to make that could be really difficult to change.

6.11
Harmful Decisions
Give an example of a decision that might be harmful to you or someone you care about in some way.

6.12
Limiting Decisions
Give an example of a decision you could make that might keep you from doing something you want to do.

6.13
Contingent Decisions
Give an example of a decision which would have an effect on other decisions.

6.14
Values
What value or values were important to you in making those decisions?

6.15

Factors Adversely Affecting Decisions

The purpose of this exercise is to investigate factors that may unfavorably influence decision making and to determine whether any patterns are evident. State three decisions and check which of the factors listed below were present, and to what extent, in making each decision. Use a check for decision 1, an X for decision 2, and an 0 for decision 3.

Decision 1 _____

Decision 2 _____

Decision 3 _____

Table 6.2
Factors Affecting Decisions

External Factors	Slightly present	Moderately present	Very present
1. Family Expectations			
2. Family Responsibilities			
3. Cultural Stereotypes			
4. Male/Female Stereotypes			
5. Other (Specify)			
6. Other (Specify)			

Internal Factors			
1. Lack of self-confidence			
2. Fear of change			
3. Fear of making a wrong decision			
4. Fear of failure			
5. Fear of ridicule			
6. Other (Specify)			

After filling in the chart, look for patterns which may appear:

a. Do you experience more internal or external factors as obstacles to making satisfying decisions?

b. If a particular factor is "Very Present" only once, but another factor is "Slightly Present" in two or possibly all three of your decisions, which of the two factors do you think is more significant in affecting your decision making?

6.16
What If . . .

If you are presently in college, suppose you lost all forms of support and had to leave school. List three things you could do.

a. _____

b. _____

c. _____

How satisfying would these alternatives be to you?

Suppose you had one year to remain in college. With one year to prepare, what would you do?

a. What alternatives might you choose?
b. What information would you need about your chosen alternatives?
c. What action would you take?
d. How satisfying would your one-year plan be?

6.17
Specific/Unspecific Objectives

The following statements are objectives. They may also be called goals or decisions. Read each objective and decide, in your own judgment, if the objective or goal is specific or unspecific. These are statements anyone may make; they don't necessarily apply to you. Suppose someone's standing in front of you in a line making each of these statements. With that in mind, please mark each objective as "S" (specific) or "U" (unspecific) to the left of the statement.

_____ 1. I want to explore my interests.

_____ 2. I want to get a good job.

_____ 3. I'd like to get an idea of the job I'm best suited for.

_____ 4. I'd like to take Spanish IA next semester and continue for at least two years so I'll have another skill to use as a teacher.

_____ 5. When I leave school, I want to get a job that pays at least $4.00 an hour.

_____ 6. Tomorrow I'm going to make a one-hour appointment to see Ms. Rogers in her office.

_____ 7. I want to get at least a B on every history exam and earn a B as my final grade this semester.

_____ 8. I'm going to ask Teresa to help me find some information about health careers in the Career Development and Placement Center right after class.

_____ 9. I plan to move to an area where there are lots of jobs.

_____ 10. I want to be accepted by the state university when I graduate.

_____ 11. I want to find out more about myself.

_____ 12. I want to get along better with other people at work.

_____ 13. Next week I'm going to see my friends more.

_____ 14. I'm going to read one good book about social service careers tonight.

_____ 15. I want to get a good education.

Answers:

1.	U	6.	S	11.	U
2.	U	7.	U	12.	U
3.	U	8.	S	13.	U
4.	S	9.	U	14.	S
5.	U	10.	U	15.	U

6.18
Test Your Assumptions

a. Try to connect the following dots with only four straight lines and without lifting your pen. (Answer at end of chapter.)

```
.   .   .

.   .   .

.   .   .
```

b. Make a 6 out of IX by adding one line.

6.19
Time Savers

List three things you do to save time. _____

_____

_____

6.20
Short and Long-Term Goals

Write a lifelong goal and list two activities you can do in the next two weeks that will contribute to that

goal. _____

_____

_____

Summary—Write a Brief Paragraph Answering These Questions:

What did you learn about yourself? How does this knowledge relate to your career/life planning? How do you feel?

_____

_____

_____

_____

_____

_____

_____

_____

_____

_____

Answers to question 6.18

a.
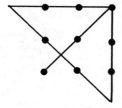

(The directions did not indicate that the lines needed to stay *inside* the dots outline.)

b. SIX

(The directions did not mandate a "straight line.")

Part I

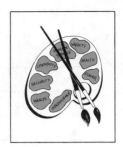

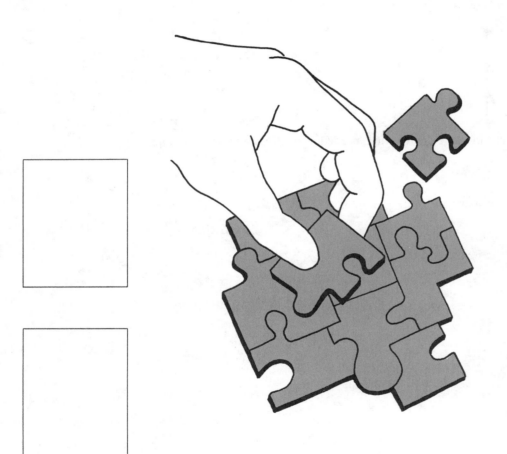

Part II

Information Integration   7

*You may be on the right track but if you just sit there
you'll get run over.*
Will Rogers

Learning Objectives   At the end of the chapter you will be able to:

Demonstrate how your interests, values, and skills
can be grouped into job clusters.

Make tentative career choices by reviewing
information gathered in previous chapters.

Familiarize yourself with printed sources of
information to use in further clarifying your career
choices.

Choosing, Changing or Confirming Your Options

By now you probably have one or several career areas in mind. This chapter will help you get more specific. It will enable you to review, clarify, and integrate the information that you've collected about your needs, desires, values, interests, skills, personal attributes, and decision-making style. It is important to put these pieces together to identify some specific occupational areas that you can begin to research.

This chapter is divided into three sections. The first section, "Job Clusters and Fields of Interests" illustrates how interests, values and skills can be grouped into job categories or clusters so that you can begin to select specific fields of interests to research.

The second section of this chapter enables you to summarize insights. First you will review and record information about yourself gained from past chapters; then you will use your powers of observation, intuition and research to identify potential fields of employment.

The third section of this chapter will introduce you to the written resources available in libraries and college career centers. By using these references you will have the information necessary to further clarify and confirm your tentative career choices. You need to make a tentative career decision to effectively use the remainder of this book.

In case you get stuck or blocked in listing specific occupations, try using the guided fantasy (exercise 7.9). Start by quickly reviewing all the written information that you've recorded (at the end of this chapter). Then close your eyes and visualize yourself in your perfect career. "Mental visualization" can sometimes focus your thoughts into areas that suit you perfectly. This technique helps you tap into and integrate the wealth of information, intuition, and wisdom that you already have about yourself. It is only natural to feel hesitant and even fearful about committing yourself to a career decision. These are the feelings that block you from making a decision and getting specific. Mental visualization is a technique to help your mind "wander" into a career choice.

In this chapter, the exercises are integrated into the text in order to help you identify your tentative career goal. This tentative goal will be confirmed or changed by additional information you will gather from written resources and information interviews (which will be discussed later in this book).

OBJECTIVES:

After reading and completing Section I you will:

1. Identify the job clusters and Holland Personality Types that interest you.
2. Match your interests to occupations using the "Worker Trait Groups" along with any other inventory you may have taken.
3. Identify and compare where your interests fall into the job clusters that are often used in career centers (U.S. Office of Career Education categories).
4. Identify other occupational interests areas and condense related job titles into three top career choices.

After reading and completing Section II you will:

1. Organize your interests, values, skills, personal qualities, and tentative career goals into a few summary pages.
2. Compare your tentative career choices from this section with your top interests from Section I.

After reading and completing Section III you will:

1. Improve your knowledge of written resources.
2. Refine your skills in gathering information about specific occupations and career related opportunities by using library materials.
3. Confirm your first impressions about your top career choices.

Section I—Identifying Job Clusters or Fields of Interest

Interest Inventories

Many interest inventories ask if you like or dislike a variety of subjects, and then return to you a profile of results. The results group your preferences into fields such as: science, technology, service, arts, communications, or other clusters such as the Guide to Occupational Explorations (GOE) worker trait groups. We have included in the following pages an interest inventory available from the Department of Labor that has results grouped according to the clusters in the G.O.E. worker trait groups. Another commonly used system was developed by Professor John Holland and is used in several interest inventories. Holland's clusters are known as "personality types" or "environments" and are based on the following assumptions: (1) People express their personalities through their vocational choices; (2) people are attracted to occupations that they feel will provide experiences suitable to their personalities; (3) people who choose the same vocation have similar personalities and they react to many situations in similar ways. The clusters are as follows.

Holland's "Environments"

REALISTIC (R) types like realistic jobs such as automobile mechanic, aircraft controller, surveyor, farmer, electrician. They like to work outdoors and to work with tools. They prefer to deal with things rather than with people. They are described as:

Doers

Conforming	Materialistic	Modest
Frank	Natural	Shy
Honest	Persistent	Stable
Humble	Practical	Thrifty

INVESTIGATIVE (I) types like investigative jobs such as biologist, chemist, physicist, anthropologist, geologist, medical technologist. They are task-oriented and prefer to work alone. They enjoy solving abstract problems and understanding the physical world. They are described as:

Problem solvers

Analytical	Independent	Modest
Cautious	Intellectual	Precise
Critical	Introverted	Rational
Curious	Methodical	Reserved

Creators   ARTISTIC (A) types like artistic jobs such as composer, musician, stage director, writer, interior decorator, actor/actress. They like to work in artistic settings that offer opportunities for self-expression. They are described as:

Complicated	Idealistic	Independent
Disorderly	Imaginative	Intuitive
Emotional	Impractical	Nonconforming
Expressive	Impulsive	Original

Helpers   SOCIAL (S) types like social jobs such as teacher, clergy, counselor, registered nurse, personnel director, speech therapist. They like to be sociable, responsible, and concerned with the welfare of others. They have little interest in machinery or physical exertion. They are described as:

Convincing	Helpful	Responsible
Cooperative	Idealistic	Sociable
Friendly	Insightful	Tactful
Generous	Kind	Understanding

Persuaders   ENTERPRISING (E) types like enterprising jobs such as salesperson, manager, business executive, television producer, sports promoter, buyer. They enjoy leading, speaking, and selling. They are impatient with precise work. They are described as:

Adventurous	Energetic	Self-confident
Ambitious	Impulsive	Sociable
Attention-getting	Optimistic	Popular
Domineering	Pleasure-seeking	

Organizers   CONVENTIONAL (C) types like conventional jobs such as bookkeeper, stenographer, instrument assembler, banker, cost estimator, tax expert. They prefer highly ordered activities, both verbal and numerical, that characterize office work. They have little interest in artistic or physical skills. They are described as:

Conforming	Inhibited	Practical
Conscientious	Obedient	Self-controlled
Careful	Orderly	Unimaginative
Conservative	Persistent	Efficient

If you review chapter 1, exercise 1.2, you will notice the Adjective Check List is based on these six types. Most interest inventories compare how your interests are similar to these six fields or types, and usually provide a list of jobs that are related to these interests. If you are in a class that uses the Self-Directed Search or the Strong-Campbell Interest Inventory your instructor will explain which jobs are related to these six environments.

If you don't have access to separate inventories, the interest inventory developed by the U.S. Department of Labor (exercise 7.1 listed below) should give you a general idea about how your interests relate to potential jobs.

7.1
Interest Check List

U.S. Department of Labor
Employment and Training Administration
U.S. Employment Service 1979

DIRECTIONS:

It is important to all of us that we like our jobs; doing so will increase our chances of success.

This Interest Check List may help you decide what kinds of work you would like to do. It lists activities that are found in a broad range of industries and occupations in the United States today.

Read each of the statements carefully. If you think you would "like" to do this kind of activity, make a check √ under the "L"; if you "don't like" the activity, make a √ under the "D"; if you are not certain whether you would like the activity or not, make a √ under the "?". After you have checked each activity, go back and double check √√ at least *five* activities that you think you would like most to do.

You may check an activity even if you do not have training or experience for it, if you think you would enjoy the work. Check the "?" *only* when you cannot decide whether you would like or dislike the activity, or when you do not know what the activity is. There are no right or wrong answers. Check each activity according to how *you* feel about it.

Table 7.1

Read each of the items below and indicate how you feel about the activity described by placing a check √ under

L (Like)	? (Uncertain)	D (Dislike)

	L	?	D		L	?	D
01.01 Write short stories or articles	___	___	___	**03.01** Manage a beef or dairy ranch	___	___	___
Edit work of writers	___	___	___	Operate a commercial fish farm	___	___	___
Write reviews of books or plays	___	___	___	Manage the use and development of forest lands	___	___	___
01.02 Teach classes in oil painting	___	___	___	**03.02** Supervise farm workers	___	___	___
Carve figures of people or animals . .	___	___	___	Supervise a logging crew	___	___	___
Design artwork for magazines	___	___	___	Supervise a park maintenance crew .	___	___	___
01.03 Direct plays	___	___	___	**03.03** Train horses for racing	___	___	___
Perform magic tricks in a theater . . .	___	___	___	Feed and care for animals in a zoo . .	___	___	___
Announce radio or television programs	___	___	___	Bathe and groom dogs	___	___	___
01.04 Conduct a symphony orchestra	___	___	___	**03.04** Pick vegetables on a farm	___	___	___
Compose or arrange music	___	___	___	Catch fish as a member of a fishing crew	___	___	___
Play a musical instrument	___	___	___	Trim branches and limbs from trees .	___	___	___
01.05 Create routines for professional dancers	___	___	___	**04.01** Direct police activities	___	___	___
Dance in a variety show	___	___	___	Issue tickets to speeding motorists . .	___	___	___
Teach modern dance	___	___	___	Enforce fish and game laws	___	___	___
01.06 Restore damaged works of art	___	___	___	**04.02** Guard inmates in a prison	___	___	___
Carve designs in wooden blocks for printing greeting cards	___	___	___	Guard money in an armored car . . .	___	___	___
Design and paint signs	___	___	___	Fight fires to protect life and property	___	___	___
01.07 Analyze handwriting and appraise personality	___	___	___	**05.01** Plan and design roads and bridges . .	___	___	___
				Design electrical equipment	___	___	___
Introduce acts in a circus	___	___	___	Plan construction of a water treatment plant	___	___	___
Guess weight of people at a carnival .	___	___	___				
01.08 Model clothing for customers	___	___	___	**05.02** Direct operations of a power plant . .	___	___	___
Pose for a fashion photographer . . .	___	___	___	Direct construction of buildings	___	___	___
Be a stand-in for a television star . . .	___	___	___	Supervise operations of a coal mine .	___	___	___
02.01 Develop chemical processes to solve technical problems	___	___	___	**05.03** Survey land to determine boundaries	___	___	___
				Make drawings of equipment for technical manuals	___	___	___
Analyze data on weather conditions .	___	___	___	Operate a radio transmitter	___	___	___
Develop methods to control air or water pollution	___	___	___	Design and draft master drawings of automobiles	___	___	___
02.02 Study causes of animal diseases	___	___	___	Direct air traffic from an airport control tower	___	___	___
Develop methods for growing better crops	___	___	___	Conduct water pollution tests	___	___	___
Develop new techniques to process foods	___	___	___	**05.04** Pilot a commercial aircraft	___	___	___
				Operate a ferry boat	___	___	___
02.03 Examine teeth and treat dental problems	___	___	___	Be captain of an oil tanker	___	___	___
Diagnose and treat sick animals	___	___	___	**05.05** Build frame houses	___	___	___
Give medical treatment to people . . .	___	___	___	Make and repair dentures	___	___	___
02.04 Prepare medicines according to prescription	___	___	___	Prepare and cook food in a restaurant	___	___	___
				Plan, install and repair electrical wiring	___	___	___
Study blood samples using a microscope	___	___	___	Repair and overhaul automobiles . . .	___	___	___
Test ore samples for gold or silver content	___	___	___	Set up and operate printing equipment	___	___	___

Go on to next page

Table 7.1 (continued)

L (Like)	? (Uncertain)	D (Dislike)

			L	?	D
05.06	Operate generators at an electric plant		___	___	___
	Operate boilers to heat a building ..		___	___	___
	Operate water purification equipment		___	___	___
05.07	Inspect fire-fighting equipment		___	___	___
	Inspect aircraft for mechanical safety		___	___	___
	Grade logs for size and quality		___	___	___
05.08	Drive a tractor-trailer truck		___	___	___
	Operate a locomotive		___	___	___
	Operate a motorboat to carry passengers		___	___	___
05.09	Prepare items for shipment and keep records		___	___	___
	Receive, store and issue merchandise		___	___	___
	Record amount and kind of cargo on ships		___	___	___
05.10	Develop film to produce negatives or prints		___	___	___
	Repair small electrical appliances ...		___	___	___
	Paint houses		___	___	___
05.11	Operate a bulldozer to move earth ..		___	___	___
	Operate a crane to move materials ..		___	___	___
	Operate an oil drilling rig		___	___	___
05.12	Recap automobile tires		___	___	___
	Operate a duplicating or copying machine		___	___	___
	Clean and maintain office buildings .		___	___	___
06.01	Set up and operate a lathe to cut and form metal		___	___	___
	Drill tiny holes in industrial diamonds		___	___	___
	Hand polish optical lenses		___	___	___
06.02	Operate a drill press		___	___	___
	Operate a power saw in a woodworking factory		___	___	___
	Assemble refrigerators and stoves in a factory		___	___	___
	Operate a power sewing machine to make clothing		___	___	___
	Operate a dough-mixing machine for making bread		___	___	___
	Assemble electronic components ...		___	___	___
06.03	Inspect bottles for defects		___	___	___
	Sort fruit according to size		___	___	___
	Test electronic parts before shipment		___	___	___

			L	?	D
06.04	Operate a grinding machine in a factory		___	___	___
	Work on a factory assembly line ...		___	___	___
	Operate a machine that fills containers		___	___	___
	Hand package materials and products		___	___	___
	Assemble parts to make venetian blinds		___	___	___
	Drive a fork-lift truck to move materials in a factory		___	___	___
07.01	Take dictation, type and handle business details		___	___	___
	Search records to verify land ownership		___	___	___
	Maintain records on real estate sales .		___	___	___
07.02	Maintain charge account records ...		___	___	___
	Keep time card records		___	___	___
	Compute average weekly production from daily records		___	___	___
07.03	Receive and pay out money in a bank		___	___	___
	Sell tickets at places of entertainment		___	___	___
	Operate a cash register in a grocery store		___	___	___
07.04	Answer questions at an information counter		___	___	___
	Operate a telephone switchboard ...		___	___	___
	Interview persons wanting to open checking accounts		___	___	___
07.05	Check typewritten material for errors		___	___	___
	Compile and maintain employee records		___	___	___
	Deliver mail to homes and businesses		___	___	___
07.06	Type letters and reports		___	___	___
	Operate a computer typewriter to send or receive information		___	___	___
	Operate a billing machine to prepare customer bills		___	___	___
07.07	File office correspondence		___	___	___
	Locate and replace library books on shelves		___	___	___
	Handstamp return addresses on envelopes		___	___	___
08.01	Sell telephone and other communication equipment		___	___	___
	Sell newspaper advertising space ...		___	___	___
	Select and buy fruits and vegetables for resale		___	___	___
08.02	Sell automobiles		___	___	___
	Demonstrate products at a trade exhibit		___	___	___
	Sell articles at auction to highest bidder		___	___	___

Go on to next page

Table 7.1 (continued)

L (Like)			? (Uncertain)			D (Dislike)		
	L	?	D		L	?	D

08.03
Sell merchandise from door to door . ___ ___ ___
Sell candy and popcorn at sports events ___ ___ ___
Persuade night club customers to pose for pictures . . . . ___ ___ ___

09.01
Supervise activities of children at vacation camp . . . . ___ ___ ___
Greet and seat customers in a restaurant ___ ___ ___
Serve meals and beverages to airline passengers . . . . ___ ___ ___

09.02
Give haircuts . . . . ___ ___ ___
Style, dye and wave hair . . . . ___ ___ ___
Give scalp-conditioning treatments . . ___ ___ ___

09.03
Drive a bus . . . . ___ ___ ___
Drive a taxi cab . . . . ___ ___ ___
Teach automobile driving skills . . . . ___ ___ ___

09.04
Wait on tables in a restaurant . . . . . ___ ___ ___
Park automobiles . . . . ___ ___ ___
Cash checks and give information to customers . . . . ___ ___ ___

09.05
Check passenger baggage . . . . ___ ___ ___
Help hotel guests get taxi cabs . . . . . ___ ___ ___
Operate a carnival ride . . . . ___ ___ ___

10.01
Plan and carry out religious activities ___ ___ ___
Work with juveniles on probation . . ___ ___ ___
Help people with personal or emotional problems . . . . ___ ___ ___

10.02
Provide nursing care to hospital patients ___ ___ ___
Plan and give physical therapy treatment to patients . . . . ___ ___ ___
Teach the blind to read braille . . . . . ___ ___ ___

10.03
Give hearing tests . . . . ___ ___ ___
Care for children in an institution . . ___ ___ ___
Prepare patients for examination by a physician . . . . ___ ___ ___

11.01
Plan and write computer programs to help solve scientific problems . . . . ___ ___ ___
Plan collection and analysis of statistical data . . . . ___ ___ ___
Apply knowledge of statistics to set insurance rates . . . . ___ ___ ___

11.02
Teach courses in high school . . . . . ___ ___ ___
Teach vocational education courses . ___ ___ ___
Manage the library program for a community . . . . ___ ___ ___

11.03
Do research to develop new teaching methods . . . . ___ ___ ___
Do research to understand social problems . . . . ___ ___ ___
Review and analyze economic data . . ___ ___ ___

11.04
Serve as a court judge . . . . ___ ___ ___
Advise clients on legal matters . . . . ___ ___ ___
Settle wage disputes between labor and management . . . . ___ ___ ___

11.05
Manage a department of a large company . . . . ___ ___ ___
Plan and direct work of a government office . . . . ___ ___ ___
Purchase supplies and equipment for a large firm . . . . ___ ___ ___

11.06
Examine financial records to determine tax owed . . . . ___ ___ ___
Approve or disapprove requests for bank loans . . . . ___ ___ ___
Buy and sell stocks and bonds for clients ___ ___ ___

11.07
Direct administration of a large hospital ___ ___ ___
Serve as principal of a school . . . . . ___ ___ ___
Direct operations of a museum . . . . ___ ___ ___

11.08
Write news stories for publication or broadcast . . . . ___ ___ ___
Broadcast news over radio or television ___ ___ ___
Direct operations of a newspaper . . . ___ ___ ___

11.09
Plan advertising programs for an organization . . . . ___ ___ ___
Direct fund raising for a non-profit organization . . . . ___ ___ ___
Lobby for or against proposed legislation . . . . ___ ___ ___

11.10
Direct investigations to enforce banking laws . . . . ___ ___ ___
Inspect work areas to detect unsafe working conditions . . . . ___ ___ ___
Inspect cargo to enforce customs laws ___ ___ ___

11.11
Manage a hotel or motel . . . . ___ ___ ___
Direct activities of a branch office of an insurance company . . . . ___ ___ ___
Manage a grocery, clothing or other retail store . . . . ___ ___ ___

11.12
Investigate and settle insurance claims ___ ___ ___
Obtain leases for outdoor advertising sites . . . . ___ ___ ___
Sign entertainers to theater or concert contracts . . . . ___ ___ ___

12.01
Manage a professional baseball team ___ ___ ___
Referee sporting events . . . . ___ ___ ___
Drive in automobile races . . . . ___ ___ ___

12.02
Perform as a trapeze artist in a circus ___ ___ ___
Perform stunts for movie or television scenes . . . . ___ ___ ___
Perform juggling feats . . . . ___ ___ ___

NOW, GO BACK AND DOUBLECHECK AT LEAST FIVE
ACTIVITIES THAT YOU WOULD MOST LIKE TO DO

Worker Trait Groups

The numbers beside each group of activities in the Interest Check List refer to a "Worker Trait Group." The Worker Trait Groups are broad, general categories of interest. The trait groups describe many of the occupational functions and factors related to these areas of interest: physical requirements, necessary academic skills, specific vocational preparation time, etc. These descriptions then lead to a listing of some possible occupations which fall within the interest categories and Worker Trait Groups. Look at the five activities that you would most like to do (the double checks √√) and identify them by the number on the side of the inventory. Find the corresponding number in the following list. This gives you some idea of the kinds of occupations that are of greatest interest to you.

More complete and detailed descriptions may be found in the *Guide to Occupational Exploration* (G.O.E.) and in the McKnight *Worker Trait Group Guide* (1980), which are found in College Career Centers. The letters to the side of the trait groups indicate the related "Holland Types."

A *01. ARTISTIC*
01.01   Literary Arts
01.02   Visual Arts
01.03   Performing Arts: Drama
01.04   Performing Arts: Music
01.05   Performing Arts: Dance
01.06   Technical Art
01.07   Amusement
01.08   Modeling

I *02. SCIENTIFIC*
02.01   Physical Science
02.02   Life Science
02.03   Medical Science
02.04   Laboratory Technology

R *03. NATURE*
03.01   Managerial Work: Nature
03.02   General Supervision: Nature
03.03   Animal Training and Care
03.04   Elemental Work: Nature

R *04. AUTHORITY*
04.01   Safety and Law Enforcement
04.02   Security Services

R *05. MECHANICAL*
05.01   Engineering
05.02   Managerial Work: Mechanical
05.03   Engineering Technology
05.04   Air and Water Vehicle Operation
05.05   Craft Technology
05.06   Systems Operation
05.07   Quality Control
05.08   Land Vehicle Operation
05.09   Materials Control
05.10   Skilled Hand & Machine Work
05.11   Equipment Operation
05.12   Elemental Work: Mechanical

R *06. INDUSTRIAL*
06.01   Production Technology
06.02   Production Work
06.03   Production Control
06.04   Elemental Work: Industrial

C *07. BUSINESS DETAIL*
07.01   Administrative Detail
07.02   Mathematical Detail
07.03   Financial Detail
07.04   Information Processing: Speaking
07.05   Information Processing: Records
07.06   Clerical Machine Operation
07.07   Clerical Handling

E *08. PERSUASIVE*
08.01   Sales Technology
08.02   General Sales
08.03   Vending

09. ACCOMMODATING
09.01   Hospitality Services
09.02   Barbering and Beauty Services
09.03   Passenger Services
09.04   Customer Services
09.05   Attendant Services

S *10. HUMANITARIAN*
10.01   Social Services
10.02   Nursing and Therapy Services
10.03   Child and Adult Care

S/E *11. SOCIAL-BUSINESS*

11.01   Mathematics and Statistics
11.02   Educational and Library Services
11.03   Social Research
11.04   Law
11.05   Business Administration
11.06   Finance
11.07   Services Administration

11.08   Communications
11.09   Promotion
11.10   Regulations Enforcement
11.11   Business Management
11.12   Contracts and Claims

R   *12. PHYSICAL PERFORMING*

12.01   Sports
12.02   Physical Feats

Career Clusters

Career centers tend to be organized by the following career clusters (These clusters were originally created by the U.S. Office of Career Education):

Agriculture and Home Economics
Arts and Letters
Business
Education and Welfare
Engineering and Architecture
Government and Law
Health
Industrial, Trade and Service (includes apprenticeships)
Science

If you are attending school and have a major, you might research the cluster in which your major falls. Otherwise, select one area that seems to relate to your interests, values, and skills, and explore it.

The following exercise (7.2) will help you to examine the various clusters and to emphasize that the ones that you repeatedly select are your definite preferences.

7.2

Confirming Occupational Interest Areas

Circle the areas or words in 1, 2, 3 that you find most interesting. If you had two hours to research careers, which area(s) would you select?

1. WHAT FIELDS INTEREST YOU?

a. *Social*: Do you like to work with people? Do you help others organize activities? Are you active in social events?

b. *Sales-Verbal*: Do you like to sell, convince, persuade, influence, lead? Do you like to talk, write, read?

c. *Mechanical*: Do you like to fix things? Do you use and repair machines, appliances, equipment? Do you like to make or build things?

d. *Scientific*: Are you curious about ideas and abstract processes? Do you like to experiment and solve problems?

e. *Clerical-Computational*: Do you like to keep things orderly? Do you like to keep records, type, be accurate?

f. *Artistic*: Do you like music, dance, art, literature, photography, decorating? Do you like to express yourself creatively?

2. OCCUPATIONAL CATEGORIES ACCORDING TO THE SIX HOLLAND TYPES.
   a. *Realistic* (R) occupations include jobs in industry, trade, and service.
   b. *Investigative* (I) occupations include jobs in the fields of science and technology.
   c. *Artistic* (A) occupations include jobs in the fields of art, music, and literature.
   d. *Social* (S) occupations include jobs in the fields of education and welfare.
   e. *Enterprising* (E) occupations include jobs in sales and management.
   f. *Conventional* (C) occupations include office and clerical jobs.

3. OCCUPATIONAL FIELDS—JOB FAMILIES OR JOB CLUSTERS (LETTERS RELATE TO HOLLAND'S TYPES DESCRIBED ABOVE).
   a. Agriculture and Home Economics—R&I
   b. Arts and Letters—A
   c. Business—C
   d. Education and Welfare—S
   e. Engineering and Architecture—R&I
   f. Government and Law—E&S
   g. Health—I&S
   h. Industry, Trade and Service—R&C
   i. Science—I&R

4. LIST SUMMARY (PUTTING IT ALL TOGETHER) OF ANY ASSESSMENT OR INVENTORIES YOU HAVE TAKEN DURING THE PAST YEAR. FOR EXAMPLE:
   a. Strong Campbell Interest Inventory: Code letters ___ ___ ___ General Occupational Themes:

   _____   _____   _____

   Three highest Basic Interest Scales:

   _____

   _____

   _____

   Similar occupational scales (job titles). List five:

   _____   _____   _____

   _____   _____

   b. California Occupational Preference Survey (COPS)
   List your three highest occupational groups from this survey or from any other inventory used:

   _____   _____   _____

   List five related job titles that sound interesting:

   _____   _____   _____

   _____   _____

5. AFTER REVIEWING YOUR TOP INTERESTS, LIST YOUR TOP THREE CHOICES:

   _____   _____   _____

6. SUMMARIZE THE THREE CAREERS THAT RELATE TO THESE INTERESTS:

   _____   _____   _____

Section II—Chapter Summaries

Fill in the blanks in the following exercise after reviewing the summary pages found at the end of each chapter: If your responses today are different from those you recorded when you initially read the chapter, record your current responses to each item.

7.3

Chapter Summaries
Complete the following summary pages on chapters 1–6.

A. Summary—Chapter 1

1. I am _____

2. I need _____

_____

3. I want _____

_____

4. My current life stage could be summarized as: _____

_____

_____

_____

_____

5. The three Holland types most like me are:

Realistic   _____

Investigative   _____

Artistic   _____

Social   _____

Enterprising   _____

Conventional   _____

6. Adjectives that best describe me:

_____   _____   _____

_____   _____   _____

7. My favorite school subjects include: _____

_____

8. Five high status occupations include:

_____

_____

_____

_____

_____

B. Summary—Chapter 2

1. I am _____

2. Five positive attitudes I bring to the job are: _____

_____

3. I admire the following characteristics in people:

_____   _____   _____

_____   _____   _____

4. I am working on developing the following qualities _____

_____

5. My affirmations are: _____

_____

_____

C. Summary—Chapter 3

1. I highly value:

_____   _____   _____

_____   _____   _____

2. A problem in society that really concerns me is:

3. My most important considerations in a job are:

_____   _____   _____

_____   _____   _____

_____   _____   _____

4. I gain energy from the following types of people:

_____   _____   _____

_____   _____   _____

_____   _____   _____

5. I am energized by the following types of activities (from my past jobs, volunteer experiences, or hobbies):

_____   _____   _____

_____   _____   _____

_____   _____   _____

6. My ideal job would be:
   (If you don't have a title, list the job specifications.)

_____

D. Summary—Chapter 4

1. Fill in the percentage of time during a day that you would like to work with data, people, or things.

   _____ data   _____ people   _____ things

2. Three of my accomplishments are:

   a.

   b.

   c.

3. List the (a) work-content skills, (b) adaptive skills, and (c) functional skills identified in chapter 4, written exercise 4.5:

4. A summary of the skills I most enjoy using:

5. The skills I want to use in my future career are:

6. The skills I hope to develop in the next few years are:

E. Summary—Chapter 5

1. The advantages of my age, sex, and background in looking for a job or working toward a career goal are:

2. The disadvantages of my age, sex, race, or physical limitations in looking for a job or working toward my career goal are:

3. Occupations that interest me:

   a.

   b.

   c.

   d.

   e.

F. Summary—Chapter 6

1. I use the following decision-making strategies:

2. My limiting beliefs include:

3. My belief about the future is:

4. The best use of my time right now is:

5. A long-range goal related to my career is:

6. A short-term goal related to my career is:

7. External influences that can affect these career decisions include:

8. Internal factors that influence these career decisions include:

7.4

Quick Impressions

Read each category and respond quickly by recording the first three thoughts that come to mind in each one.

Values	Interests	Skills/Abilities	Possible Occupations	Related Leisure Time Pursuits

7.4 (*continued*)
Quick Impressions

Short Term Goals and Objectives	Long Term Goals and Objectives	Support People to help you implement your goals
1.	1.	
2.	2.	
3.	3.	
4.	4.	
5.	5.	

Review exercise 7.4, Quick Impressions, with three supportive people in your life. Ask for their responses, input, and help in working toward your goals.

Section III—Written Information Sources

Occupations are related and naturally fall into clusters or groupings such as Hollands types, the U.S. Office of Career Education's Career Clusters, or the G.O.E. Worker Trait Groups. To improve your skills in gathering job information, we will describe job clusters designed by the American College Testing Program (A.C.T.). They divide job clusters by the educational preparation needed. Additionally, to help you choose your specific career direction, we will explain how to examine career paths and common organizational divisions in business and industry.

Occupational Classification System

Career Clusters

The American College Testing Program (A.C.T.) has devised a useful system of organizing jobs into job clusters (table 7.2). A valuable aspect of this cluster system that differentiates it from the U.S. Department of Career Education's system is that it refers to educational preparation needed by cluster. Table 7.3 provides you with a further breakdown of the business, sales, and management cluster including educational preparation information. At some point you will have to decide how much education you will need to enter the career of your choice. This example allows you to see which jobs require only high school education and which require higher education.

Career Paths

Career ladders

Sometimes a greater awareness of the job market can be gained by researching career paths or career ladders in a specific industry (Stair 1980). Most career centers and libraries have books that outline career paths. Table 7.4 illustrates how jobs are related in the insurance field. Once you've assessed where you currently fit in you can start preparing to move up the ladder. The insurance industry is recognized as a field where a person can obtain entry-level employment with a high school diploma and work up the ladder. If you are currently working, your immediate supervisor and the personnel department can provide information about routes for advancement, e.g., in-house workshops, institutes, community college associate degrees, bachelor's degrees, etc.

Common Organizational Divisions

Although the world of work includes a number of different broad fields (e.g., business; education; government, including the military, health care, and nonprofit agencies), all of these fields share certain common functional needs and have some common departmental organizations. As an example, all four of the fields mentioned above need the accounting functions of payroll computation and disbursement, budgeting, and servicing of accounts payable and receivable. Administration, finance, human re-

Table 7.2
A.C.T. Job Clusters

Business, Sales & Management
Job Cluster

A. Promotion and Direct Contact Sales

Public relations workers, fashion models, travel agents, sales workers who visit customers (for example—real estate brokers, insurance agents, wholesalers, office supplies sales workers)

B. Management and Planning

Hotel, store, and company managers, bankers, executive secretaries, buyers, purchasing agents, small business owners

C. Retail Sales and Services

Sales workers in stores and shops, auto salespersons, retail sales workers

---

Business Operations
Job Cluster

D. Clerical and Secretarial Work

Typists, file clerks, mail clerks, office messengers, receptionists, secretaries

E. Paying, Receiving, and Bookkeeping

Bank tellers, accountants, payroll clerks, grocery check-out clerks, ticket sellers, cashiers, hotel clerks

F. Office Machine Operation

Adding, billing, and bookkeeping machine operators, computer and data processing machine operators, telephone operators

G. Storage, Dispatching, and Delivery

Shipping and receiving clerks, stock clerks, truck and airplane dispatchers, delivery truck drivers, cab drivers, mail carriers

---

Technologies & Trades
Job Cluster

H. Human Services Crafts

Barbers, hairdressers, tailors, shoemakers, cooks, chefs, butchers, bakers

I. Repairing and Servicing Home and Office Equipment

Repairing and servicing—TV sets, appliances, typewriters, telephones, heating systems, photo copiers

J. Growing and Caring for Plants/Animals

Farmers, foresters, ranchers, gardeners, yardworkers, groundskeepers, plant nursery workers, animal caretakers, pet shop attendants

K. Construction and Maintenance

Carpenters, electricians, painters, custodians (janitors), bricklayers, sheet metal workers, construction laborers, (buildings, roads, pipelines, etc.)

L. Transport Equipment Operation

Long haul truck and bus drivers, bulldozer operators, crane operators, forklift operators

M. Machine Operating, Servicing, and Repairing

Auto mechanics, machinists, printing press operators, sewing machine operators, service station attendants, laborers and machine operators in factories, mines, lumber camps, etc.

N. Engineering and other Applied Technologies

(For science and medical technicians, see Job Families O and P.) Engineers and engineering technicians, draftsmen and draftswomen, pilots, surveyors, computer programmers

---

Natural, Social, & Medical Sciences
Job Cluster

O. Natural Sciences and Mathematics

Biologists, chemists, lab technicians, physicists, geologists, statisticians, agricultural scientists, ecologists

P. Medicine and Medical Technologies

Dentists, doctors, veterinarians, medical technologists and lab workers, pharmacists,

Table 7.2 (continued)

X-ray technicians, optometrists, dental hygienists, dietitians

Q. Social Sciences and Legal Services

Sociologists, lawyers, political scientists, historians, psychologists, home economists

---

Creative & Applied Arts Job Cluster

R. Creative Arts

Authors, concert singers, musicians, actresses and actors, dancers, artists

S. Applied Arts (Verbal)

Reporters, technical writers, interpreters, newswriters, newswriters, ad copy writers

T. Applied Arts (Visual)

Interior decorators, architects, commercial artists, photographers, fashion designers

U. Popular Entertainment

Night club entertainers, popular singers and musicians, disc jockeys, circus performers

---

Social, Health, & Personal Services Job Cluster

V. Education and Social Services

Teachers*, counselors, social workers, librarians, athletic coaches, recreation workers, clergymen and clergywomen

W. Nursing and Human Care

Child care aides, nurses, dental assistants, physical therapists, hospital attendants

X. Personal and Household Services

Waiters and waitresses, airline stewardesses and stewards, housekeepers, porters, car hops, butlers and maids

Y. Law Enforcement and Protective Services

Police officers; building, food and postal inspectors; watchmen; plant guards; firefighters

*NOTE—Teachers: Students thinking about high school or college teaching should consider whether their main goal is *teaching students* (mark Job Family V) or *doing work or research in the subject area*: for example—chemistry, (mark Job Family O), art (mark R or T), economics (mark Q), etc.

There are more than 21,000 job titles in the world of work. This page is meant to illustrate how a sample of jobs can be clustered into related categories.

Source: Reprinted with the permission from The American College Testing Program (American College Testing Program 1977)

sources, marketing and public relations, management information systems, and research and development are departmental functions common to almost all work fields. The list below explains the general functions of these and other departments in typical business-area operations; however, you will find identical or very similar departments performing very similar functions in the fields of education, government, nonprofit agencies, or health care.

If you have been concentrating on specific industries in your search for job possibilities, you can gain a fresh perspective by selecting functions interesting to you and then researching jobs in those departments in different industries.

■ **Administration**

An organization's top executive officers and other managers. Secretarial and word-processing personnel are also included in this function.

■ **Corporate Relations**

Responsible for advertising, public relations, community relations.

- **Distribution**

  Sometimes called transportation department. Oversees warehousing and shipping of the company's products.

- **Engineering**

  Product design and modification; often oversees manufacturing of product (process engineers).

- **Finance**

  Accounting functions which include payroll, budgets, accounts payable and receivable.

- **Human Resources Development (HRD)**

  Sometimes called personnel or industrial relations. In charge of hiring, firing, training employees, administering equal employment law.

- **Management Information Systems (MIS)**

  All tasks involving handling information, including computer operations and record keeping.

- **Marketing**

  Responsible for sales of a product or service and possibly market research.

- **Operations**

  The line workers who assemble product, sales clerks, nurses in hospitals.

- **Production Management**

  Responsible for securing parts, supplies, inventory; also called purchasing or buying.

- **Quality Assurance**

  Responsibility for maintaining a certain quality standard for the product manufactured.

- **Research and Development**

  Designs and develops new products.

- **Strategic Planning**

  Looks at long-range economic forecasts, plans strategies for company's advancement.

Written Information Sources for Researching Specific Jobs

Now that you have a clearer idea of the jobs that best suit your personality it is necessary to research the actual requirements of the job. There are several ways to obtain job information. Basically you can search either through written materials in the library or contact people who already work in your area of interest. This section will focus on books and written materials while Chapter 10 will focus on people and contacts. Your local library or the local college career development and placement center should be able to provide you with some or all of the following resources.

Library research

Table 7.3

Business, Sales & Management Cluster

Typical Formal Preparation

The left arrow (←) for certain jobs means that may workers *also* enter that job with the type of preparation shown in the column at the left. The right arrow (→) refers to the type of preparation shown in the column at the right.

	High School Graduation Desirable	Up to Two Years of Preparation beyond High School	Three or More Years of Preparation beyond High School	Related High School Courses
A. Promotion and Direct Contact Sales	House-to-house salesperson Sample distributor Promotion worker Peddler Demonstrator Interviewer Survey Worker Telephone solicitor Car rental clerk Sound truck operator	Fashion model Photographer's model Travel clerk or agent Radio–TV time salesperson → ← Auctioneer Encyclopedia salesperson → Bridal consultant Wholesale salesworkers → who visit customers to sell *products*, such as—computers, medical and dental supplies, machinery, printing supplies, office machines, food products, petroleum products	Fashion coordinator ← Lobbyist ← Public relations worker ← Advertising worker ← Business agent ← Salesworker who sells services to customers, for example—stocks and bonds salesperson, insurance agent, account executive, real estate agent, and investment analyst	General business Speech Bookkeeping General math Economics Distributive education programs such as sales, marketing, and product information
B. Management and Planning	See note below	Credit manager → Buyer → Import-export agent → Store or hotel manager → Sales manager → ← Automobile parts manager ← Apartment house manager Postmaster → City planning aide Funeral director ← Manager or owner of → small business such as—skating rink, record shop, dance studio, beauty shop, donut shop, hobby shop, restaurant, theatre, hardware store	Bank officer Assessor Controller Treasurer City manager Urban planner ← Purchasing agent Hospital administrator Personnel manager Airport manager Traffic manager Athletic director	Business law Bookkeeping Speech Economics General business Distributive education programs such as business operation and product information

C. Retail Sales and Services

Concession attendant	See note below	← Sales clerks and retail salesworkers in stores selling products such as—furniture, drapery, radios, televisions, gas and electric appliances, hi-fi, sporting goods, automobiles, mobile homes, hearing aids, photographic supplies, musical instruments, jewelry	Economics General math General business Distributive education programs such as product information, sales and marketing
Newspaper carrier			
Will-call clerk			
Lost-and-found clerk			
Counter attendants in restaurants, dry cleaning shops, and snack bars			
Sales clerks and retail salesworkers → in stores selling products such as—shoes, clothing, flowers, lawn and garden equipment, floor coverings, hardware, books, pets, food, china and glassware, cosmetics			

Source: Reprinted by permission of American College Testing Program.

Note—Workers with this type of job preparation are sometimes employed in jobs listed in the other columns of this chart. Jobs in another column might have arrows (←, →) pointing toward this column. Check with your counselor if you want to know about other jobs with this type of preparation. Remember that the jobs on these charts are listed under the type of preparation typical of *most*, but not all, workers entering the jobs.

Table 7.4
Career Paths

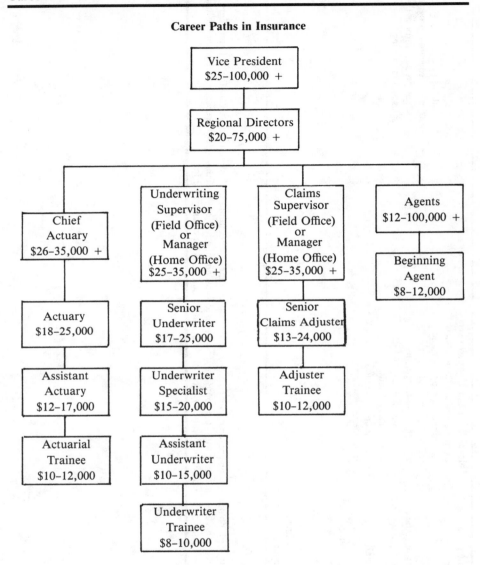

Career Paths in Insurance

Organization charts listing career paths are sometimes found in files in personnel offices. (1986 salaries, however, would not be included. The salaries in this table are 1980 national averages.)

Federal Government Offices and Publications

You may obtain employment with the federal government by applying for a position announcement. Printed job information is available at your Federal Job Information Center. Table 7.5 lists the positions.

Government listings

Did you know that the federal government hires some 1500 people each day? No one in the federal government knows all the positions vacant on a particular day, week, or month. Thus, you must contact the personnel offices of each agency for a complete listing of vacancies in that agency. An alternative to walking the blocks to each agency is using a private publication. *The Federal Research Service, Inc.* (a private firm) publishes some 2500 vacancies every two weeks in its *Federal Yellow Pages*, which also outlines the organization of all executive agencies and gives names, addresses, and phone numbers of key officials. The *Congressional Yellow Book* is a similar volume on congressional agencies as well as personal and committee staff in the House and Senate.

Federal Job Information Centers may also have access to a national computerized job bank. This would be especially useful for those of you who want to know about job opportunities located some distance from you.

U.S. Department of Labor Publications.

The Dictionary of Occupational Titles (D.O.T.) lists over 35,000 job titles and over 20,000 different occupations. This reference has been mentioned previously in this book and will be referred to in Chapter 9 as a tool to use in writing resumes. It is especially useful because it lists specific tasks to be done on a job, e.g., COPY WRITER:

> COPY WRITER
> *Writes advertising copy for use by publication or broadcast media to promote sale of goods and services: Consults with sales media, and marketing representatives to obtain information on product or service and discuss style and length of advertising copy. Obtains additional background and current development information through research and interview. Reviews advertising trends, consumer surveys, and other data regarding marketing of specific and related goods and services to formulate presentation approach. Writes preliminary draft of copy and sends to supervisor for approval. Corrects and revises copy as necessary. May write articles, bulletins, sales letters, speeches, and other related informative and promotional material.*

The Occupational Outlook Handbook (OOH) includes information on job descriptions, places of employment, training, educational requirements, and salary ranges. This is updated every other year and represents a national survey of occupations. Salary information should be compared with local salaries and local cost of living factors. For example, Los Ange-

Table 7.5
Federal Employment

Federal Employment Positions Previously Covered by Exams	Federal Employment Positions Covered by Announcements	
Administrative Trainee	Accountant	Physicist
Alcohol Tax Inspector	Aerospace Technologist	Pest Controller
Archivist	Air Traffic Controller	Plant Scientist
Budget Analyst	Animal Husbandry	Prison Administrator
Claims Examiner	Architect	Range Conservationist
Community Planner	Astronomer	Refuge Manager
Contract Negotiator	Attorney	Social Worker
Customs Specialist	Bacteriologist	Soil Conservationist
Customs Inspector	Biologist	Special Agent
Customs Technical Aide	Cartographer	Speech Pathologist
Computer Programmer	Chemist	Teacher
Economist	Dietitian	Therapist
Financial Examiner	Education Officer	Urban Planner
Food and Drug Inspector	Engineer	Veterinarian
Geographer	Entomologist	
Historian	Equipment Specialist	
Housing Intern	Estate Tax Examiner	
Intelligence Analyst	Forester	
Investigator	Geodesist	
Loan Examiner	Geophysicist	
Management Analyst	Hospital Administrator	
Management Intern	Hydrologist	
Manpower Specialist	Illustrator	
Marketing Specialist	Internal Revenue Agent	
Museum Curator	Landscape Architect	
Park Ranger	Librarian	
Personnel Specialist	Manual Arts Therapist	
Psychologist	Mathematician	
Public Information	Medical Record Librarian	
Realty Assistant	Metallurgist	
Revenue Officer	Meteorologist	
Social Insurance	Microbiologist	
Sociologist	Nurse	
Statistical Assistant	Oceanographer	
Supply Specialist	Occupational Therapist	
Tax Technician	Patent Examiner	
Writer and Editor	Pharmacist	

les tends to pay $1,000-$2,000 more per year than many of the generalized estimates in the OOH.

Between editions of the OOH, *The Occupational Outlook Quarterly* provides updates of occupational projections as well as compensation ranges and cost of living comparisons throughout the United States.

The Guide to Occupational Exploration (G.O.E.) provides detailed information about the interests, aptitudes, skills, and job activities of various occupational groups. The data in this publication are organized into 12 interest areas, 66 worker trait groups, and 348 subgroupings. The worker trait groups were listed after the interest inventory.

State and Local Government

State and local governments hire the majority of people in public work. Local government alone hires over 50 percent of all public employees. Table 7.6 lists the types of positions generally available. State personnel offices have applications, tests, job descriptions, and occupational outlook data for their state. For example, in California there is a "Guide to the Use of Labor Market Publications." It is important to consider that it takes six to nine months to complete the application, test, interview, and hire process. This is not a resource for one who needs immediate employment. Many college students start the application and test process during their senior year in college.

Local government is a large employer

Directories

Information about a variety of enterprises, from foundations to corporations, can be found in directories. Directories list names and addresses of employers, product, and geographic location, as well as other information, including size in terms of volume of sales, number of employees, and names of top-level executives. *Don't forget to use your local telephone directory*. The white pages list government agencies and departments while the yellow pages list other places of employment. A phone call will get you specific information!

Let your fingers do the researching

- *California Manufacturers Directory:* Lists companies by location and product with an additional section on companies that have import/export business.
- *Dun and Bradstreet Middle Market Directory:* Lists companies with assets between $500,000 and $1 million.
- *Dun and Bradstreet Million Dollar Directory:* Lists names and addresses of thousands of trade publications from companies earning more than $1 million annually.
- *Encyclopedia of Associations:* Lists names of 15,000 associations in every field with names of officers, telephone numbers, and brief descriptions of orientations and activities.
- *Encyclopedia of Business Information Services:* Lists source materials on businesses.
- *Geographical Index:* Lists companies by cities and towns.
- *Guide to American Directories:* Describes 3,300 directories subdivided into 400 topical areas.
- *Poor's Register of Corporations, Directors, and Executives:* Gives names and addresses of 260,000 leading executives by company and product.

Table 7.6
State and Local Government Departments and Independent Government Organizations

State	Independent Government Organizations	Local Government
Conservation	Energy Research and	Tax Assessment
Criminal Justice	Development	Tax Collection
Education Programs	Administration	Elections
Elections	Board of Governors of the	Courts
Employment Services	Federal Reserve System	Law Enforcement
Financial Operations	Central Intelligence Agency	Urban Planning
Health Services	Federal Bureau of	Sanitation
Highway Operations	Investigation	Health
Law Enforcement	Foreign Service of the U.S.	Social Work
Legislative Liaison	International Monetary Fund	Welfare
Mental Health Services	National Science Foundation	Roads and Streets
Parks and Recreation	National Security Agency	Parks and Recreation
Prison Operations	Organization of American	Fire Protection
Social Welfare	States	Public Records
Transportation Systems	Tennessee Valley Authority	Financial Services
Unemployment Services	United Nations Secretariat	
	U.S. Mission to the U.N.	
	U.S. Nuclear Regulatory	
	Commission	
	U.S. Postal Service	
	World Bank and IFC	

■ *Regional and community magazines:* Most large cities and metropolitan areas have community magazines which focus on business, industry, education, the arts, and politics; states and regions also have their own magazines.

■ *Standard Directory of Advertisers:* Lists 50 major industries with names, addresses, and telephone numbers.

■ *The Standard Periodical Directory:* Describes 50,000 periodicals and directories.

■ *Standard Rate and Data Business Publications Directory:* Lists names and addresses of thousands of trade publications.

■ *State Directories:* Each state has a directory of trade and industry. If not in your library, contact your local or state chamber of commerce or write to U.S. Chamber of Commerce, 1615 H Street, N.W., Washington, D.C. 20006.

■ *Thomas' Register of American Manufacturers:* Lists 100,000 manufacturers by location and product.

■ *Who's Who in Commerce and Industry:* Gives names and biographical sketches of top executives.

■ *World Trade Academy Press:* Lists U.S. firms in 85 countries. (The U.S. Embassy and U.S. Chamber of Commerce also list U.S. companies overseas.)

Newspapers

Check out all the newspapers in the geographical area in which you would be interested in working. Read the help-wanted section for openings as well as local wage and fringe benefit information. There may be a separate business section that advertises for professional jobs. Read everything in terms of your own job target. Keep a file. Beware that only 15 percent of job openings are listed in want ads. Therefore note other parts of the paper such as articles that announce business expansion, personnel changes, and new ideas. Planning commission announcements usually mention new industrial plazas and the expected number of employees to be located in the plaza. Marriage announcements which usually list bride and groom's occupations, may give you the name of an important executive of a firm that interests you. "Living Sections" may profile leaders in the community; gossip columns may suggest where to find trend setters.

Look beyond the want ads

Trade Journals

Almost every trade and profession has at least one regularly published journal. The business section of your library should have references. The following three resources are useful in tracking down particular trade journals: *Ulrich's International Periodical Directory*; the *Encyclopedia of Business Information Sources*; and the *Encyclopedia of Associations*. Use these trade journals to locate job ads, familiarize yourself with the people, products, current trends, and specific vocabulary of that field.

Become aware of trends in a specific field

Magazines

The Reader's Guide to Periodicals, available at any library, can be used both to locate names of magazines and to find out informative and useful titles of articles about any field you wish to research. Do you want to learn the latest in word-processing careers, the outlook for engineers in the western United States, opportunities for liberal arts graduates? It's been covered in some magazine recently! Also business magazines provide profiles of both businesses and their executive officers which is information that you might use in comparing companies.

Keep current

A. Useful magazines for business information:
   Business Week
   Executive Female
   Forbes
   Fortune
   Kiplinger's Changing Times
   SAVVY, Magazine for Executive Women
   Working Women
   Wall Street Journal
   Inc.
   Success

B. Specialized magazines for college graduates:
Business World, the Career Magazine for College Students (University Publications Inc., P.O. Box 1234, Rathway, N.J. 07065)
Black Collegian (Black Collegian Service Inc., New Orleans, La.)
College Placement Annual, Check with local college placement office. (P.O. Box 2263, Bethleham, Pennsylvania 18001)
Business Week's Guide to Careers
Hispanic Times Magazine, P.O. Box 6368, Westlake Village, CA 91359
Womens' Careers (Equal Opportunity Inc., Chicago, Illinois)

In-House Bulletins and Announcements

Personnel offices in virtually every business, agency, school, or hospital post jobs as they become available. Job posting best serves the person already employed at such places; however, some of the jobs may be open to anyone.

?? Written Exercises

The following written exercises serve to help you digest the contents of section 3. They can be completed by using the local library or college career center and exploring some of the resources mentioned in this chapter. Exercise 7.5 requires that you investigate written resources utilizing the local library, college library, and local newspaper. Exercise 7.6 asks that you learn what your college career center and local state employment office or other employment offices might have available. Exercise 7.7 is a summary sheet for exercises 7.5 and 7.6. Lastly, exercise 7.8 gives you the format by which you can gather the facts about your three top choices.

7.5
Library Research

a. What directories are most helpful to you now, what do you need to know? Where are directories found?

b. What are the names of three trade journals related to your field of interest? Where are they found?

   1. _____

   2. _____

   3. _____

c. What are some of the current trends reflected in these journals?

d. Name one professional association related to your field. Also list where and when the local meetings are held. (What about the national conference - can you attend or join as a student?) For example:

   Association: American Society of Women Accountants (ASWA)
   　　　　　　　Local Contact: Joan Smith–phone (805) 555–1213
   　　　　　　　Meeting time & location: 3rd Thursday of each month
   　　　　　　　7:00 pm (dinner)
   　　　　　　　Colonial House Restaurant, Oxnard

e. Study the newspaper for three weeks and make a scrapbook of articles that relate to your field. (Include want ads as well as feature articles or names of executives in your field whose names appeared anywhere in the paper.)

7.6
Local Resources

a. Investigate the local career and placement centers. Ask whether they place people in your field or whether they can give you referrals.

b. Visit the state employment office and private employment agencies to find out how they place people and how long it might take to get a job.

7.7
Printed Information Work Sheet

Name _____

Job Target _____
Using the resources explained earlier, use your own job target and list the sources in each category.

a. Newspapers, Bulletin Boards, Magazines.

b. Trade Journals.

c. Directories.

d. Placement Centers.

e. Career Centers.

7.8
Gathering the Facts

Select three jobs to research in a library or career center utilizing the following outline in this exercise. You may either select three different jobs (i.e., teacher, social worker, personnel manager); three jobs that are related (i.e., lawyer, paralegal, legal secretary), or three that represent the same field but vary in degree of education or experience (i.e., marketing executive, graphic artist, display assistant).

Once you identify some interesting job titles, you need to gather the following information from a library or a college career center:

1. Title of career
2. Salary
3. Hours
4. Benefits
5. Outlook (Will there be jobs in the future?)
6. Educational requirements
   Minimum training necessary:
   If college is necessary, what types of classes available in my local area.
7. Schools or colleges offering the training
8. Personal requirements
9. Physical demands
10. Work description
11. Working conditions
12. Where employed
13. Opportunities for advancement
14. Related occupations
    No additional training needed:
    Some college needed:
    BA or BS degree needed:
    Other training (i.e., masters degree or special licenses):
15. Sources:
    May include written resources in the career center or names of people whom you have contacted.
16. After researching the specifics, are you still interested; how does this mesh with your vision of a life style?

If you've identified more than one career goal and are confused about which to pursue, work with exercise 7.9, a guided fantasy. Try to visualize yourself in each career. Which one feels most comfortable, most consistent with who you are?

7.9
Guided Fantasy

Close your eyes, take a few deep breaths and relax. Remove all feelings of tension from your body, and erase all previous thoughts and worries from your mind. . . .

Imagine that you are getting up on a typical workday about five years from now. You're sitting on the side of your bed trying to decide what kind of clothes you are going to wear. Take a moment and look over your wardrobe. What type of clothing do you finally decide to wear? . . .

Imagine yourself getting ready for work. . . . Any thoughts while you're getting ready about the day to come? . . . What kind of feelings do you have as you look forward to your workday? . . . Do you feel excited? Bored? Apprehensive? . . . What gives you these feelings? . . .

It's time for breakfast now. . . . Will you be sharing breakfast with someone, or will you be eating alone? . . .

You've completed your breakfast now, and are headed out the door. Stop for a moment and look around your neighborhood. . . . What does it look like? . . . What does your home look like? . . . What thoughts and feelings do you experience as you look around? . . .

Fantasize now that you're heading toward work. How are you getting there? . . . How far is it? . . . What new feelings or thoughts are you experiencing? . . .

You're entering your work situation now. . . . Pause for a bit and try to get a mental picture of it. Think about where it is and what it looks like. . . . Will you be spending most of your time indoors, or outdoors? . . . How many people will you be working with? . . .

You are going to your specific job now. Who is the first person you encounter? . . . What does he or she look like? . . . What is he or she wearing? . . . What do you say to him or her? . . .

Try to form an image of the particular tasks you perform on your job. Don't think about it as a specific job with a title such as nurse or accountant. Instead, think about what you are actually doing such as working with your hands, adding figures, typing, talking to people, drawing, thinking, etc.

In your job, do you work primarily by yourself or do you work mostly with others? . . . In your work with others, what do you do with them? . . . How old are the other people? . . . What do they look like? . . . How do you feel towards them? . . .

Where will you be going for lunch? . . . Will you be going with someone else? Who? What will you talk about? . . .

How do the afternoon's activities differ from those of the mornings? . . . How are you feeling as the day progresses? . . . Tired? . . . Alert? . . . Bored? . . . Excited?

Your work day is coming to an end now. Has it been a satisfying day? . . . If so, what made it satisfying? . . . What about the day are you less happy about? . . . Will you be taking some of your work home with you? . . .

As a final step in confirming your career goal, complete exercise 7.10, the Information Integration and Goal-Setting Form. Refer to the following page if you need a sample to help you along.

7.10
Information Integration & Goal Setting
Complete the "Information Integration & Goal Setting" form below using Exhibit 7.1 as a guideline and sample.

Life Goal: _____

_____

Present Short Range Occupational Goal (One-to-Five-Year Goal):
   Fill in the blanks.

   I look forward to becoming a _____

   _____

   because I value _____

   _____

   and my interests include _____

   _____

   and this career would allow me to _____

   _____

   _____

Personal Strengths	Personal Weaknesses (Need to improve)
Favorable External Conditions	Unfavorable External Conditions
Strategies to Reach Goal	Resources

Alternative short range goals that would be mutually satisfying:

_____

_____

Exhibit 7.1

Information Integration and Goal Setting (sample)

Life Goal: *To enable people to use their resources.*

Present Short Range Occupational Goal (One-to-Five-Year Goal):
   Fill in the blanks.

I look forward to becoming a   *social worker or counselor*

because I value   *helping others, serving people, being resourceful, variety, creativity and continually learning*
and my interests include: *communications, holistic health, adult development, higher education, and career counseling.*

and this career would allow me to   *share, keep informed, serve people, be an expert*

Personal Strengths	Personal Weaknesses (Need to improve)
Have a B.A. *Willing to study* *Quick learner* *Self confident* *Able to present before a group* *Eligible for credential programs* *Already have volunteered*	*Impatient* *Lack money for further education* *Fear taking graduate record exam* *Need time management*
Favorable External Conditions	**Unfavorable External Conditions**
Many education programs available *Many counselors retiring in next three years* *Already working* *Volunteer experiences are available* *Graduate Programs exist*	*Not many openings now* *Not many paid positions available now* *Many people with this degree out of work*
Strategies to Reach Goal	**Resources**
*Talk to graduate advisor **Obtain application to grad school* **Disucss alterntives with advisor* **Identify volunteer possibilities* **Volunteer* **Seek part-time job related to counseling (i.e., teacher's aide, etc.)*	**Faculty* **Counselors* **College Career and Placement Center*

Alternative short range goals that would be mutually satisfying: _____

1.   Personnel Assistant   2.   Employment Interviewer   3.   Community Services ssistant _____

I   look   forward   to   becoming   a _____ because I value

_____ and this career would allow me to _____

_____

If you are still confused about which career to focus on, start with the one that is most easily attainable and work through your job search strategy in Part II of this book using this career as your focal point. Once you understand the job search process, you can use it to explore additional career goals.

Congratulations! You are now in the process of exercising your options. You have identified a possible career goal and you are about to begin Part II of this book, Job Search Strategy. This will help you further clarify your goals and move you toward the career of your choice. Remember that the clarification process is ongoing throughout your career search. Every new contact and piece of information opens new possibilities and options.

Part Two

Job Search Strategy— Maintaining Momentum

Part I →

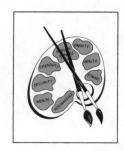

← **Part II**

Focusing in on Your Target

A wise man will make more opportunities than he finds.
Sir Francis Bacon

Learning Objectives   At the end of the chapter you will be able to:

Identify the components of a successful job search.

Differentiate between the traditional and non-traditional approaches to the job search.

Begin the process of searching for a job.

Congratulations! You have just completed the qualifying trials for the Olympics! In other words, you have finished the personal assessment portion of your career fitness program. You have reviewed and analyzed your potentials, your interests, and your values and you have tentatively selected some career alternatives. They are tentative because you may find reason to alter your initial decisions as you continue to gather further information. Just as adjustments occur in a physical fitness program based on your body's responses, so must adjustments occur in your career fitness program based on your "gut-level" responses.

The next step is to begin to design your job search strategy, which comprises the second part of the career-planning process. Job search strategy involves the long-term process of acquiring the training, background, and experience needed to be competitive in the job market. Simultaneously, you need to begin to identify potential employers for your skills, and develop a resume that reflects your background and your particular career goal. Finally, you need to learn how to present yourself in the best light in job interviews.

The winning edge

Your job search must be conducted consistently over a period of time. The U.S. Department of Labor has estimated that it can take nine months

163

of searching to obtain the job that's best suited to your desires. Regardless of how certain or tentative you are currently feeling about your career alternatives you must have a specific occupation in mind in order to benefit maximally from the remainder of this book. By the end of this chapter you should choose one of the occupations that you have been considering and keep it in mind as you read and work through the following chapters.

A job search requires focus

The rest of this chapter will provide you with information and skills that will enable you to gain control over a competitive job market. In other words, you will learn many techniques to put yourself in the right place at the right time and to present yourself as the best candidate for your desired job. The underlying and most important concept, however, is that you must become focused on what you want. Without this concentration you run the risk of being swayed into random opportunities and jobs that don't live up to your expectations. *Focusing* means that all new information should be evaluated and compared with your needs, values, interests and skills. Remember, the first job you are seeking should not be considered an end in itself. It is one job on the way to several more that will comprise your total career. As Webster's Dictionary defines *career*, it is a "pursuit of consecutive progressive achievement in public, professional, or business life." Additionally, career experts predict that the average worker can expect to make three or four career changes in a lifetime.

This approach assumes that you have identified a job objective for which you feel *100 percent enthusiasm*, that you will go after it with *100 percent determination*, and that you will interview for it with *100 percent of your heart*. This approach charges you with the responsibility to make things happen!

Designing a Comprehensive Job Search Strategy

A comprehensive job search strategy involves much more than just researching to decide what your ideal job is, and to discover areas of employment where you could expect to find such jobs. It encourages you, once having made these basic decisions, to assertively locate and actually become employed in your ideal job. A comprehensive job search strategy stimulates you to consider a variety of aspects associated with attaining your ideal job, such as whether you are likely to find your job in the geographical area where you live or want to live, and what sorts of activities and experiences will better qualify you for your career objectives. Equally important, job search strategy helps you to select and become involved in volunteer and entry-level activities that are the vital first steps toward your ultimate job or career goal. You can't always start right out in your ideal job, but, guided by job search strategy, you can almost always start out in jobs and activities that will lead to your goals. Assuming that you have adequate skills and background and that you have identified a job for which you are 100 percent enthusiastic, the following approach is for you.

The assertive approach

A Comprehensive Job Search

1. Be 100 percent committed to your job objective.
2. Compare the tasks and responsibilities required in your chosen job at different companies and organizations.
3. Get involved in voluntary and entry-level jobs related to your ultimate goal.
4. Identify the hidden job market through personal contacts.
5. Utilize both the traditional and nontraditional search resources.
6. Utilize professional assistance, if necessary.
7. Conduct informational interviews with people who are in a position to hire you. Approach all contacts with enthusiasm and sincerity and send thank-you letters to all contacts.
8. Network: Let everyone know you are looking for a job (friends, neighbors, dentists, etc.).
9. Identify the needs of the organization. If the exact position you would like is not available, your task is to define a problem within the organization that you can help to solve with your own unique skills.
10. Convince an employer that you have the skills that the employer needs.

First you must commit yourself, make a contract with yourself, that you will complete all the tasks necessary to get the job. Next, you must become totally informed about the tasks and responsibilities of the job you are seeking. Much of this information can be gained from the written materials previously cited. Additionally, you will need to amplify the written information by making personal contacts with insiders.

Once you have identified your ideal job situation, an important part of your job search strategy is to investigate associated activities that may be indispensible first steps toward your goal. Such activities may be temporary or volunteer or entry-level jobs in your chosen field. They can be very important in adding to your experience and making you a better candidate for your preferred job. For example, one teacher wanting to move into the advertising business took a job as a secretary in the executive suite of an advertising agency in New York. Of course, he had brushed up on his typing and shorthand skills to get this entry-level job, but he didn't plan to remain at that level for long. Being male, he had high visibility as a secretary. But even more important, he kept his eyes and ears open for ways that he could contribute to the efficiency of the business. Within six months he had learned enough about the advertising business to interview at a competing firm and become assistant to the president.

One final suggestion before you conduct further research. You may find that your ideal job is years of education and experience away from you, or that you don't have the dedication or talent to make it in your ideal field. If so, possibly you can be just as happy if you work in some job *related to* the career of your dreams. For example, behind every President of the United States there are advisors, speech writers, guards, secretaries, chefs, press representatives, chauffeurs. Behind every rock musician there are disc jockeys, public relations representatives, recording technicians, piano tuners, album cover designers, sound editors, cutting designers, concert coordinators, costume and make-up artists, background musicians, etc.

There is some merit to the idea that if you stay around the field, constantly adding to your experience, you may be at the right place at the right time and get the job of your dreams. Every understudy in a play or musical has a chance to become a star some day!

The Traditional Job Search

To increase your chances of getting the job of your choice, consider using traditional job search strategy as well as the nontraditional strategy described thus far. There are three prime sources in the traditional search strategy: (1) want ads (2) direct mail (3) employment agencies.

Want ads

Want ads are found in local newspapers, newspapers from your desired geographical area, trade journals, a supplement from the *Wall Street Journal,* and association magazines. Some newspapers have business sections with separate "Help Wanted" sections. You should become familiar with the specialized meanings of words and phrases used in these ads. Other job listings are also to be found in your state employment department, county and city personnel offices, placement centers, private employment offices, and the personnel office of each individual organization.

Understanding want ad headings

Much important information is given in these headings. Here are a few hints to help you understand the terminology.

HELP WANTED ——— Employment Agencies
You, the jobseeker, will usually pay the agency fee.

HELP WANTED ——— Fee-Paid Jobs
The employer pays the fee.

HELP WANTED ——— Canvassers—Solicitors
May be salary or commission (no sales, no pay!)

HELP WANTED ——— Commissions, Bonus, etc.
Some jobs listed here pay a salary.
Some jobs may require an investment by you.
"Draw"—is an advance against future commission earnings.
"Guarantee"—generally means you will receive a certain amount of money from the company although you make no sales.

DOMESTIC HELP WANTED ———
Work to be done in the employer's home
Compensation may be salary or room and board only.

Answering ads promptly and efficiently

> CLERK TYPIST
> *Type 40 wpm, familiar with office practices, telephone procedures, high school graduate. Apply at Personnel Dept. HOME STORES, VENTURA*

Apply in person. No phone number in the ad.

> GROCERY STORE
> *In Oxnard - In need of box boy experienced in store pricing and display methods. $4.50 per hour. Call Sunday 9:00 am to noon or Monday 9:00 am to 4:00 pm 488-4215.*

Call (at time indicated) for an appointment.

> PET STORE ASSISTANT
> *Neat, ambitious young man or lady to assist in pet care, sales, and store clean-up. 2000 S. Victor Rd. Moorpark. 684-2152*

A good idea to call first for an appointment. NEVER inquire about salary over the phone!

> OFFICE TRAINEE
> *Young and aggressive high school graduate to learn financial firm office procedures. Must type and be capable of using standard office calculating machines and copying equipment. Send Résumé to Box 24 w, Blade Tribune.*

This is a blind ad, since you don't know who placed it. Send your letter and resume to the box number, in care of the newspaper. Use "Dear Sir/Madame" or "To whom it may concern" as a salutation.

It has been found that in larger cities regularly reviewing the want ads over several months can lead you to meaningful employment leads. Although it has been estimated that only 15 percent of jobs are found through want ads there are thousands of ads in large newspapers. You can increase your chances of obtaining a job by applying for different job titles in the want ads. People with accounting degrees may be eligible for Junior Accountant, Management Trainee, Accounts Payable, Stock Broker, as well as Accountant.

Only 15 to 20% of all available jobs appear in the want ads

An additional way to increase your chances to find a good job involves mixing the traditional search in the want ads with your active accummulation of information about companies. When you see a job opening in the paper from a firm that you've visited you should have a contact in that company to call and ask for more information about the opening. You may find that the want ad is written with absolute qualifications but that the specific department will accept alternative experiences in lieu of some of the specific qualifications. Only people who have personal contacts would know such information.

Direct Mailing

If you fail to find your ideal job in the want ads, you may try two kinds of direct mailings: (1) to all companies in a desired geographical area; or (2) to specific organizations or companies most likely to need your qualifications.

Direct mailing can be expensive, depending on how many companies you address in your search. The prime objective is to find job openings. Once the opening is found you should follow up with a telephone call to arrange for an interview. Since the return rate is very low, it is a good idea to enclose a stamped, self-addressed post card. The post card can include check-off statements such as "sorry, no openings"; "opening possible within one month"; "opening available, please contact: _____"; as well as blank spaces for the name, address, and telephone number of the organization.

Although this approach sounds quite sophisticated, you may get less than 10 replies per 100 mailed. Traditionally, people have only gotten 15 replies out of 1000 mailings! You are more likely to get more replies if you have targeted an audience. In order to target the audience either you need to have read about the company or organization (in any of the resources previously mentioned) to discover that the company is expanding in your specialty area, or you need to have heard that the company needs your expertise through a contact. Annual reports available through the company, a stock broker, or your local library are excellent sources for identifying companies with potential openings. For example, recently Bank of America indicated in its annual report that it would be expanding its human resources development function at its headquarters in San Francisco. Upon seeing that information an interested job seeker called the headquarters Staff Development Department, sent her resume to the person identified by the switchboard as the head of the department, and got an interview!

Employment Agencies

Before you register with an agency, check carefully their fees, the types of positions they handle, and their reputation. There is some controversy over the merits of a system which makes a profit by simply placing you on a job with limited concern for your satisfaction. However, there are good agencies that are very concerned about matching people with a job that suits them.

Temporary Employment Agencies

These provide excellent ways to get back into the work force or to test the climate in a variety of companies. The jobs primarily available are clerical or entry-level computer jobs unless the temporary employment agency specializes in a field like accounting or nursing. Some agencies place people part-time, some place people for short-term assignments. The only drawback is that you are under contract to the temporary agency and cannot be hired by the employer using you, for a specified period of time.

The Nontraditional Job Search

The nontraditional approach to job hunting involves putting yourself in the right place at the right time. It involves strategies that assist you to find openings in your target area before the openings are publicly announced. In situations when you do not appear to be the ideal candidate, the nontraditional approach will assist you in getting noticed and getting an interview.

Many times it is best to try this approach while you are still employed because potential employers tend to defer any unemployed inquirers to the personnel office. This approach requires you to have a specific field and job objective in mind. Let's say you selected Real Estate Development and majored in Business Administration specializing in finance and real estate. An important decision would entail whether you want to work for a commercial bank, private developer, government appraisal office or government bureau of land development, or a related association that employs people to interact with the government. Following is an example:

> Susan was an assistant to a county supervisor and just happened to find many of her assignments related to land development. While finishing her Bachelors in Business (attending college after work hours), she increasingly represented her supervisor when land developers appealed to the Board of Supervisors for zoning and code changes. When her supervisor did not run for reelection, Susan was hired as a Director for the Business-Industry Association to lobby the county for the industrialization of farm land. Within a few years, Susan became a consultant to land developers and interacted with her present boss who hired her into his prospering real estate development firm as a Vice President of Government Relations.
>
> Even while working in an entry level job, Susan met people working in the field of her interest, real estate. As an Assistant to the County Supervisor, she met people in government, associations, and private industry. Susan maintained high visibility by speaking at community events, representing the Supervisor in his absence, and joining related organizations and community clubs. When she needed to make a job change, she had already identified and made contact with the types of places and people with whom she wanted to work. She had contacts who were insiders who could recommend her for jobs before they were announced. But even more important, she had discovered the "hidden job market." She knew the needs of the Business Industry Association and could tell them how her skills and contacts could benefit them. She was able to sell herself. She knew she had skills and contacts with government that could enhance her present employer's expansive plans. She was hired because she was able to describe the job she wanted to do in his firm and her ideal job meshed with the vision of the president of the company. She created her current position.

Visibility

*Hidden
Job Market*

Volunteering

> Ms. Lee found she was tired of going to college. She was beginning work on a master's degree in anthropology when she realized that studying native tribes in the wilds of Africa would not allow her to make the personal contribution to other people's lives that she felt necessary for her own job satisfaction. With the help of a career counselor at the local YWCA and talking with people working in her ideal setting,

she became aware that working in a family-planning clinic would best suit her personal needs. So she volunteered for one year in such a clinic and additionally conducted some studies on pregnancy and childbirth. Within the next year she had a full-time job in the Education Department of the Planned Parenthood organization.

The importance of getting job-related experience cannot be overestimated. As can be seen in Lee's story, she got volunteer experience to supplement her previous training. Many people have negative images of volunteering. They think volunteering means doing paper work or "go-fer" *Apprentice-* work. However, you can create meaningful volunteer positions for your-*ships,* self rather than taking whatever is available. To optimize your chances for *internships* obtaining such useful experience, go through a community voluntary action center (VAC), a college volunteer services office (sometimes part of the college placement office), or a college cooperative education office. There may even be some classes at your local college called *internships*. Internships are usually restricted to students who have studied in the subject area of the internship. For example, a history major or a political science major may be most eligible for an internship in local or state government; a graphic arts, public relations, English, or communications major may be most eligible for an internship in an advertising agency. Such internships are generally closely supervised by college professors to insure that they are educational learning experiences as well as free labor for employers.

An even more intense volunteer experience for those who have the time and resources may be through the Peace Corps, VISTA, or the UN Volunteers. Such volunteer work requires a commitment of one to three years and provides room, board, benefits (including government service experience), and a living allowance. A good resource for identifying volunteer programs is *Invest Yourself* (obtainable from Susan Angus, P.O. Box 117, New York, NY 10019, $3) which lists names of most volunteer organizations in the United States.

Volunteering adds visibility and experience to your job search. However volunteering does not only relate to jobs. Think about becoming a student member of a professional association. Student membership usually gives all the benefits of regular membership but costs half as much. Once in an organization, *volunteer* for committees and leadership positions and gain visibility and recognition. The people in these organizations will soon be your peers. This is also an excellent method to make contacts for both jobs and letters of recommendation.

As a graduate student in counseling, Terry wanted to focus on human resources development and training in industry. So he joined the American Society for Training and Development (ASTD). He volunteered to chair the student recruitment subcommittee and joined the Career Development Special Interest group. Two years later when interviewing for a job as assistant to a director of training, he found he knew people who had worked with the director, was able to learn about the firm from the former employees who were ASTD members, and made an excellent impression in his interview.

Starting Your Own Business

One final way to get a job, of course, is to start your own business. Career centers and libraries have useful information on starting a business. Additionally the Small Business Administration (SBA) provides seminars and low-cost materials to local communities. A group called SCORE (Service Corps of Retired Executives) is composed of local retired business people who lead low-cost workshops and offer free technical advice. Contact your local chamber of commerce for information about these resources. Also your local community college or the extension/continuing education division of your local university may offer courses in small business administration or marketing. If they offer such courses they may also have students available who get class credit by giving free technical assistance to new small businesses.

Become your own boss

Many people find that owning their own business feels more secure than working for another person. Often people don't take the chance until they have been forced out of an old job. Stories abound in the *Wall Street Journal* of ex-factory supervisors who started their own sales or repair or remodeling businesses. Then there are others who wait until retirement and use their savings to launch a new business.

> Ely Callaway invested in land and planted a vineyard three years prior to retirement from Burlington Industries. He now has a flourishing winery. Mr. Callaway also has expanded into several other small business operations which serve to satisfy him during his "retirement years."

Information Interviewing and Networking

Survey after survey on job hunting confirms a basic fact about job search strategy. Namely, that the one best way to find out about a job and to get a job is through people. Now that you have reviewed the written sources of information on jobs, and have your own polished resume prepared, you are ready to begin conducting information interviews. These interviews help you to develop contacts. Your contacts become a source of knowledgeable and experienced people in a field. Your contacts form your network of people who will keep you informed and connected to possible job openings. Once you gain some experience through information interviewing and networking, you will be ready to master the techniques involved in interviewing for a job.

Cultivating contacts

Information Interviewing—The Purpose

Information interviewing involves learning to identify people who are doing what you want to be doing and asking them questions related to their current job. Information interviewing serves several purposes. It helps you further refine your knowledge and understanding of the field you are exploring. It enables you to develop social skills related to your feeling comfortable and knowledgeable when you are being interviewed. Information interviewing creates the setting to develop contacts. These contacts are often helpful to your specific job search. The people you interview may themselves be in a position to hire someone like you for a job or they may simply hear about a job opening and pass on the information to you. Remember your specific purpose in information interviewing is *not* to look for a job but to confirm your information about the field and to develop contacts that may be helpful in the future. When doing an information interview, *you* are asking the questions. When doing a *job interview* you are being *asked* the questions.

Information interviewing is based on the premise that you have already read much of the written information related to a specific type of job and now need a confirmation from people who are already doing that job. You basically want them to tell you what the field is really like before you commit your time, effort, and finances to the pursuit of a new field. Or, if you are already in the field, you want to know if one employer's environment would be more appealing to you than another's. Other information you can gain from such an interview involves much more than simply confirming the skills needed and the salary range. On one hand, you can find out if you like the people, if the atmosphere feels comfortable, if the people are friendly and helpful. On the other hand, you may find that no one has time to talk to you, or they keep you waiting, or they let the telephone constantly interrupt your interview, or they work in noisy cubicles. This information is only available through on-site visits. Thus the overt goal of information interviewing is to collect information, but the covert goal is to make contacts and determine whether you have made an appropriate match between your personal needs and your career goal.

Information Interviewing—The Process

Identify people who are doing what you would like to do

The first step in the process of information interviewing is to identify people who are working in the fields that you've decided are interesting to you. It's especially helpful if you know a relative, friend, or neighbor involved in the field, or at least someone who can refer you to a potential contact; it's always easier to talk to someone whose name you know. The hardest step is making the first phone call to a stranger or, even worse, a strange firm and asking for the name of a person doing that interesting job! Strangers will be receptive to talking to you if you demonstrate the following characteristics:

1. Indicate that you are seeking personalized information about their field before you decide to enter it.
2. Confirm the person's job title by asking.
3. Sound enthusiastic and delighted to reach this person.
4. Refer to the research you've already reviewed about this field or company.

5. Ask if you can have a specific amount of time to interview this person (i.e., 15–30 minutes).
6. Try to arrange the interview at the person's work site, so you can determine first hand how it might feel to work there.
7. Keep to your agreed-upon time frame.
8. Thank your interviewer and follow up with a thank-you note.

As we noted, it's tough making that first phone call. Here are some specific examples of telephone "lead-ins" to help you get started. Remember to identify yourself, state your purpose, and ask for an appointment with the appropriate person. This straightforward approach is generally effective.

Getting through on the telephone

Example:

> *Hello, Mr. Jones, my name is Diane Smith from Moorpark College. I'm doing some research in the field of houseplant maintenance service, and I'd like to stop by at your convenience to ask you a few questions. Is Thursday at 2:00 P.M. all right?*

or:

> *Hello, this is . . . . and the other day in a conversation with . . . . your name was mentioned and . . . . suggested that I should meet you. So I am calling to find out when you will have a few minutes to see me. Would it be convenient in the morning or afternoon?*

or:

> *Hello . . . . this is . . . . This morning I talked to . . . . about the opportunities in . . . . and he spoke very highly of you. I'm calling to find out when you will have a few minutes to see me. Would it be convenient to meet with you in the morning or afternoon?*

Information Interviewing Outline

Now that you have located your contacts and made definite appointments to interview them, you need to consider in specific detail the most efficient ways and the best questions to ask to gain the maximum useful information as quickly and pleasantly as possible. Remember, you will be talking to busy people with many demands on their time; they will expect you to be, and it's to your advantage to be, as businesslike as possible. Finally, having made the telephone contact and set the date to meet, you should send a note confirming the information interview appointment.

Here is a framework to help you design your Interview for Information-Field Survey. You may think you already have answers to some of the questions, but personal interviews should help to fill out details, and possibly fill some blanks in your information that you don't realize are there. Try to choose your questions from the general categories of type of business, position classification, position description, work environment, benefits, and entrance requirements, as follows:

Type of Business

What are the services, products, or functions of the organization?

Who utilizes their services or products?

Who are the competitors in this field?

What sets your company apart or distinguishes it from others in the same industry?

What are the projections for future development or new directions?

Position Classifications

In each major corporate division, what types of positions are available?

What are the qualifications for entry-level and experienced positions? (Consider education, skills, abilities, etc.)

Position Description

What duties and responsibilities are performed in the area in which you are interested?

What are some examples of the projects currently in work and problems currently being solved?

What is a typical day like?

What contacts would there be (personal . . . data . . . machine . . . other) with other organizations?

Work Environment

What type of physical localities are involved. . .outdoors. . .indoors . . . travel? Is there pressure? Routine? Variety? How much supervision? Do flexible work schedules exist? Is overtime typical or atypical?

Benefits

How does compensation compare to education and ability level?

What are the opportunities for advancement, promotions, or lateral mobility?

What opportunities are available for advanced training, on-the-job training or academic coursework? Is there a tuition reimbursement plan?

What other benefits are available? Possible benefits might include:

Medical/Dental Insurance	Recreation, Personal Health Services
Life, Disability Insurance	
Vacations, Holidays	Profit Sharing
Retirement	Expenses for moving, travel
Pre-Retirement Planning	Outplacement
Employee Assistance Programs (counseling for work related problems)	Child Care Facilities
	Job Placement Assistance (for a spouse)

Entrance

What suggestions do you have for an individual wishing to enter this field of employment?

What other companies might employ individuals to perform this type of work? Could you refer me to someone else for more information about opportunities in this field?

Moving from a general categorical framework to more specific detail, here is a sample list of typical questions you might ask in your information-al interviews.

Specific sample questions

1. What do you like most about your job and why?
2. What do you like least about your job and why?
3. How did you decide to get into this field and what steps did you take to enter the field?
4. What training would you recommend for someone wanting to enter this field now?
5. What is the salary range for a person in this field? Entry level to top salary?
6. What personal qualities do you feel are most important in your work and why?
7. What are the tasks you do in a typical work day? Would you describe them?
8. What types of stress do you experience on the job?
9. What types of people survive and do well in this field?
10. What are the opportunities for promotion?
11. Is this field expanding? Taking any new directions?
12. What related occupations might I investigate?
13. Can you give me the names of three other persons who share your enthusiasm for this kind of work? How can I contact them?

Exhibit 8.1 presents an outline/guide/review format which lists all the points we have discussed about information interviewing. You should use this form as a guide in preparing for each interview you make.

If you approach professionals in your field of interest from a research point of view and *not* as if you want a job, they will often be happy to talk with you. Even the busiest executives will often find time for you. If one person doesn't have time, ask to be referred to another professional in the field. It is the secretary's job to protect the boss from distractions. When a secretary asks "What is this call regarding?" you might respond: "This is a personal call," or "Mrs. Smith is expecting my call," or "May I talk to Jane," or "I was referred to Jane by her associate, Don Reid." Whatever you do, sound confident and friendly. It's best to call on a Tuesday, Wednesday, or Thursday between eight and eleven o'clock in the morning. If the person isn't in and you must leave a message, just leave your name, phone number, and the message "personal."

Once you start interviewing people who work in a field that interests you, the information gained should confirm or revise your views. But even better, you will make contacts who may be able to help you actually find a job in the future. These contacts can suggest groups or associations to join, colleges to attend, and classes to take, as well as the current status of employment activity in their field. If you use this information wisely, you too can become visible in these inner circles. It's never too early to start.

Exhibit 8.1
Review Guide on Informational Interviewing

1. FIND SOMEONE WITH WHOM TO START THE INTERVIEW PROCESS. MAKE SURE YOU GET THE PERSON'S NAME. CALL THE PERSON DIRECTLY, BY NAME.

   What is the name of the person you're going to call? _____

2. MAKE A SPECIFIC APPOINTMENT, FOR A SPECIFIC LENGTH OF TIME.

   When is your appointment, where?   _____

   _____

3. MAKE A LIST OF SPECIFIC QUESTIONS, THINGS YOU WANT TO KNOW ABOUT THE JOB.

   Your questions for this interview. (See list in this section) _____

   _____

   _____

   _____

   _____

4. EXPLAIN WHY YOU'RE CALLING FOR THE INTERVIEW. SOME EXPLANATIONS:

   a. You want to know more about this kind of work before you decide that you're interested, or before you decide you should choose it as a career.

   b. You are getting ready for a job interview and would like to get some advice from someone in the field before the interview.

   c. You are interested in the field but haven't found much information on it and would appreciate someone filling you in on it.

   d. You are doing some research for a career class and would like some specific information in this field.

   Which explanation will you give when you call? _____

   _____

   _____

   (Make up your own if you wish.)

5. TELL THE EMPLOYER WHO RECOMMENDED THAT YOU CALL. A REFERENCE HELPS.

   Who is your reference for this interview? _____

6. AFTER THE INTERVIEW, SEND A NOTE THANKING THE PERSON FOR THE TIME AND HELP.

Practice Information Interviews

Some people find it easier to practice information interviews until they become confident in approaching people about their careers. If you need to practice you might try one of the following approaches. Either you can interview someone you already know about a hobby that sounds interesting or you can try to consistently ask people about their hobbies and careers at any informal gathering you attend. These informal activities tend to build your self-confidence in asking questions. Once you get started you might find you enjoy searching for leads through other people.

Two interesting success stories may help you get started. Thomas Shanks, assistant professor for communications in a California college, relates how one of his students moved from California to New York. For three months, he sent his resume everywhere, knocked on the doors of every friend, relation, and remote acquaintance that he could find. He even found out which after-hours spots the television crowd preferred and he frequented those places. He eventually got offers from all three networks. Another student, a freshman at Moorpark College, was a business major with an interest in art. She heard the vice-president of industrial relations of an engineering firm talk in her leadership class in November. After class she asked him about summer jobs with his firm (notice how early she asked). By January he had arranged for her to interview in the graphic arts department of his firm. She got the summer job, a job many art graduates would have envied.

Information interviewing leads to contacts and careers

Lastly, if you are a student, or have access to a college campus, teachers often make fine resources. Many faculty members have had interesting summer jobs and temporary positions prior to becoming teachers. They are valuable contacts. If you are a teacher interested in a career change you might find a lead through a student. Many times a teacher can design a lesson plan to find out the occupations of parents and invite parents to speak in their classes about their careers. These parents can become future contacts for both students and teachers!

Networking

Networking refers to the process of developing contacts. While you are conducting information interviews you will meet many people. Besides gathering information you are making contacts. Contacts, if cultivated and used wisely, can lead to or be your potential employers. In a tight and competitive job market, contacts often make the difference between your being selected or being passed by. This is true for several reasons. Often jobs need to be filled before there is time to advertise. Additionally, as has been mentioned, the majority of new jobs that are available each year come from businesses that start off with relatives and neighbors. Most people hear about jobs by word of mouth. You need to let people know that you are looking.

*Networking
provides the
edge*   One state employment agency in San Diego tried an experiment in trying to place some of its "hard-core unemployed" applicants. First, the staff taught the applicants to be positive and confident about their ability to get a job, and trained them in using the telephone to make contacts. Then, for one week, the applicants used the yellow pages and called prospective employers from 8:00 A.M. to 5:00 P.M. At the end of seven days, 80 percent of the applicants had at least three interviews! So there were jobs out there!

How do you find those hidden jobs if you don't plan to make fifty-six hours worth of phone calls? You meet people face to face and let them know you are available before a job may be available. On the next page, exercise 8.1 suggests some likely people to contact.

If you really want to get your preferred position, you need to make it your business to let everyone know you are looking (except maybe your current employers, if they aren't expecting to be losing you!). One caution on this approach is that it works best if you have six months to two years in which to make a change. Contacting people may give a prospective employer the idea to create a job for you, but job creation within a company also takes time.

Networking and practice interviewing not only give you contacts but also personal experience with people working in your desired job environment. Additionally however, they allow you to hear the answers professionals in your chosen field give to the sort of questions that you may be asked in a job interview. While conducting information interviews or discussing people's careers at a conference, try asking people what kind of questions they were asked in interviews; try asking what they considered to be the most difficult questions in their interviews.

Summary

This chapter has discussed traditional and non-traditional job search. It is important that you confirm your impressions about your ideal job. When you first start an exercise program you are unsure about the correct movements and the results of your labors. After several months of workouts you learn to know how each workout affects your body. Similarly, you won't know the accuracy of your researched information until you volunteer in the field, find part-time work in the field, or find a job that will put you around the people doing the type of job you really desire. Only then will you know how you feel about the real job environment. It also takes practice to remember to ask everyone about their jobs. The more jobs you learn about the more alternative choices you will have.

There is a hidden job market out there. The people you meet through the process of information interviewing may inform you about potential jobs before they are advertised.

?? Written Exercises

8.1

Support Network Checklist

a. Fill in the names of people who might help you (use checklist below).
b. Specifically, ask yourself what am I going to ask this person to do for me? (Provide information, introduce me to someone, offer advice, write a reference, etc.)

Former Employers:	Bankers:
Former Co-workers:	Accountants:
Present Employer:	Financial Planners:
Relatives:	Insurance Agents:
Friends:	Real Estate Agents:
Civic Group Members:	Stock Brokers:
Professional Association	Sales People:
Members:	Retail Store Owners:
Alumni Group Members:	Medical Professionals:
Religious Group Members:	Other:
Clients:	Other:
Counselors:	Other:
Teachers:	Other:
Clergy:	Other:
Neighbors:	Other:
Classmate:	

8.2

Select three individuals who work in fields that are interesting to you and conduct brief informational interviews using the list of sample information interview questions given earlier as your guide. Write up a brief report of each.

8.3

Prepare a log of personal contacts (at least five) using the approaches described under "Information Interviewing" and "Practice Information Interviews." Use your own job target and see how much information and how many new contacts you acquire. Use the following outline format.

Name_____Job Target _____
Using the approaches described under Information Interviewing and Practice Information Interviews, use your own job target and see how much information and how many new contacts you acquire.

a. Practice Information Gathering _____

    Hobby or Interest _____

    Contact _____

    Information gathered as a result of the interview _____

    _____

    _____

Other possible contacts _____

b. Expert Information Gathering _____

Occupational Interest _____

Contact (who, where employed, how you found this person) _____

_____

Information Gathered _____

_____

New Contacts _____

_____

Any contradictions _____

_____

Conclusions _____

_____

c. Interviewing for Employment, Apprenticeship, Volunteer Experience _____

Choice of possible work site _____

_____

What do you want (job, apprenticeship, or volunteer experience) _____

_____

Who is in a position to hire you _____

Your approach (telephone, letter, or in person) _____

_____

Outcomes and follow up _____

_____

Exhibit 8.2   **SAMPLE CONTACT FILE FORMAT**

1. Company: _____ Phone No.: _____ Contact Person & Title: _____ Type of Contact & Date:
   _____   Letter _____
                            Referred by: _____   Phone _____
                                                                                                  Resume _____
   Address: _____   Application _____
   _____   Job Target: _____   Interview _____

   Follow-up: _____   Conclusions: _____

2. Company: _____ Phone No.: _____ Contact Person & Title: _____ Type of Contact & Date:
   _____   Letter _____
                            Referred by: _____   Phone _____
                                                                                                  Resume _____
   Address: _____   Application _____
   _____   Job Target: _____   Interview _____

   Follow-up: _____   Conclusions: _____

3. Company: _____ Phone No.: _____ Contact Person & Title: _____ Type of Contact & Date:
   _____   Letter _____
                            Referred by: _____   Phone _____
                                                                                                  Resume _____
   Address: _____   Application _____
   _____   Job Target: _____   Interview _____

   Follow-up: _____   Conclusions: _____

4. Company: _____ Phone No.: _____ Contact Person & Title: _____ Type of Contact & Date:
   _____   Letter _____
                            Referred by: _____   Phone _____
                                                                                                  Resume _____
   Address: _____   Application _____
   _____   Job Target: _____   Interview _____

   Follow-up: _____   Conclusions: _____

5. Company: _____ Phone No.: _____ Contact Person & Title: _____ Type of Contact & Date:
   _____   Letter _____
                            Referred by: _____   Phone _____
                                                                                                  Resume _____
   Address: _____   Application _____
   _____   Job Target: _____   Interview _____

   Follow-up: _____   Conclusions: _____

Summary—Write a Brief Paragraph
Answering These Questions

What did you learn about yourself? How does this knowledge relate to your career/life planning? How do you feel?

_____

_____

_____

_____

_____

_____

_____

_____

_____

_____

_____

_____

_____

_____

_____

_____

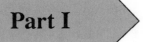 Part I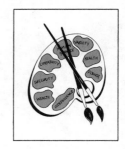

  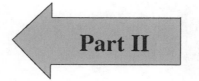 Part II

Preparing Your Resume

9

*Life is a mirror and gives back to us
the reflection of our own self.*
Joseph Batten, *Expectations & Possibilities*

Learning Objectives   At the end of the chapter you will be able to:

Understand the advantages for developing a resume.

Identify guidelines for resume preparation.

Write a resume and cover letter.

Resumes

Every good fitness program includes a chart which visually indicates where you started, where you are currently, and where you are going. In a career fitness program this chart is called a resume (pronounced "res-u-may'"). Eventually, in the course of job hunting, you will be asked to present a resume to a prospective employer. Some career counselors feel that the resume isn't going to get you an interview unless you already have a good contact inside the company; others suggest that a good resume can help you get your "foot in the door." In either case, a resume can be a useful tool. A resume is:

1. A systematic assessment of your skills in terms of a specific job objective.
2. An invaluable memory aid to refer to in an interview in answering the following questions commonly asked by interviewers:
   a. Tell me about yourself?
   b. Why should I hire you?
   c. What skills do you bring to this job?
3. An aid in filling out application forms.

This chapter will give you guidelines for writing a resume and will present you with three sample formats: functional, chronological, and a creative combination. Additionally the importance of cover letters and application forms will be addressed. Once you have finished this chapter you should be able to compile your own resume. It is often useful to have a career counselor or a potential employer review a draft of your resume before duplicating your final copy.

Purpose

An effective resume can get you an interview

The purpose of the resume is to get an interview. Like an advertisement, the resume should attract attention, create interest, describe accomplishments, and provoke action. Brevity is essential; one page is best, two is the limit. The resume tells the prospective employer what you can do and have done, who you are, and what you know. It also indicates the kind of job that you desire. The resume must provide enough information for the employer to evaluate your qualifications and it must interest the employer enough to invite you for an interview.

Writing a well-constructed resume requires that your research has been completed before compiling the resume. You need to keep in mind the type of employer and position as well as the general job requirements in order to tailor your resume to the specific requirements and the personality of the employer. To be most effective, your resume should be designed to emphasize your background as it relates to the job being sought. Additionally the resume should look neat, clean, and organized. This means typed, and photocopied on good quality paper with no errors.

By now you should have completed all the necessary research. Utilize the information gathered in chapter 7, "Information Integration," and chapter 8, "Job Search Strategy." Integrate your answers with the categories listed on the following Resume Review Sheet.

Resume Review

Review this information mentally. It will help you write a complete resume.

A. PERSONALS
   1. Name
   2. Address
   3. Phone
B. CURRENT JOB OBJECTIVE
C. EDUCATION
   1. High school and college
      a. Favorite subjects
      b. Best grades
      c. Extracurricular interest
      d. Offices held
      e. Athletic achievements
      f. Other significant facts (i.e., honors, awards)
   2. Other (military, volunteer, correspondence, summer, languages, technical skills, licenses and/or credentials.)
D. HOBBIES
E. WORK EXPERIENCE
   Refer to your experiography or your skills analysis.
      a. Employer
      b. Length of employment
      c. Position
      d. Skills & accomplishments
F. PUBLICATIONS
G. ASSOCIATIONS OR COMMUNITY INVOLVEMENT

Preparation for Composing Your Resume

Although stating an objective is considered optional by some experts (because it can be stated in your cover letter), it is to your advantage to include it on the resume. In actuality, one resume should be designed for each job objective. Remember, there are no jobs titled "Anything."

The job objective is a short concise statement about the position you are seeking. This may include the type of firm in which you hope to work (i.e., a fast-growing small company). A clear objective gives focus to your job search and indicates to an employer that you've given serious thought to your career goals. In a limited number of cases, where time does not allow you to develop a resume for several different jobs that interest you, the job objective may be emphasized in the cover letter (which will be discussed at the end of this chapter) and deleted in the resume.

Job objectives are sometimes referred to as "Goal," "Professional Objective," "Position Desired," or simply "Objective." They can be as specific as "Community Worker," "Personnel Assistant," "Junior Programmer," or as general as "management position utilizing administrative communications and research skills" or "To work as an administrative assistant in a creative atmosphere and have the opportunity to use my abilities." Generally speaking, the more specific the objective statement, the better, because a clear objective enables you to focus your resume more directly to the objective. The effect is pointed, dramatic, and convincing.

As you can see, a resume summarizes your particular background as it relates to a specific job. It summarizes your career objectives, education, work experience, special skills, and interests. Visualize a pyramid or triangle with the job objective at the top, and everything else supporting that objective.

In writing the rough draft of your resume create 5″ × 8″ index cards for each job you've held. (Exhibits 9.1, 9.2) The index card should contain the following:

Front of card
1. Name, address, phone number of employer, and immediate supervisor at worksite.
2. Dates employed (month and year).
3. Job title.
4. Special skills utilized.

Back of card
   Duties divided into functional areas.

Guidelines for the Resume

The appearance of this document is important. To be acceptable, the resume must be typed clearly, well spaced, and visually attractive. Remember that many employers only skim the first page of a resume. Thus it is crucial that your material be strategically placed so that what is most likely to be read is most relevant to the job desired. Employers have been known to receive hundreds of resumes each day giving them only minutes to review each one. Therefore, even if you must use two pages, the first is most crucial. Experts advise against using a "resume service." An employer can usually spot a "canned" resume and might assume that the applicant lacks initiative or self-confidence. The time you spend writing your resume will be time well spent. It will give you the opportunity to summarize what you have to offer to an employer.

Put the most relevant information first

Avoid anything that may not be considered in a positive light or that has no relationship to your ability to do the job (e.g., marital status such as divorced or separated; children; political or religious affiliation; age; photos). When in doubt, leave it out. One clue: In the next chapter you will be given information about illegal questions in an interview. If it's illegal in an interview then it's unnecessary in a resume.

Exhibit 9.1
Front of Resume Index Card

Joe's Bar 'n Grill
555 Stevens Circle   April 1, 1988 –
Simi, Calif. 93065   December 1989
(805) 555–1211

Supervisor: *Duties:*
Joe Smith   Bookkeeping & waitressing

Special Skills Utilized:
   Related well with continuous flow of people.
   Attentive to detail; organized; energetic.

Exhibit 9.2
Back of Resume Index Card

Functions:

Management   —Coordinated service with customer needs,
                        calculated wages, scheduled employees.
Communications   —Welcomed guests. Directed busboys toward
                        performing courteous and rapid service.
                        Responded to complaints.
Bookkeeping   —Maintained records of financial transactions.
                        Balanced books. Compiled reports to show
                        statistics.

Action words

Remember that your writing style communicates the work *activity* with which you have been involved. Use phrases and document experiences that involve the reader and make your resume outstanding and active.

Basic guidelines for selecting your "power" words are:

Select "power" words

- Choose short, clear phrases.
- If you use sentences throughout, keep them concise and direct.
- Utilize the acceptable jargon of the work for which you are applying. Remember: You want your prospective employer to READ your resume.

Table 9.1
Sample Resume Guidelines

Name
Address
Phone Number

Job Objective	State and describe as specifically as possible. Refer to the *Dictionary of Occupational Titles* for appropriate descriptive vocabulary.
Education	Depending on your job objective and the amount of education you have had, you may want to place this category directly after Job Objective. Most recent education should be listed first. *Include relevant credentials and licenses.*
	Example: Educational institutions are usually more concerned with appropriate degrees than other employers. Include special workshops, noncredit courses, self-taught skills when appropriate to job objective.
Experience	Describe *functionally* (by activities performed) your experience relevant to the particular job for which you are applying; start with the most relevant and go to the less relevant. Include without distinction actual job experience, volunteer experience, and work in class projects and school and class offices held. Alternatively, list your experience *chronologically*, giving your most recent experience first.
	There is no need to stress dates unless they indicate that you have been continuously advancing toward this job objective.
	Use action verbs (see below); do not use full sentences, unless you decide to write your resume as a narrative.
	Use the *Dictionary of Occupational Titles* to help you describe accurately what you have done, always keeping in mind how your experiences relate to your job objective.
Special Skills	Put this optional category directly after Job Objective if you feel that your experiences do not adequately reflect the talents you have that best support this job objective.
	Example: Facility with numbers, manual dexterity, patience, workshops you have led, writing ability, self-taught skills, language fluency.
References	Available on request. (Only use references if you have space and if the names are well known to potential employers.)

- Avoid general comments such as "my duties were . . . " or "I worked for . . ." Begin with action words that concisely describe what your tasks were, i.e.:
  Organized new filing system
  Developed more effective interviewing procedure
  Evaluated training program for new employees
- List the results of your activities, i.e.:
  Time for completing office filing was reduced twenty-five percent.
  A concise interview evaluation summary form was developed.
  A training class was begun.
- Don't dilute your action words with too many extraneous activities. Be SELECTIVE and sell your BEST experiences.
- Target your words around the employer's needs.

Here are some examples of action verbs that could be used in your resume:

accomplished	evaluated	negotiated
achieved	expanded	organized
analyzed	facilitated	oriented
arranged	guided	planned
built	implemented	processed
controlled	improved	produced
created	increased	proved
demonstrated	initiated	raised profits
designed	inspired	reduced costs
developed	interpreted	researched
directed	invented	sold
effected	led	supervised
encouraged	managed	supported
established	motivated	wrote

For additional action verbs see the skills analysis section, chapter 4, table 4.1.

Types of Resumes

There are three general types of resumes: functional; chronological; and combination. Comparing the following two sample work experience entries (taken from exhibits 9.3 and 9.7) will give you some idea of the basic difference between functional and chronological resumes, which we referred to in table 9.1, Sample Resume Guidelines. The next part of this chapter will discuss all three types in detail. The combination resume, as the name implies, is a combination of functional/chronological.

Sample "FUNCTIONAL" entry under work experience:
Budgeting/Financial

> Analyzed and coordinated payroll record keeping, budgeted expenditures, requisitioned supplies, prepared attendance accounting reports, and initiated budget system for $10,000 of instructional monies.

Sample "CHRONOLOGICAL" entry under work experience:
1983 Cashier

> Builders Emporium
> Wadsworth, Texas 90090
> (212)666-0000
> Operated cash register and made change. Worked well with public, motivated fellow employees, encouraged customers to buy products.

The Functional Resume

A functional resume presents your experience and job history in terms of the functions you have actually performed rather than as a simple chronological listing of the titles of jobs you have held. Like any resume, it should be tailored to fit the main tasks and competencies required by the job you are seeking. Essentially, you redefine your past experiences according to the functions in the job for which you are applying. You should select and emphasize those activities from previous employment that relate to that specific job and deemphasize or omit irrelevant background.

For example, an administrative assistant might perform some administration, communication, and clerical functions. A secretary for an elementary school rewrote her resume to highlight these categories. In order to better define the skills used in her secretarial job she researched the job description of executive secretary and office manager in her school personnel manual and located the description of administrative assistant in the D.O.T. (Dictionary of Occupational Titles). (See "Suggestions for job descriptions" below.) She then compiled her resume to show how her executive secretarial responsibilities related to the administrative assistant position desired. (See Functional Resume—exhibit 9.3 at the end of this chapter.) Review organizational divisions described in chapter 8, to access how your past work or life experience can be described in such categories as marketing, human resources, finance, community services, or research and development.

Suggestions for job descriptions

Descriptions in the *Dictionary of Occupational Titles* and in some personnel manuals provide a source of helpful phrases and statements to use in writing up your job history and experience. The following three descriptions, for example, would be especially useful in composing a functional resume for a job in business. However, you would only use relevant sentences and adapt them to your background.

Examples:

OFFICE MANAGER
Coordinates activities of clerical personnel in establishment or organization. Analyzes and organizes office operations and procedures, such as typing, bookkeeping, preparation of payrolls, flow of correspondence, filing, requisitioning of supplies, and other clerical services. Evaluates office production, revises procedures, or devises new forms to improve efficiency of work flow. Establishes uniform correspondence procedures and style practices. Formulates procedures for systematic retention, protection, retrieval, transfer, and disposal of records. Plans office layouts and initiates cost reduction programs. Reviews clerical and personnel records to insure completeness, accuracy, and timeliness. Prepares activity reports for guidance of management. Prepares employee ratings and conducts employee benefits and insurance programs. Coordinates activities of various clerical departments or workers within department.

ADMINISTRATIVE ASSISTANT
Aids executive in staff capacity by coordinating office services, such as personnel, budget preparation and control, housekeeping, records control, and special management studies. Studies management methods in order to improve work flow, simplify reporting procedures, or implement cost reductions. Analyzes unit operating practices, such as record-keeping systems, forms control, office layout, suggestion systems, personnel and budgetary requirements, and performance standards to create new systems or revise established procedures. Analyzes jobs to delimit position responsibilities for use in wage and salary adjustments, promotions, and evaluation of work flow. Studies methods of improving work measurements or performance standards.

EXECUTIVE SECRETARY
Coordinates collection and preparation of operating reports, such as time and attendance records, terminations, new hires, transfers, budget expenditures, and statistical records of performance data. Prepares reports including conclusions and recommendations for solution of administrative problems. Issues and interprets operating policy. Reviews and answers correspondence. May assist in preparation of budget needs and annual reports of organization. May interview job applicants, conduct orientation of new employees and plan training programs. May direct services, such as maintenance, repair, supplies, mail, and files.

Creative functional resume

Married women who have had no paid experience often find it hard to make their activities sound transferable to the world of work. All they see is domesticity which they mistakenly think differs markedly from work in business. But usually they have been performing business functions without realizing it. People without paid work experience, and people returning to the job market after taking time out to be homemakers can persuade employers to recognize their ability and practical experience if they describe their life in categories such as these:

Management

■ Coordinated the multiple activities of five people of different ages and varying interests, keeping within tight schedules and continuous deadlines.

■ Established priorities for the allocation of available time, resources, and funds.

Office Procedures

■ Kept lists of daily appointments, reminders, items to be purchased, people to be called, tasks to be accomplished.

■ Handled all business and personal correspondence—answered and issued invitations, wrote stores about defective merchandise, made hotel reservations.

Personnel

Creative Functional Resume

■ Recruited, hired, trained household staff; negotiated wages.

■ Motivated children to assume responsibilities and helped them develop self-confidence.

■ Resolved problems caused by low morale and lack of cooperation.

Finances

■ Established annual household budget, and monitored costs to stay within expenses.

■ Balanced the checkbook and reconciled monthly bank statements.

■ Calculated take-home pay of household staff, made quarterly reports to the government on social security taxes withheld.

Purchasing

■ Undertook comparison shopping for food, clothing, furniture, and equipment, and purchased at various stores at different times, depending upon best value.

■ Planned meals according to specials at different food stores.

■ Shopped for insurance and found lower premiums than current coverage, resulting in substantial savings.

Pros and cons

The functional resume is especially useful if you have limited work experience or breaks in your employment record. You need not include dates or distinguish paid activities from nonpaid voluntary activities. By deleting previous employers' names, you avoid any stereotyped assumptions a future employer may have about previous employers (McDonalds, the P.T.A., or a school district, etc.). Similarly, omitting job titles helps direct the future employer to the fact that you are a person with specific skills that are useful in the present job opening. This format also can emphasize your growth and development.

Some disadvantages to using this format include the fact that you need to be able to identify and write about your achievements. This sometimes requires the assistance of an expert resume writer. Additionally, some employers are not familiar with this format and may want dates and job titles.

Exhibits 9.3, 9.4, and 9.5 (at the end of this chapter) are examples of functional resumes for various positions.

The Chronological Resume

The chronological resume is considered the traditional and most often used resume. Basically, it lists your work history in reverse chronological order with the most recent listed first. The work history should include dates employed, job title, job duties, employer's name, address, and telephone number.

Pros and cons

The chronological resume is most useful for people with no breaks in their employment record for whom each new position indicates continuous advancement or growth. Recent high school and college graduates also find this approach simpler than creating a functional resume.

As dates tend to dominate the presentation, any breaks or undocumented years of work are glaring. If your present position is not related to the job you desire, you may be eliminated from the competition by employers who feel that current experience is the most important consideration in reviewing resumes.

Exhibits 9.6, 9.7, 9.8, and 9.9 (at the end of this chapter) are examples of chronological resumes for various positions.

The Combination Resume

If you have major skills important for success in your desired job as well as an impressive record of continuous job experience with reputable employers, you can best highlight this double advantage with a *combination* of the functional and chronological styles of resume. This combination style usually lists functions followed by years employed with a list of employers. The combination style also satisfies the employer who wants to see the dates that you were actually employed. See exhibits 9.10 and 9.11.

Cover Letter Guidelines

Want to turn off a prospective employer? Send a resume with no cover letter. Or send a form letter addressed to "Personnel Manager."

An original, personalized cover letter, accompanying every resume you send, should explain why you are writing and why your qualifications would be of interest. It's your best opportunity to communicate on a personal level with an employer you're asking to hire you. The employer is more than a position title just as you, certainly, are more than a resume. Use your cover letter to spark added interest in you as an individual. Challenge the employer to read your resume before reading the other forty-nine that also arrived in the morning mail.

Cover letters

How to do it? For one, address your letter to a specific person. Spell his or her name correctly and use the proper title. These details count. Your opening paragraph should contain the "hooker." Arouse some work-related interest. Explain (very briefly) why you are writing. How did you become interested in that company? Summarize what you have to offer. Details of your background can show why you should be considered as a job candidate. The self-appraisal that went into preparation of your resume tells what you can do and like to do, where your strengths and interest lie. Your research on your prospective employer should have uncovered the qualifications needed. If your letter promises a good match—your abilities with the company's needs—you've attracted attention.

Keep your letter short and to the point. Refer to your resume highlighting relevant experiences and accomplishments that match the companies stated needs. Ask for an interview. Indicate when you will be calling to confirm a convenient time for the interview. Let your letter express your individuality but within the context of the employment situation.

The cover letter should be individually typed for each job desired in contrast to the fact that resumes can be printed (mass produced). Always review both cover letter and resume for good margins, clarity, correct spelling, and accurate typing. Appearance does count! Review the sample cover letters in exhibits 9.13 through 9.18.

Application Forms

A final type of form, accepted sometimes as a substitute for a resume, is an *application form*. The employment application is a form used by most companies to gain necessary information and to register applicants for work. This information becomes a guide to determine a person's suitability both for the company and the job which needs to be filled. You should observe carefully the following guidelines.

You will probably be asked to fill out an employment application form, usually before the interview takes place. Therefore, it is good practice to arrive at the employment office a little ahead of the time of your interview. Bring along your pen and your resume or personal data sheet. You will be asked to list your name, address, age, training or education, experience, special abilities, hobbies, and preferences. Practically all application forms request that you state the job you are seeking and the salary you have received in the past. All firms require an applicant to fill out an application form.

Many times the employer wants to make rapid comparisons and therefore makes up a company employment application. For example, Mr. Ford needed a stenographer who could type fast. He examined several application blanks filled out by people applying for stenographic jobs. *By referring to the same blanks each time,* he quickly thumbed through dozens of applications, eliminating all candidates who had average speed. Thus, there was no need for Mr. Ford to examine resumes or read dozens of letters to find out exactly how fast each candidate could type.

Neatness Counts

The way in which an application form has been filled out indicates neatness, thoroughness, and accuracy on the part of the applicant. If two applicants seem to have equal qualifications, but one form is carelessly filled out, the application itself might tilt the scale in favor of the other applicant. Unless your handwriting is especially clear, print or type all answers.

Sometimes you may apply for a job by mail and a form will be sent to you. The application form should be carefully, completely, and accurately filled out. You should then send it to the company. You may also attach a copy of your resume. When you have completed the application, go over it again. Have you given the information asked? When an item asked for is "not applicable," have you written in N/A?

Filling Out Application Forms

1. Fill out the application form in ink—or use a typewriter.
2. Answer every question that applies to you. If a question does not apply, or is illegal (see chapter 10) you may write N/A, meaning, "not applicable," or draw a line through the space to show that you did not overlook the question.
3. Give your complete address, including your zip code.
4. The question on marital status simply means whether you are single, married, divorced, separated, or widowed.
5. Spell correctly. If you aren't sure about how to spell a word, use the dictionary or try to use another word with the same meaning.
6. The question on place of birth means the city and state in which you were born—not the name of the hospital.
7. A question on job preference or "job for which you are applying" should be answered with a specific job title or type of work. Do not write "anything." Employers expect you to state clearly what kind of work you can do.
8. Have a list prepared of previous schools attended and employers. Include addresses and dates of your attendance or employment.
9. Be prepared to list several good references. It is much better to ask permission of those you plan to list. Those considered good references include:

    a. A recognized community leader.
    b. A former employer or teacher who knows you well.
    c. Friends who are established in business.
10. When you write or sign your name on the application, use your correct name—not a nickname. Your first name, middle initial, and last name is usually preferred.
11. Be as neat as possible. The employer expects that your application will be an example of your best work.

Summary

This chapter has tried to provide models of dynamic and concise resumes, cover letters, letters of introduction, and application form reminders. Putting the resume together is now your job. Use the forms and ideas in the following written exercises as well as the samples throughout the chapter to assist in getting your resume into shape.

?? Written Exercises

9.1

Fill in the following Resume Review Sheet. It will help you write a complete resume.

A. PERSONALS

  1. Name _____

  2. Address _____

  3. Phone _____

B. CURRENT JOB OBJECTIVE _____

C. EDUCATION

1. High school and college _____

  a. Favorite subjects _____

  b. Best grades _____

  c. Extracurricular interest _____

  d. Offices held _____

  e. Athletic achievements _____

  f. Other significant facts (i.e., honors, awards) _____
     _____

2. Other (military, volunteer, correspondence, summer, languages, technical skills, licenses and/or credentials) _____

D. HOBBIES _____

E. WORK EXPERIENCE
   Refer to your experiography or your skills analysis

  a. Employer _____

  b. Length of employment _____

  c. Position _____

  d. Skills & accomplishments _____

F. PUBLICATIONS _____

G. ASSOCIATIONS OR COMMUNITY INVOLVEMENT _____

9.2

Create a card file describing your work experiences using exhibits 9.1 & 9.2 as a guide. This gives you a chance to write your job tasks in functional terms.

9.3

Choose the format desired and write your own resume.

9.4
Use the Resume Checklist and Critique Form to evaluate your resume. (Table 9.2.)

9.5
Have other people give you feedback about your resume (e.g., career counselors, people who have been receptive to you during informational interviews, teachers, friends, etc.)

Table 9.2
Resume Checklist & Critique Form

	Strong	Average	Weak	Plans for Improvement
1. Resume format. Does it say "READ ME"?				
2. Appearance. Is it brief, did you use an interesting layout, type clearly, use correct layout formats?				
3. Length. Are the key points concise and descriptive?				
4. Significance. Did you select your finest experiences?				
5. Communication. Do your words give the "visual" impression you want? Is the job objective clearly stated?				
6. Conciseness. Does your information focus on the experiences that qualify you for the position?				
7. Completeness. Do you include *all* important information? Have you made the connection between the job desired and your experience?				
8. Reality. Does the resume represent you well enough to get you an interview?				

Summary—Write a Brief Paragraph
Answering These Questions

What did you learn about yourself? How does this knowledge relate to your career/ life planning? How do you feel?

_____
_____
_____
_____
_____
_____
_____
_____
_____
_____
_____
_____
_____
_____
_____

Exhibit 9.3
Functional Resume for Administrative Assistant

```
JANE P. DOE
P. O. Box 1111                                          (805)   555-1212
Simi Valley, Calif. 93065                               (805)   522-1111
```

GOALS

To work as an administrative assistant in a
creative atmosphere and have the opportunity
to use my abilities.

SUMMARY OF EXPERIENCE

Twenty years of increasing responsibility in the area of office management involving organization, problem solving, finances, and public relations.

MANAGEMENT

Initiated and organized procedures used in the office, coordinated activities of
clerical personnel, formulated procedures for systematic retention, protection,
transfer, and disposal of records. Coordinated preparation of operating reports,
such as time and attendance records of performance data. Reviewed, composed, and
answered correspondence. Directed services, such as maintenance, repair, supplies,
mail, and files. Aided executive in staff capacity by coordinating office services, such as personnel, budget preparation and control, housekeeping, records
control, and special management studies.

PUBLIC RELATIONS

Interfaced with state, county, and district officials; district and local employees, student body, staff members, and parents in our community. Planned and
coordinated social functions for school, staff, and two social clubs. Promoted
sales of jewelry, gourmet foods, and liquors in sales-related jobs.

PROBLEM SOLVING

Made decisions according to district policy in the absence of the principal.
Worked under constant pressure and interruption while attending to student problems regarding their health and welfare. Liaison between school and community,
resolving as many problems as possible before referring them to superior.

BUDGETING/FINANCIAL

Analyzed and coordinated payroll record-keeping, budgeted expenditures, requisi-
tioned supplies, prepared attendance accounting reports, and initiated budget
system for $10,000 instructional monies allocated to the school.

CREATIVE

Typed newscopy on varitype machine, composed on headliner, and assisted in copy
paste-up. Designed flyers, posters, calendars, and bulletins sent home from school
to parents. Personal hobbies include ceramics, oil painting, sculpturing, interior
decorating, and needlecraft.

EMPLOYERS

```
Simi Valley Unified School District        So. California Blue Cross
1115 Old School Road                       5900 Erwin Road
Simi Valley, Calif. 93065                  Woodland Hills, Calif. 91360
(805) 555-2345                             (213) 622-1212
```

Exhibit 9.4
Functional Resume for Management Position

MARGARET C. PEARLSON
2406 Adams Avenue
Los Angeles, CA 90025
(213) 555-1212

PROFESSIONAL OBJECTIVE:
Management position utilizing administrative, communications, and research skills.

SUMMARY OF SKILLS:

Administrative
Designed and implemented disbursement and evaluation program for compensatory education project.
Co-authored grant proposal.
Maintained liaison between volunteers and university administration.
Directed registration program and coordinated staff at registration desk, Western Psychological Association Annual Convention, 1988.
As student senator, initiated Earth Day activities, and helped generate faculty evaluation program.

Communications
Planned discussion sections, provided office hours, co-wrote and graded examinations for undergraduate courses in developmental psychology and statistics.
Prepared tutorials in science and study methods, and offered educational guidance to economically disadvantaged high school students.
Participated in human growth seminar led by clinical psychologist, trained in therapy methods, helped devise therapy program for young people.

Research
Designed and conducted study investigating memory in four-year-olds.
Studied mathematical structure underlying Piagetian developmental theory.
Implemented computer simulation model of certain cognitive behaviors in children.
Analyzed and categorized data for cognitive anthropologist and psychologist.

EDUCATION:
M.A., August 1988 Developmental Psychology, University of California, Los Angeles, California. California State Graduate Fellow, National Science Foundation Honorable Mention.
B.A., 1982. Psychology, University of California, Irvine. Summa Cum Laude, Outstanding Scholar, Honor Scholar.

EXPERIENCE:
Teaching Assistant and Reader. Psychology Department, University of California, Los Angeles, January 1984–1988.
Administrative Assistant. Psychology Department, California State University, Fullerton, February–June, 1984.
Business Manager, Education Motivation. Community Projects Office, University of CA, Irvine. August 1982–January 1984.
Research Assistant. Departments of German and Russian. University of California, Irvine. October 1980–June 1982.

REFERENCES WILL BE FURNISHED ON REQUEST

Exhibit 9.5
Functional Resume for Teacher Changing Careers

STACY L. MOLLARD

1001 Gainsborough Street   (312)990-0000 (home)
Chicago, IL 70664   (312)555-1212 (work)

POSITION OBJECTIVE:

    Employee Training Specialist

QUALIFICATIONS IN BRIEF:

    B.A. in English, Mundelein College, Chicago, 1982.
    Six years elementary teaching with experience in communications, human
    relations, instruction, and supervision.
    Bilingual.

EXPERIENCE SUMMARY:

    COMMUNICATIONS:

        Conducted staff development workshops. Presented new curriculum plans
        to parent groups; sent periodic progress reports to parents; developed
        class newsletter. Presented workshops in Parent Effectiveness at state
        and local conferences.

    HUMAN RELATIONS:

        Did effective problem solving/conflict resolution between individual
        students and student groups; initiated program of student self-
        governance; acted as liaison between families of diverse cultural,
        ethnic, and economic backgrounds and school personnel/services; con-
        ducted individual and group conferences to establish rapport with parents
        and discuss student progress.

    INSTRUCTION:

        Developed instructional modules to solve specific learning problems,
        developed instructional audio-visual material, used audio-visual equip-
        ment such as overhead, opaque, and movie projectors, audio and video
        cassettes; did extensive research in various curricula; member of cur-
        riculum development committee; introduced new motivational techniques
        for students.

CURRENTLY EMPLOYED:

    Austin Elementary School, Chicago, Illinois

COMMUNITY INVOLVEMENT

    Board member, Chicago Community Services Center
    Allocations Committee, Chicago United Way

REFERENCES:

    Available upon request

Exhibit 9.6
Chronological Resume for Public Relations

MEGAN N. SCOTT

000 Castillian Court   (805)000-0000 (Home)
Westlake, CA 91360   (805)200-0000 (Work)

OCCUPATIONAL OBJECTIVE:

   Seeking an entry-level position in sales or public relations leading to advanced responsibilities.

SUMMARY OF QUALIFICATIONS:

   Three years of increasingly responsible experience, in different positions.

      BOOKKEEPER   Hungry Hunter and El Torito Restaurants
                                      Thousand Oaks, CA 1985-present

   Kept records of financial transactions, entering them in account and
   cash journals. Balanced books and compiled reports to show statistics,
   such as cash receipts and expenditures, accounts payable and receivable,
   and other items pertinent to operation of business. Calculated employee wages from time cards and operated calculating, bookkeeping, and
   adding machines.

      RESTAURANT HOSTESS   Hungry Hunter Restaurant
                                      Thousand Oaks, CA 1984-1985

   Welcomed guests, seated them in dining area, maintained quality of
   facilities. Directed busboys toward performing courteous and rapid
   service, also assisted in settling complaints. Related well with the
   continuous flow of people, coordinating the service with the customers'
   needs.

SPECIAL ACCOMPLISHMENTS:

   National Forensic League, Vice President (third place, statewide oratory com-
   petition); Varsity cheerleader; Women's Athletic Association (gymnastic team);
   Honor Roll and Dean's List; Alpha Gamma Sigma; and recognized in Who's Who
   Among American High School Students, 1984-1985.

EDUCATION:

   Moorpark College   Moorpark, CA
      Majoring in Business Administration
      G.P.A.: 3.5 on a 4.0 scale

REFERENCES:

   Available upon request.

Exhibit 9.7
Chronological Resume for Bank Teller

Eleanor Rutledge
3388 N. Dallas
Wadsworth, Texas 88000
(909)777-0000

JOB OBJECTIVE: An entry-level position as a bank teller
                      which affords opportunities to learn and
                      progress.

EDUCATION: 1988--Moorpark College, Moorpark, CA.
                      Courses included:

                      Typing 1   Sociology 1
                      Calculating Machines   English 1A

                      1983-1987--Wadsworth High School,
                      Wadsworth, Texas.
                      Courses included:

                      Typing 1   Algebra 1
                      English 1 & 2   Geometry 1
                      Public Speaking

SPECIAL SKILLS: Facility with numbers, manual dexterity,
                      patience, excellent telephone communicator,
                      organized fund-raisers for church group,
                      planned a ski trip with friends.

EXPERIENCE: 1986 to present--Builders Emporium. Wadsworth, Texas.
                      Operated cash register and made change,
                      worked well with public, motivated fellow
                      employees, encouraged customers to buy
                      products.

                      1981-1984--Miscellaneous Employment:
                      Babysitting for local families. Assumed
                      full responsibility while parents were
                      away, helped children with their homework.

REFERENCES: Available upon request.

Exhibit 9.8
Chronological Resume for New Graduates with Limited Experience (High School)

1050 Your Street	John Jones
Simi Valley, CA 93063	(805) 527–1221

OBJECTIVE: An entry-level position as a (list one or two related job titles) which affords opportunities to learn and progress.

SUMMARY: Three years of part-time and summer employment while attending high school, related to sales, public contact, accounting.

EDUCATION: (*List your most recent education first*)
1986   Valley Vista High School, Zenith, California
Graduated with double major in mathematics and business. Courses included:

Typing 1 & 2	Algebra 1 & 2
Bookkeeping 1 & 2	Trigonometry 1 & 2
Business Machines	Geometry 1
English 1, 2, 3	Business Math 1
Journalism 1 & 2	

EXPERIENCE: (*List most recent experience first*)
1985–1987   Moorpark General Store. Moorpark, California.
<u>Salesperson</u>. Sold ready-to-wear in ladies', men's, and children's departments.

1983–1984   Taco Bell. Simi Valley, California.
<u>Counterperson</u>. Assembled customers' orders and packaged orders to go. Operated cash register and made change.

1979–1983   Miscellaneous employment: Babysitting for four local families with up to four children each. Stayed with children weekends and while parents on vacation, assuming full responsibility for normal household routines.

HONORS: *If you had a high grade point average, list it. (See above) List any offices held in a student or community organization. List any publications. If none, omit this section from your resume.*

EXTRA-
CURRICULAR
ACTIVITIES: Future Business Managers Association
Journalism Club
Student Tutoring Association
Young Republicans Club

Exhibit 9.9
Chronological Resume for Community Worker

Mary Smith
980 Victory Blvd.
Simi Valley, California 90063
805/000–0000

OBJECTIVE:	Public Representative or Community Service Worker.
SUMMARY OF QUALIFICATIONS:	Three years experience in public relations, media work, press releases and newsletters. Organized concerts, rallies, walk and volunteer-a-thons. Basic qualifications in office procedures: phone networking, mailing, leafletting, outreach and public speaking.

EDUCATION:

1985   Moorpark College—still attending
Sociology Major. Additional specialized institute from
Loyola Marymount in "Social Organizing."

1983   Alemany High School—graduated
Two years as teacher's aid in L.A. City School System.
Interrelated with variety of cultural groups.

EXPERIENCE:

1983–1987 Community Service Organizations in Los Angeles
Organized, educated, convinced, created social change,
and involved in security work.

1977–1983 Self-employed
Cleaned and maintained family residence.

1981–1983 Receptionist and secretary
Interviewed applicants for positions of sales personnel
and maintained records.

SPECIAL SKILLS:	Interact easily with diverse people while under pressure. Knowledge of fund-raising practices. Self-motivated. Experience in analyzing and working with issues and strategies underlying a particular campaign.
REFERENCES:	Available Upon Request

Exhibit 9.10
Combination Resume for Sales Executive

John W. Doe
304 Amen St.
San Francisco, Calif. 94102
(415) 778-0000 (w)
(415) 588-1111 (h)

OBJECTIVE

MARKETING DIRECTOR

SALES PROMOTION

Designed and supervised sales promotion projects for large business firms and manufacturers, mostly in the electronics field. Originated newspaper, radio, and television advertising. Coordinated sales promotion with public relations and sales management. Analyzed market potentials and developed new techniques to increase sales effectiveness and reduce sales costs. Created sales training manuals.

As sales executive and promotion consultant handled a great variety of accounts. Sales potentials in these firms varied from $100,000 to $5 million per annum. Raised the volume of sales in many of these firms 25 percent within the first year.

SALES MANAGEMENT

Hired and supervised sales staff on a local, area, and national basis. Established branch offices throughout the United States. Developed uniform systems of processing orders and sales records. Promoted new products as well as improving sales of old ones. Developed sales training program. Developed a catalog system involving inventory control to facilitate movement of scarce stock between branches.

MARKET RESEARCH

Devised and supervised market research projects to determine sales potentials, as well as need for advertising. Wrote detailed reports and recommendations describing each step in distribution, areas for development, and plans for sales improvement.

SALES

Retail and wholesale. Direct sales to consumer, jobber, and manufacturer. Hard goods, small metals, and electrical appliances.

EMPLOYERS

1976-1988	B.B. Bowen Sales Development Co., San Francisco, Calif.	Sales Executive
1966-1975	James Bresher Commercial and Industrial Sales Research Corp. Oakland, Calif.	Sr. Sales Promotion Mgr.
1958-1965	Dunnock Brothers Electronics Co., San Francisco, Calif.	Order Clerk, Salesworker, Sales Mgr.

EDUCATION

University of California, Berkeley, B.S. 1959; Major: Business Admin.

REFERENCES AVAILABLE UPON REQUEST

Exhibit 9.11
Combination Resume for Programmer Trainee

John Smith

111 East Maple

Moorpark, CA 93021

(805) 555-1122

OBJECTIVE: Applications programmer trainee.

QUALIFIED
BY: Flowcharted, coded, tested and debugged interactive COBOL and
BASIC programs for the HP 3000. Created a system of five COBOL
programs from a system problem statement and flowchart. Built
a KSAM file for use by the system. Wrote JCL for the five-
program job stream. Designed system flowcharts and wrote other
documentation for improved payroll system for previous employer,
as Systems Analysis class project.

Tutored students in BASIC and COBOL, working with Hispanics,
Vietnamese, and re-entering adults, as well as with more conventional students.

Currently searching a bibliographic data base, as a volunteer
at Simi Valley Public Library.

EDUCATION: 1987 Associate in Science in Computer Science, Moorpark College
      3.6 GPA in Computer Science classes.

1981 B.A. in English, Florida Southern College.

Post-graduate work in research methods.

Supported self through college by security work at various firms.
Gained Secret clearance while at IBM Federal Systems Division.

SPECIAL
SKILLS: Attentive to detail, organized, work well with little supervision,
enterprising, enjoy problem solving and interacting with others
to plan projects, work well under pressure, able to see relationships between abstract ideas, good at communication, concise.

COMMUNITY
SERVICE
EXPERIENCE: Organized CROP Walks (fund-raisers for Church World Service)
which resulted in raising $6,000 in 1980 and $10,000 in 1982.

Chaired the Planning Committee, recruited members, chose walk
route.

Obtained parade permits and business tax exemptions.

Wrote press releases and walkers' instruction sheets.

REFERENCES: Available upon request.

Exhibit 9.12
A Poor Resume

PERSONAL:
Age: 26
Marital Status: Single
Height: 5'9"

Henry O'Neil
617 Barclay Street
Carbondale, Illinois

Job Objective:

I am looking for any position dealing with the design and manufacture of
furniture. Would prefer a position in the midwestern United States.

Education:

Carbondale High School--graduate 1970--academic courses

Lehigh University--Bethlehem, Pennsylvania--BS Industrial Engineering,
1981, finished top half of class.

Experience:

1981: Traveled extensively in Europe.

1981 to present: White Shoe Company, 1783 Fairlawn Drive, Cicero, Illinois.
                 I started there as time and motion study consultant on as-
                 sembly line operations, reporting to the cheif Industrial
                 Engineer. I was promoted to Equipment Analysis and pur-
                 chasing section after one year. In this position I handled
                 several new equipment installations and start-ups, and in-
                 cluding a 140,000 PPH boiler and solvent recovery system.

                 In 1984 was promoted to Product Supervisor for a special
                 new line of cork-soled deck shoes which were successfully
                 marketed in U.S. and foreign markets. In this position I
                 was in charge of several junior engineers and a large pro-
                 duction staff.

Miscellaneous: Have won several awards for furniture design.
               Finished first in Lake Michigan Class E Sailboat races.
               Fluent in French and Italian.

Hobbies: Furniture design and repair.
               sailing
               music

References: On request

Exhibit 9.13
Resume Cover Letter Guidelines

                                                    Address
                                                    City, State, Zip Code
                                                    Date

Name of Person or Company
Street Address or P.O. Box
City, State, Zip

Salutation: (Dear M... ....: or Greetings:)

THE FIRST PARAGRAPH SHOULD INDICATE WHAT JOB YOU ARE INTERESTED IN AND HOW
YOU HEARD ABOUT IT. USE THE NAMES OF CONTACT PERSONS HERE, IF YOU HAVE ANY.

SAMPLE
ENTRY

Your employment advertisement in Tuesday's News Chronicle indicating an
opening for an administrative assistant is of special interest to me. Mary
Smith, who presently is employed at your firm, suggested I write to you. I
have heard that Rohn Electronics is a growing company and wants dynamic employees who also want to learn and contribute to the firm.

THE SECOND PARAGRAPH SHOULD RELATE YOUR EXPERIENCE, SKILLS, AND BACKGROUND
TO THE PARTICULAR POSITION. REFER TO YOUR ENCLOSED RESUME FOR DETAILS AND
AND HIGHLIGHT THE SPECIFIC SKILLS AND COMPETENCIES THAT COULD BE USEFUL TO
THE COMPANY.

SAMPLE
ENTRY

During the last five years, I worked as an office manager and was able to
redesign the office by investigating and selecting word-processing equipment. I understand that your opening includes responsibilities for super-
vising and coordinating word-processing procedures with your home office.
I was able to reduce the operating costs over 30 percent by selecting the
best equipment for our purposes.

THE THIRD PARAGRAPH SHOULD INDICATE YOUR PLANS FOR FOLLOW UP CONTACT AND
THAT YOUR RESUME IS ENCLOSED.

SAMPLE
ENTRY

I am excited about the opportunity of discussing with you the information
I have gathered about your company and why I feel I would be a valuable
asset. I have enclosed a resume of my education and work experience, for
your examination. I will call your office early next week to determine a
convenient time for an appointment to further discuss employment opportunities.

Sincerely,

Your first and last name

Enclosure or Attachment

Exhibit 9.14
Cover Letter for Community Health Worker

Date

Mr. Harvey J. Professional
Executive Director
Lung Association of Alma County
1717 Opportunity Way
Santa Ana, California 92706

Dear Mr. Professional:

I am interested in the position of Community Health Education/Program Coordinator
with the Lung Association of Alma County. I feel that my education, skills, and
desire to work in this area make me a strong candidate for this position.

My education has helped me develop sound analytical abilities and has exposed me
to the health care field. My involvement with health care and community organizations has provided me with the working knowledge of various public and private
health institutions which has increased my ability to communicate effectively
with health care professionals, patients, and the community at large. This combination of education and exposure has stimulated my interest in developing a
career in the health field.

Please review the enclosed resume and contact me at your convenience regarding a
personal interview. If I do not hear from you in the next week, I will contact
you.

Sincerely yours,

Denise M. Jobseeker
18411 Anticipation Drive
Northridge, California 91330
(213) 886-0000

Enc.

Exhibit 9.15
Cover Letter for a Teacher with Some Business Background

April 1, 1989

Mr. John Smith
Director of Personnel
ABC Corporation
Anytown, CA 90000

Dear Mr. Smith:

I am applying for the administrative assistant position currently
available in your firm. I have been impressed for some time with
the outstanding reputation your firm holds in our community.

As you read my resume, please note that my twelve years of business
experience directly relates to the needs of your company. One of
my greatest assets is seven years in motivational psychology related
to personnel management and public school teaching. I am aware how
important strengths in business and management are in your firm, and
I would like the opportunity to discuss with you, at your earliest
convenience, how we might work together for our mutual benefit.

Enclosed is my resume for your review. I will telephone your secretary next week to see when we might set up an appointment to further
discuss the administrative assistant position and any other ways that
I could serve your corporation.

                              Sincerely,

                              Gerald Anybody

GA:

Encl: Resume

Exhibit 9.16
Cover Letter for Electronic Technician

000 Melbrook Avenue
Westlake Village, CA 91361
June 17, 1989

Mr. Lloyd Price
Sonar Technical Supervisor
Lear Electronic Company
0000 Van Owen
Rosemead, CA 91770

Dear Mr. Price:

I am interested in working for your company as an electronics technician
in the field of customer installation and calibration.

During my tour of duty in the submarine service, I became acquainted
with many of your electronic systems aboard ship. I was extremely impressed with your system's design and documentation. I have since
pursued a course of studies at Moorpark College to increase my competence in the field of electronics. For these reasons I feel I would
be an asset to your company.

I am planning to contact you by telephone next week to set up a meeting
to discuss employment opportunities with your company.

Sincerely yours,

John Fish

Exhibit 9.17
Cover Letter for Public Relations

0000 Evanston Avenue
Kambridge, IL   80080
June 17, 1989

Mr. Harrison MacBuren
Director of Personnel
The North Hills Mall
Kambridge, IL   80080

Dear Mr. MacBuren:

I am very interested in the position which is currently available in your Public Relations Department for an assistant to the Director of Public Relations.

As you can see by my resume, my previous administrative experience would be a definite asset to your company. I feel a vital part of any public relations job is the ability to deal with people. This is a skill I have acquired through many years of volunteer work.

I would like to meet with you to discuss how we might work together for our mutual benefit. I will be contacting you within the week to arrange a convenient meeting time.

Sincerely,

Janet Ellsworth

Exhibit 9.18
Cover Letter for Marketing Manager

1736 D. Street N.W.
Washington, D.C. 20006
(202) PO 7-8192
February 1, 1989

Mr. Edward Major, President
Vendo Corporation
1742 Surf Drive
Fort Lauderdale, Florida

Dear Mr. Major:

I was intrigued by the write-up of your new portable vending centers as described in Sales Management magazine. Frankly, I think it is an extremely good idea.

As you will note from the enclosed resume, my marketing, planning, and sales management experience could be of great assistance to you at this early stage in your project.

Because of my familiarity with the types of locations and clients you are seeking, I am sure that if we were able to work together in this new venture, the results would reflect my contribution.

I have roughed out some specific marketing ideas which you might like to review, and would like to make arrangements to meet with you in Florida during the week of February 15th.

I am looking foward to meeting with you. I will call next week to arrange for an appointment.

Very truly yours,

John W. Doe

Exhibit 9.19
Letter of Introduction

TO WHOM IT MAY CONCERN:

This will introduce Mary Smith, a trusted and valued member of my staff for the past two and a half years.

During this time she has held a key position, performing a variety of secretarial tasks, as well as having full charge of the ordering, maintenance, and updating of our career resources library. She is keen at spotting deficiencies and was instrumental in developing a more efficient system for updating our materials.

She has been recognized by other members of the staff, including the counselors and our program director, the Dean of Student Personnel, as being outstanding in poise, appearance, and reliability. Additionally, and probably most important, she has been exceptionally effective in working with students, faculty, and professionals using the resources of our Center.

Mary is a good organizer, capable of dealing with concepts and goals and devising a systems approach to problem solving. She is highly loyal and discreet in dealing with unusual situations and those calling for confidentiality.

If there is anything more you feel you would like to discuss regarding Mary's qualifications, please feel free to contact me.

Very truly yours,

Her Past Employer

Part I

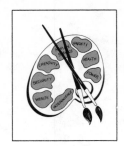

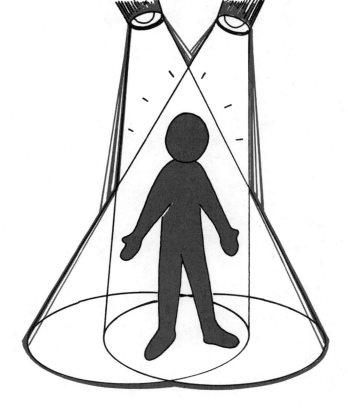

Part II

Selling Your Product 10

The person who gets the job isn't always the person who is best qualified but rather the person who is best prepared to find potential jobs and interview for them.

Learning Objectives   At the end of the chapter you will be able to:

Understand the art of interviewing.

Develop guidelines and techniques for good interviewing.

Learn how to prepare for an interview.

The Job Interview

Once you begin to feel comfortable with the notion of networking and practice interviewing, you are ready to begin preparing for the "Olympic Finals," the interview.

Before the Interview

Here are some tips to take into consideration as you approach your first interview or refine your current interviewing style.

Some of the best preparation for the interview is research about the prospective employer. You must be able to show the employer why you will be the best person for the job. Relate your personal strengths and past accomplishments to this particular enterprise. Specifically, tell how you can help with current problems, or function as a valuable member of the organization.

Before the interview, or at least early in it, try to find out what the essential responsibilities of the job are. Make a mental note of them, and throughout the interview, feed back the kind of information from your background that shows that you can handle these responsibilities.

Don't let the formal job description disqualify you for the job. Remember that job descriptions are only guidelines, and once in the job, you are allowed to imprint your own style. Additionally, over 50 percent of any job is expected to be learned on the job. Thus, your ability to express what your skills are, how you can contribute to the company, and your willingness to learn new skills are as important as being able to do each task described in the job description. In fact, if you already can do each task described, you might be labeled as overqualified and not get the job!

Your resume and cover letter become the written and mental outline upon which you elaborate to translate your skills into potential benefits to the employer. Use your resume as a point of reference; write on index cards key points you want to convey and remember during the interview. It's *appropriate* to bring these cards with you to your interview.

Consider non-traditional jobs

In applying for jobs, a male increases his chances by trying for a field that has previously been primarily a female domain (i.e., nursing). Similarly, a female increases her chances if she applies for a position that has been previously primarily a male domain. However, it must be remembered that it will not always be easy to be the "first one" in any position.

Don't be afraid to reapply and reinterview at the same company. Hopefully, your interview skills will have improved in the meantime, and different people may be interested in you.

Be creative if you are applying for a creative job (advertising, design, sales, art) but be conservative if you are applying for a conservative job (banking, insurance, accounting).

Before the interview, verify the particulars. Write down the interviewer's name, the location, and the time and date of your appointment. Last-minute nervousness can block such details from your memory. Plan on arriving fifteen minutes early.

Apprehension, tension, and anxiety are a normal part of the pre-interview jitters. Relaxation techniques, deep breathing, and chatting with the receptionist may help.

Ask for feedback

If you are turned down, consider calling to get information to improve a later interview: "I realize that this is a bit unusual and I am aware that you've chosen someone else for the job, but could you spend a few moments giving me some ideas as I continue my job search?" You could end up with some valuable leads; it's worth a try!

Interviewing becomes easier as you get practice. Don't be overly discouraged if you don't get the first job for which you interview. Interviews and even rejections are actually invaluable opportunities to reassess and reaffirm your qualifications, strengths, weaknesses, and your needs.

In the competitive job market of today, you can maximize your chance of successful interviewing doing practice interviews and being prepared to answer an employer's typical questions. Always be prepared to support your general answers with specific examples from your experience. Your interviewers will remember your examples!

There are several types of questions generally asked in an interview. Be prepared beforehand with your answers.

1. Tell me about yourself. . . .

   Refer mentally to your resume; do not assume that the interviewer has even read it! Briefly recap your skills and experiences as they relate to this particular job.

2. Why do you want this job? Why did you apply here?

   Refer to information about this job and this company or institution that makes it particularly appealing to you. Do not give the impression that you're here just because there's a job opening here. Refer to the company's history, products, and services. Let your interviewers know that you have researched the company.

3. Why should I hire you?

   "Because I, with my skills, experiences, positive attitude and enthusiasm am obviously the best person for the job. I agree with your philosophy, I feel that I will fit in. I will be an asset to your enterprise." (Reemphasize your strengths.)

4. What are your career plans? Where do you see yourself five years from now?

   Employers generally like to think you will be with them forever; you can't make any promises, but you can indicate you would like to be with a company that allows you to grow, to assume more responsibility, and one that challenges you continuously. That challenges them to be that kind of place!

5. Are there any questions?

   You might ask just what kind of person the interviewer is really looking for. Then show how you fit the bill. You may need clarification on salary. "When can I expect to hear about the position? Oh, yes, I forgot to mention earlier that . . . .I would like to reiterate that. . . ." (See exhibit 10.2)
   Leave the interviewer convinced that you are ready and able to do the job.

Never answer a question "no" without qualifying it positively. "Have you operated a cash register before?" "No, but I have good finger dexterity and I won't have any problems learning."

"Can you type?" "No, I didn't realize it was part of the job description. If it is necessary, I can learn. Just how much typing will be involved?"

6. What salary do you expect?

If you have done your homework, you should have an idea of the general range for the position. Find out whether this company has a fixed salary schedule. You may want to defer the matter until you know more about what the job entails.

7. Don't you think you are too young/old for this position?

In either case phrase your answer so it is an advantage. Example:
Too young: Show how the job best lends itself to a young person—one who can face the challenges with youthful vigor and a fresh point of view.
Too old: Point out how your years of experience and previous success give you the confidence and wisdom to carry full responsibility with the mature judgment required by this position.

8. Why did you leave your last job?

If asked why you left your last position, avoid mentioning a personality conflict. Rather say, "I felt I had gone as far in that company as possible and I was ready for more responsibility, challenge, hours" (etc.). If your work history reflects many job changes, explain how you have transferred existing skills and learned new skills that can now benefit these employers.

Guidelines

The interview is the goal of your job search strategy. Generally, people who are interviewed are assumed qualified to do the job; the question becomes one of the most appropriate meshing of personalities. Both the interviewer and interviewee are relying on their communication skills, judgment, intuition, and insight. It is a two-way process. While you are being evaluated, you should be evaluating the position and the people offering it. Remember that a good interview is a dialogue, an exchange of information.

Two-Way Process

Take a good look at yourself. Employers are becoming increasingly broad-minded about clothes and hair, but few are totally "liberated." If you are serious about getting a job, then you had better look and dress the part. No interviewer will tell you what you are supposed to wear, but the person will partially measure your maturity and judgment by your appearance. Remember the first impression is often a lasting one. It's often not the best-qualified person who gets the job but the one who makes the best impression. *You never get a second chance to make a good first impression*!

There are some trick or stress questions that you may have to handle; be prepared beforehand with a response that feels comfortable to you. (See sample questions below.) If a question seems inappropriate you may ask: "How does this information relate to or affect my employment here?" This may prompt an employer to express the real concerns, such as your record of stability on the job, age, child care needs, or commitment to the job and company. You may even consider bringing up these relevant issues. Often seemingly unimportant conversation is an attempt to put you and the interviewer at ease or to assess your ability to socialize.

Remember that many interviewers are just as nervous about the process as you. Feel free to make the first attempts to "break the ice"; when you try to relieve another's anxiety, yours becomes secondary. Note the office decor, the cordial welcome, whatever makes sense. If you are nervous, you will find that focusing on the question, "What would it be like to work here?" rather than "How am I being perceived by them?" will relax you. Relax in the chair; a rigid posture reinforces your tenseness. Actually, a slightly forward position with head erect indicates interest and intimacy. Maintain eye contact. In answering questions, use your knowledge of yourself to transmit the idea that you are the best person for the job; allow strengths such as good will, flexibility, enthusiasm, and a professional approach to surface. Bring samples of your work if they are related. On an index card, note your strengths or key selling points, also the questions you may have and some cue words like "smile, speak up, relax"; refer to them from time to time, especially just before you go into the interview. Forthright statements about what you do well, with examples of accomplishments are of key importance. Talk with pride, honesty, and confidence about your accomplishments and your potential, your interest and commitment, and your readiness to learn on the job.

Body language can speak louder than words

Express yourself *positively*. You are selling yourself; allow your personal *energy* and *enthusiasm* to surface.

Breakdown of an Interview

Although every interview is different, most follow a general pattern. A typical half-hour session can be roughly divided into four segments:

1. The first five or ten minutes are usually devoted to establishing some rapport and opening the lines of communication. Instead of wondering why the interviewer is taking valuable time chatting about the weather, your parking problems, etc., relax and enjoy the conversation. S/He'll get to deeper subjects soon enough. The interview begins the moment you introduce yourselves and shake hands. Don't discount the initial period. Your ability to converse, expressing yourself intelligently, is being measured.

Establish initial rapport

2. The adept interviewer will move subtly from a casual exchange to a more specific level of conversation. The second part of the interview gives you a chance to answer some "where, when and why" questions about your background—to supply information left out of your resume.

Now is the time to describe some extra-curricular activities or work experience that may explain your less-than-perfect GPA. Or to talk of changes you effected as president of a campus organization or community group. This is your chance to elaborate upon your strong points and maximize whatever you have to offer. Don't monopolize the conversation; let the interviewer lead. But don't confine your statements to yes or no answers.

The interviewer will be interested not only in what you say, but how you say it. Equally important as the information you communicate will be the demonstrated evidence of a logical organization and presentation of thoughts. S/He'll be mentally grading your intelligence, leadership potential, and motivation.

3. Part three begins when the interviewer feels s/he's identified your skills and interests and can see how they might fit his/her organization. If a good match seems possible, s/he will discuss the company and the openings available.

Ask questions 4. At the end of an interview try to find out where you stand. "How do you feel I relate to this job?" "Do you need any additional information?" "When can I expect to hear from you?"

After you leave, take ten or fifteen minutes to analyze how you did. What questions did you find difficult? What did you forget to say? How can you improve on the next interview? You might even keep a diary or log with written notes on each of these concerns as well as listing the specific interview questions asked and how you responded. Also list any specific things that you can do to follow up with an employer to increase your chances of getting the offer you want. If you feel you forgot to mention something or there was a misunderstanding, correct or elaborate on these points in a letter or telephone call. Write a thank-you letter to the interviewer, recalling a significant fact or idea of the interview that will set you apart from the other applicants.

Practice questions

The following are types of questions that have been asked during interviews, intended to create a *stress* response. They are asked out of pattern, designed to throw you. The interviewer sometimes is more interested in *how* you respond than in what you say. S/He wants to see how you react and how you "think on your feet." Determine which of the following questions are likely to be asked of you in your situation. PRACTICE!!

1. What kind of job do you expect to hold five years from now? Ten years? Twenty years?
2. Why do you want to work for this company?
3. Why did you choose your particular field of work?
4. What do you know about this company?
5. Do you feel that you have a good general education?
6. What qualifications do you have that make you feel that you will be successful in your field?
7. What are your ideas on salary? Don't you feel that you would be dissatisfied with a job paying less than you were previously making?
8. What do you think determines a person's progress in a good company?
9. Do you prefer working with others or by yourself?
10. What kind of supervision do you prefer?
11. Can you take criticism without feeling upset?
12. What interests you about our product/service?
13. How long do you expect to work?
14. Do you like routine work?
15. What is your major weakness? (or what are three of your strong points? Three of your weak points?)
16. Have you had any serious illness or injury?
17. Are you willing to go where the company sends you? Travel? Relocate?
18. What kinds of people annoy you?
19. What are your own special abilities?
20. Do you object to working overtime?
21. What arrangements do you have for child care?
22. How would your spouse feel about your accepting this job if it were offered?
23. What is your philosophy of life?
24. Do you have any objections to a psychological test or interview?
25. Don't you feel a little too old (or young) for this position?
26. Will you take an aptitude test?
27. Tell me about yourself.
28. What are your personal goals?
29. In what ways will this company benefit from your services?
30. If you were me, why would you hire you?
31. Have you ever been fired?

Illegal Questions

There are certain hiring practices, employment application form questions, and specific interviewing procedures which are now illegal under the Fair Employment Practices Act. Review table 10.1 on the following pages to familiarize yourself with the subject matter and specifics of this issue.

Table 10.1
Preemployment Inquiries: Lawful and Unlawful

Subject	Acceptable Preemployment Inquiries	Unacceptable Preemployment Inquiries
Photographs	Statement that photograph may be required after employment.	Requirement that applicant affix a photograph to application form. Request applicant at his option to submit photograph. Requirement of photograph after interview but before hiring.
Race or Color		Complexion, color of skin, or other questions directly or indirectly indicating race or color such as color of applicant's eyes and hair.
Citizenship	Request applicant to state the status of his/her residency. (a) Citizen of U.S. (b) Legal right to remain permanently in the U.S. Statement by employer that, if hired, applicant may be required to submit proof of citizenship.	Of what country are you a citizen? Inquiry whether an applicant or his/her parents or spouse are naturalized or native-born U.S. citizens; the date when the applicant or his/her parents or spouse acquired citizenship. Requirement that applicant produce his/her naturalization papers or first papers.
National Origin	An inquiry into applicant's proficiency in foreign language must be job-related.	Applicant's nationality, lineage, national origin, descent or parentage. Date of arrival in U.S. or port of entry; how long a resident of U.S. Nationality of applicant's parents or spouse; maiden name of applicant's wife or mother. Language commonly used by applicant, "What is your mother tongue?" How applicant acquired ability to read, write, or speak a foreign language.
Education	Inquiry into the academic, vocational or professional education of an applicant and the schools he/she has attended.	Any inquiry asking specifically the nationality, racial or religious affiliation of a school.
Name	Have you ever worked for this company under a different name? Maiden name of married female applicant, assumed name or change of name, if necessary to check educational or employment records.	Former name of applicant whose name has been changed by court order or otherwise.
Address or Duration of Residence	Inquiry into place and length of current and previous addresses.	Specific inquiry into foreign addresses that would indicate national origin.
Sex		If not based on a bona fide occupational qualification. (It is extremely difficult for "sex" to be considered a lawful preemployment inquiry.)

Table 10.1 (continued)
Preemployment Inquiries: Lawful and Unlawful

Subject	Acceptable Preemployment Inquiries	Unacceptable Preemployment Inquiries
Birthplace	Requirement that applicant submit a birth certificate or other proof of legal residence after employment.	Birthplace of applicant's parents, spouse, or other relatives.
Age	Requirement that applicant submit a birth certificate or other document, after employment, as proof of age.	Requirement that applicant produce proof of age in the form of a birth certificate, baptismal record, or Employment Certificate or Certificate of Age issued by school authorities.
Religion		Inquiry into applicant's religious denomination or affiliation, church, parish, pastor, or religious holidays observed. Applicant may not be told "This is a Catholic/Protestant/Jewish/atheist, etc. organization."
Work Days and Shifts	Request applicant to state days, hours, or shift that he/she can work.	It is unlawful to request applicant to state days, hours, or shift that he/she can work if it is used to discriminate on basis of religion.

How to Handle Illegal Questions

If the question is on an application, you always have the option to put N/A in the blank. If you are asked illegal questions in an interview, you should anticipate what concerns a potential employer might have about hiring you and bring them up in a manner that is comfortable for you.
Example:

Interviewer: "Do you have any children?"

Interviewee: "I guess you are wondering about the care of my school-age children. I'd like you to know I have an excellent attendance record. (You are welcome to check with my past employer) and besides, I have a live-in sitter, etc. Additionally, I have researched the needs of this position and can assure you that I have no family responsibilities that will interfere with my ability to do this job."

Not only will an employer appreciate your sensitivity to her/his concerns but your statement provides you with an additional opportunity to sell yourself and to evaluate whether this position is one that you want to consider. It is often advisable for you, the interviewee, to bring up any issue that may be on the employer's mind but because of legal concerns, will not be addressed unless you mention it. Such issues as age, children, spouse's feelings about this position, gender, disabilities, qualifications can all be addressed by you in such a way as to enhance your chances of getting the

Anticipate concerns and address them

job. Basically, you want to show how your age, qualifications, gender, or disability will be an advantage to your employer. This requires some thinking on your part before the interview, and the payoff, getting the job you want, is well worth the effort.

Body Language

Present yourself assertively

Your body language speaks just as loudly as your words. Eye contact is crucial. Remember that at a distance of five or six feet from another person, you can be looking at the person's nose or forehead or mouth and still maintain the feeling of eye contact. Try it with friends.

Voice tone, volume, and inflection are important. A soft wispy voice will seldom convince another that you mean business, while a loud or harsh voice tends to be blocked out. Listen to yourself on a tape recorder, or preferably on videotape. How do you sound to yourself? Ask others for their comments. Lessons in voice and diction are available in most schools. Try varying your voice pitch and volume while reading something into a tape recorder. You may find a range that sounds better.

Gum is a sticky subject—throw it out!

Try accenting your words with appropriate hand gestures to gain emphasis.

Before the interview, you should analyze your practice interviews. Consider the option of being videotaped during a practice interview. The instant feedback is very helpful, particularly if you use the format laid out in table 10.2 to critique your performance. If you are in a class, practice with one or more classmates, evaluating your own and your classmates' interview techniques according to the critique form.

Learning From the Interview

You are interviewing the representatives of the company as much as they are interviewing you. In fact, you will only do about 40 percent of the talking. In the remaining time you can listen and assess whether or not you want to work for that company. Although an interview tends to be rather formal, you can still gain a feeling about the climate of the organization. Entering the building you can observe the receptionist, support staff, people talking or not talking in the hallways. The colors or decor in the building should generate a positive or negative impression.

Take note of the punctuality of the interview, assuming you are on time or early, the arrangement of the seating in the interview room, and the dress of the interviewers. The entrance and hand shake are important first impressions. Some companies deliberately set up awkward or uncomfortable situations to observe your response. They may ask tough questions just to see how well you "think on your feet." If you can maintain your composure and enthusiasm in the interview they will probably think that you are able to work equally as well under stress.

In selecting your own questions you might ask who was the last person in the position and what happened to them; if the person resigned, you may

Table 10.2
Interview Critique Form

Name _____ (Individual being interviewed)	Very good	Satisfactory	Fair—could be better	Needs improvement	Comments
1. Initial, or opening presentation. (Impression)					
2. Eye contact.					
3. Sitting position.					
4. General appearance: grooming—hair, make-up, shave, beard, mustache, etc., clothing.					
5. Ability to describe past work experiences, education and/or training.					
6. Ability to explain equipment, tools and other mechanical aids used.					
7. Ability to explain skills, techniques, processes, procedures. Ability to stress how skills related to job.					
8. Ability to explain personal goals, interests, desires.					
9. Ability to explain questionable factors in personal life. (Functional limitations, frequent job changes, many years since last job.)					
10. Ability to answer questions or make statements on company or job applying for.					
11. Ability to listen attentively to interviewer's questions and to notice his/her body language.					
12. Manner of speech or conversation understandable? (Voice, tone, pitch, volume, speed.)					
13. Physical mannerisms (Facial expressions, gestures).					
14. Enthusiasm, interest in this job.					
15. Attitude (positive?) Confident.					
16. Overall Impression? Would you hire this applicant?					

ask why. Another related question would be "Given the current economy, how have careers at my level been affected?" You may also ask about the background of your potential supervisor and the mobility within the company. Although you want to emphasize your interest and commitment to the position for which you are interviewing, the previous questions can illustrate your interest in a future with the company.

What is the corporate culture?   A final bit of information you should gather or confirm about the company relates to its *corporate culture*. Corporate culture refers to the personality of the potential employer. Primarily you want to seek employment with a firm that is likely to meet your personality needs. Do you need a competitive environment to thrive? Most likely a job in a high school or government position won't satisfy those needs. Do you need security? The aerospace field may be a bit too unsteady for you. The prime questions related to corporate culture to ask during an interview would include "Can you explain the management style or philosophy of your company?" If you want to have the opportunity for input into management you might ask about the use of quality circles or the potential for the use of quality circles in the organization. If you are hoping to enter the field of business but have little relevant background, it might help to take a college class or read a book on the world of business so that you can ask educated questions about business practices.

Exhibit 10.1
Sample Questions to Ask at the Interview

Going one step further than just *answering* the interviewer's questions, you should be prepared to take the initiative in *asking* several questions:
* Could you describe the duties of this job?
* Where does this position fit into the organization?
* What type of people do you prefer for this job?
* Is this position new?
* What experience is ideally suited for this job?
* Was the last person promoted?
* Whom would I be reporting to? Can you tell me a little about these people?
* Are you happy with them?
* What have been some of the best results you have received from these people?
* Who are the primary people I would be working with?
* What seem to be their strengths and weaknesses?
* What are your expectations for me?
* May I talk with present and previous employees about this job?
* What are some of the problems I might expect to encounter on this job, i.e., efficiency, quality control, declining profits, evaluation?
* What has been done recently in regards to . . .?
* How is this program going?
* Can I tell you anything more about my qualifications?
* What is the normal pay *range* for this job?
* If you don't mind, can I let you know by (*date*)?
* What kind of on-the-job training is allocated for this position?

Factors Influencing Hiring

There are many things to consider in preparing for an interview.

There are some factors over which we have control; other considerations are beyond our control. Look over this list to distinguish between the two.

IN OUR CONTROL

1. Poor personal appearance.
2. Overbearing—overaggressive—conceited—"superiority complex"—"know-it-all."
3. Inability to express him/herself clearly, poor voice, diction, grammar.
4. Lack of planning for career—no purpose and goals.
5. Lack of interest and enthusiasm—passive, indifferent.
6. Lack of confidence and poise—nervousness—ill-at-ease.
7. Overemphasis on money—interest only in best dollar offer.
8. Poor scholastic record—just got by.
9. Unwilling to start at the bottom—expects too much too soon.
10. Makes excuses—evasiveness—hedges on unfavorable factors in record.
11. Lack of courtesy—ill-mannered.
12. Condemnation of past employers.
13. Fails to look interviewer in the eye.
14. Limp, fishy handshake.
15. Sloppy application blank.
16. Merely shopping around.
17. Wants job only for short time.
18. No interest in company or in industry.
19. Emphasis on whom he knows.
20. Unwillingness to go where we send him.
21. Intolerant—strong prejudices.
22. Narrow interests.
23. Late to interview without good reason.
24. Never heard of company.
25. Failure to express appreciation for interviewer's time.
26. Asks no questions about the job.
27. High pressure type.
28. Indefinite response to questions.

OUT
OF
OUR
CONTROL

Looking for more experience.

Looking for less experience.

Too many applicants.

Your skills are more than needed for the position.

Cannot pay you what you are making now.

The company management decided that morning on a temporary freeze on hiring—for many business reasons.

Indecisiveness on part of business owner.

Only trying to fill a temporary position.

Illness of interviewer.

An old employee changed his mind and decided not to leave.

Introduction of new personnel policies.

Change in management.

Death in company management.

Looking only for a certain type person.

Further consideration of all applicants.

A more important post must be filled first.

Lack of experience on part of interviewer.

Only accepting applications for a future need.

Finally, experts in the field agree that people don't get the job for the following six reasons (Johnson 1981):

1. Lack of clearly defined career goals.
2. Little or no knowledge of basic business principles.
3. Inability to see (and describe) how their skills and training can serve the company desired.
4. Lack of information about the firm.
5. Failure to convey a solid sense of self-awareness and confidence.
6. Lack of assertiveness and dedication.

More and more firms will be requiring a college degree. Degrees will be required primarily because so many people have degrees. Even a liberal arts degree can compete with a specialist degree in business if the following factors are taken into consideration:

1. You have an excellent grade point average.
2. You have a record of extracurricular activities (club or community involvement). It's especially good to have had leadership positions.
3. You worked your way through college (it helps even more if you worked for the company with which you seek full-time employment).
4. You've made some contacts within the firm who can serve as positive references.
5. You either minored in business or, at least, selected business courses as electives (i.e., accounting, economics, marketing, information systems).
6. You have defined goals, exude enthusiasm and confidence, and can verbalize these characteristics in an interview.

For example, ATT employs 6,000 new college graduates a year and more than one-third are liberal arts graduates. More business graduates are currently being hired to meet the needs of the sales staff who are working with deregulation.

Generally attributed to all college graduates, but especially to liberal arts graduates, are intellectual ability (verbal and quantitative), and skills in planning, organizing, decision-making, interpersonal relations, leadership, and oral communication.

Summary—Reviewing the Interview Process

PREPARATION

- Resume—contacts—letters of reference.
- Interview log—contacts—initial contact letters written.
- Thank-you letters—contacts—know your resume.
- Letters out—make appointments—contacts.
- 3″ x 5″ cards on each interview.

- Attitudes—"You can do it"—visualize that you have the job.
- Dress the part.
- Know your resume—bring extra copies to the interview.
- Know something about the company (*Dunn and Bradstreet—Moodys—Standard & Poor—Fortune 500*—annual report—magazine articles).
- Have five or six good questions—know when to ask them.
- Keep control.
- Be on time! ! !

THE INTRODUCTION

- Good posture, shake hands, breathe.
- Use good eye contact and posture.
- The first four minutes are key—establish rapport—generate the proper chemistry.
- What can I do for you?—major strengths question—tell me about your background.
- Be positive—convert negatives to pluses.

THE INTERVIEW

- Smile.
- Supply information, refer to your resume.
- Seek the next interview (or the job).
- Overcome any objections—try to anticipate objections.
- Keep answers brief.
- Ask questions about the field.
- Know the rules—when a decision will be made.
- Ask for the job if it exists.
- Be positive.
- When would you like my answer?

AFTER THE INTERVIEW

- Debrief yourself—write notes (name, address, phone number, impressions; if a panel of interviewers, write down names and positions of all panel members).
- Formally thank the employer or chairperson of the panel by letter. See exhibit 10.2.
- Plan a follow-up strategy—if you don't hear from them, call and ask if a decision has been made.
- Don't be defeated!—keep interviewing!

Use the sample thank-you letters (exhibit 10.2) as a guide and write your own to an imaginary or real interviewer.

Exhibit 10.2
Sample Thank-you Letters

19574 Delaware
Detroit, MI 48223
February 8, 1989

Mr. John Smith
Michels' Manufacturing Corporation
1928 N. Berry Street
Livonia, MI 48150

Dear Mr. Smith:

Thank you for the time you spent with me this morning. I was certainly impressed with the efficiency, friendliness, and overall climate of Michels' Manufacturing Corporation.

Now that you've told me more about Michels' recent contact with the U.S. Tank Command, I feel my degree in industrial engineering and my two years of part-time work in task force analysis should really be of value to you.

I hope you will consider me favorably for the position of junior project engineer.

Sincerely,

Steven B. Boyd

1010 Yourstreet Avenue
Simi Valley, CA 93063
July 12, 1989

Mr. John Jones
Widget Manufacturing Company
345 Widget Avenue
Los Angeles, CA 95006

Dear Mr. Jones,

Thank you for the interesting and informative interview of July 12, 1989. The position of manufacturing representative as you described it is of considerable interest to me as I am most impressed with Widget's excellent growth record. One point not brought out in our interview which may be of interest to you is that in my previous position with Ferrals Manufacturing I also had ten weeks of intensive training in billing and credit, skills which would directly relate to the position as you described it.* Again, thank you for the time you spent in interviewing me.

Your truly,

(Ms.) Terry Hamilton

*NOTE _____
This is your chance to mention anything helpful to you that you forgot to tell the employer in the interview. However your letter should be brief and to the point.

?? Written
? ? Exercises

10.1
Review the interview questions listed under "Guidelines" and be prepared to answer all of them.

10.2
Arrange a practice interview with a friend, colleague, career counselor, or potential employer (someone you've met during your information interviewing). Try to have the practice videotaped so you can review your performance. Use the interview critique form table 10.2 to evaluate your practice session.

Summary—Write a Brief Paragraph Answering These Questions

What did you learn about yourself? How does this knowledge relate to your career/life planning? How do you feel?

_____

_____

_____

_____

_____

_____

_____

_____

_____

_____

_____

_____

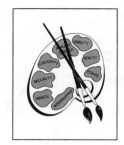

Part I

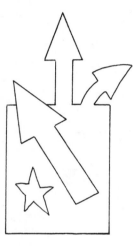

Part II

Future Focus 11

*It is a very funny thing about life; if you refuse to
accept anything but the best, you very often get it.*
W. Somerset Maugham

Learning Objectives   At the end of the chapter you will be able to:

Recognize the role of the future in your current career
planning efforts.

Understand the philosophy of personal
empowerment and career flexibility.

Because the world is changing so rapidly, the future is unpredictable. Once
career counselors could guide clients into growth areas predicted by the Bureau of Labor Statistics. Then we found that such statistics were based on
the assumption that past trends would continue into the present and future; this assumption proved to be totally mistaken. In the late 1960s teaching and engineering were still being promoted as growth fields for the
1970s. The overexpansion in hiring teachers and engineers was not expected. Next, career counselors turned to futurists to predict the future. We
heard about robotics, genetic engineering, telecommuting, and scenarios
depicting most people working thirty hours per week, many working at
home, with flexible working hours.

For some of us, this vision of the near future offers enough guidance   *Predicting your*
to begin our planning. For many others, these predictions are still too "far-   *future career*
out" to be useful to us today. Selecting a major or pursuing a career just because it's the current trend can be disillusioning. You may enjoy neither the
course work nor the job you get later. The careers in demand when you are
a freshman in college may not be in demand when you graduate. Factors
that influence job market demand are frequently unpredictable. New career fields and jobs emerge every year as a result of changes in technology,
public policy, and economic trends.

241

Create your own
career future

The only predictable future is the one that you create for yourself! Hopefully, this book has assisted you to identify who you are, define what you want to do, to research, identify, and develop your skills and create a context in which you are able to seek work which is meaningful for you. Following these guidelines, you are in full control, you are creating your own possibilities instead of spending time preparing for the "predicted future" only to find that it does not exist.

Your future is created by the choices that you make in the present. For this reason, a major emphasis of this book has been on assisting you to develop your decision-making skills. This takes the focus away from your predicting the future and puts the emphasis on your creating the future. The world is changing, you are continually changing, so why shouldn't your career be changing as well? No longer are people staying in one job until retirement. Unfortunately, it is human nature to resist change. Thus, many people do not turn to career counselors or books about career change until they are terminated from supposedly secure jobs. If you are among the fortunate who are seeking change before it is forced upon you, you have a head start. The time to seek the career of your choice is when you are already employed or when you are still in high school! Unemployment in and of itself can lead to desperation and a closed or confused mind. The anxiety and confusion generated by a life crisis makes career planning difficult, if not impossible. If you are unemployed or underemployed, you are likely to feel depressed, lethargic, and hopeless about the future. It is precisely during this time that you need to be totally immersed in the career-planning process rather than stuck in your depression.

Exercise your
options!

In the course of evaluating your personal strengths and skills, your self-confidence will blossom. You will regain a sense of purpose and direction by setting some reasonable and achievable goals. Your interaction with people through networking, informational interviewing, and volunteering will enable you to confirm or change your current goals. Most importantly, you will be energized and inspired by people who are doing the kind of jobs you find challenging and rewarding.

Exercising your options may take more effort than crystal-ball gazing, but we believe the results are worth it! As you can see from your workout, finding a career is a full-time job. We hope you have pulled, stretched, and grown in the process!

RISKING

To laugh is to risk appearing the fool
To weep is to risk appearing sentimental
To reach out for another is to risk involvement
To expose feelings is to risk exposing your true self
To place your ideas, your dreams before the crowd
  is to risk their loss
To love is to risk not being loved in return
To live is to risk dying
To hope is to risk despair
To try is to risk failure

But risks must be taken because the greatest hazard in life is to risk nothing. The person who risks nothing, does nothing, has nothing, is nothing. One may avoid suffering and sorrow, but one simply cannot learn, feel, change, grow, live or love. Chained by certitude and safety, one becomes enslaved. Only the person who risks is free.

Anonymous

References

Chapter 1

Gould, R. 1978. *Transformation: Growth and Change in Adult Life*. New York: Simon and Schuster.

Levinson, D. J. 1978. *The Seasons of a Man's Life*. New York: Knopf.

Sheehy, G. 1976. *Passages*. New York: E. P. Dutton.

Super, D. E. 1957. *The Psychology of Careers*. New York: Harper.

Chapter 2

Gelatt, H. B., et al. 1973. *Decisions and Outcomes*. College Entrance Examination Board.

Kauffman, Draper L., Jr. 1976. *Teaching the Future: A Guide to Future Education*. Palm Springs, CA.: ETC Publishing Co.

Success Magazine. October, 1983.

Sunshine, Leo. 1975. "Affirmations: Fundamentals of Prosperity." Seminar.

Waitley, Denis. 1984. *The Psychology of Winning*. Chicago, Illinois: Nightengale-Conant Corp.

Chapter 3

Herzberg, F. 1966. *Work and the Nature of Man*. New York: World Publishing Co.

Maslow, Abraham. 1970. *Motivation and Personality*. 2nd edition. New York: Harper and Row.

Raths, L., Simon, S., Harmin, M. 1966. *Values and Teaching.* Columbus, Ohio: Charles E. Merrill.

Chapter 4

Bolles, Richard Nelson. 1979. *Quick Job Hunting Map* (Advanced version). Berkeley, CA: Ten Speed Press.

Elliott, Myrna. 1982. *Transferable Skills for Teachers.* Statewide Career Counselor Training Project, Moorpark, CA.

Chapter 5

Bodner, Janet, et al. 1987. "Your Brilliant Career." *Changing Times Magazine* November, pp. 26–33.

Braden, Paul. 1987–88. "The Impact of Technology on the Work Force." *Community, Technical, & Junior College Journal* December/January, pp. 24–29.

Cetron, Marvin. 1983. "Getting Ready for the Jobs of the Future." *The Futurist* June.

Jones, Robert. 1987–88. "Influence Beyond the College Gates." *Community, Technical, & Junior College Journal* December/January, pp. 21–23.

National Forum Foundation. 1984. *Guide for Occupational Exploration.* Distributed by the American Guidance Service, Publications Building, Circle Pines, MN 55014.

U.S. Dept. of Labor, Women's Bureau. 1986. "20 Facts on Women Workers, *Statistical Abstracts of the United States* Washington, DC: U.S. Bureau of the Census, pp. 24, 69, 134, 393, 419.

Chapter 6

Kauffman Jr., Draper L. 1976. *Teaching the Future: A Guide to Future Oriented Education.*

Lakien, Alan. 1973. *How to Get Control of Your Time and Your Life.* New York: The New American Library, Inc.

Chapter 7

National Forum Foundation. 1984. *Guide for Occupational Exploration.* Distributed by the American Guidance Service, Publications Building, Circle Pines, MN 55014.

Hispanic Times, 6355 Topanga Canyon, Suite 307, Woodland Hills, CA 91367 (818) 889-3281.

Chapter 8

Bolles, Richard N. 1988. *What Color Is Your Parachute? A Practical Manual for Job Hunters and Career Changers.* Revised edition. Berkeley, CA: Ten Speed Press.

Other References for Stressful Circumstances:

Allan, Jeffery G., J. D. 1986. *Surviving Corporate Downsizing How to Keep Your Job.* New York: Wiley and Sons.

Hirsch, Paul. 1987. *Pack Your Own Parachute, How to Survive Mergers Takeovers and Other Corporate Disasters.* Menlo Park: Addison-Wesley.

Chapter 9

Brennan, Serard, & Gruber. 1988. *Resumes for Better Jobs.* New York: ARCO.

Coxford, Lola. 1989. *Resume Writing Made Easy.* Scottsdale, AZ: Gorsuch Scarisbrick, Publishers.

Parker, Jana. 1988 *Resume Catalog, 200 Damn Good Examples,* Ten Speed Press.

Chapter 10

"Career Planning." 1982. *CAM Report,* February 1.

Johnson, David. 1981. "Employability." *The Collegiate Career Woman* Spring, p. 21

Bibliography

Alberti, Robert E., and Emmons, Michael L. *Your Perfect Right*. California: Impact Press, 1974.

American College Testing. *Career Planning Program Handbook,* 1077, p. 12. *Planning Your Career,* ACT Adult Booklet, p. 14. 1981.

Appalachia Educational Lab., Inc. *Worker Trait Group Keysort Deck*. Bloomington, Illinois: McKnight Publishing Co., 1980.

Biegeliesen, J. I. *How to Go About Getting a Job with a Future*. New York: Grosset & Dunlap, 1967.

Black Collegian: The National Magazine of Black College Students. New Orleans, LA: Aug./Sept. 1982.

Bolles, Richard N. *What Color Is Your Parachute? A Practical Manual for Job Hunters and Career Changers*. Revised edition. Berkeley, CA: Ten Speed Press, 1988.

_____.*Quick Job Hunting Map*. Berkeley, CA: Ten Speed Press, 1979.

_____.*Newsletter*. January, 1982.

CAM Report. *Career Planning*. Feb. 1982.

Cetron, Marvin. *The Great Job Shakeout: How to Deal with the Coming Crash*. New York: Simon & Schuster, 1988.

Crystal, John, and Bolles, R. *Where Do I Go from Here with My Life: The Crystal Life Planning Manual*. New York: Seebury Press, 1974.

Elliott, Myrna. *Transferable Skills for Teachers*. Statewide Career Counselor Training Project. Moorpark, CA. 1982.

_____.*Transferable Skills for Liberal Arts Graduates*. Statewide Career Counselor Training Project. Moorpark, CA. 1982.

Gelatt, H. B. *Decisions and Outcomes.* College Entrance Examination Board. 1973.

Haldane, B. *Career Success and Satisfaction.* New York: AMACOM, 1974.

Herzberg, Fredrick. *Work and the Nature of Man.* New York: World Publishing Co., 1966.

Hill, Napoleon. *Think and Grow Rich.* New York: Fawcett Press, 1979.

Holland, John. *Making Vocational Choices: A Theory of Careers.* New Jersey: Prentice Hall, 1973.

Interest Checklist. Developed by U.S. Department of Labor, Employment and Training Administration, U.S. Employment Service, 1979.

Irish, Richard K. *Go Hire Yourself an Employer.* New York: Doubleday.

Johnson, David. "Employability." *The Collegiate Career Woman.* Spring 1981. p. 21.

Jones, John E., and Pfeiffer, William J. *A Handbook of Structured Experiences for Human Relations Training.* Vol. VI. California: University Association Publishers and Consultants, 1977.

Kauffman Jr., Draper L. *Teaching the Future: A Guide to Future Oriented Education.* Palm Springs, CA: ETC Publishing Co., 1976.

Kreigel, Robert, and Harris, Marilyn. *The C Zone.* Garden City, New York: Doubleday and Co. 1984, pp. 100–101.

Lakein, Alan. *How to Get Control of Your Time and Your Life.* New York: The New American Library, Inc., 1973.

Levinson, *The Season's of a Man's Life.* New York: Alfred A. Knopf, 1978.

Loughary, John W., and Ripley, Theresa M. *Career and Life Planning Guide: How to Choose Your Job, How to Change Your Career, How to Manage Your Life.* Illinois: Follett, 1976.

Markus, Marian. *The Working Woman Success Book, "Your First Job: How to Find a Good One".* New York: Ace Books, 1981.

Maslow, Abraham. *Motivation and Personality.* 2nd edition. New York: Harper and Row, 1970.

Murphy, Michael. *The Psychic Side of Sports.* Addison Wesley Publishing Co., 1978.

Naisbitt, John. *Megatrends, Ten New Directions Transforming Our Lives.* Warner Books, 1982.

Peters, Tom, & Waterman, Robert. *In Search of Excellence.* New York: Harper & Row, 1982.

Phelps, Stanlee and Austin, Nancy. *The Assertive Woman, A New Look.* San Luis Obispo, CA: Impact Publishers, 1988.

Raths, L., Simon, S. Harmin. *Values and Teaching.* Columbus, Ohio: Charles E. Merrill, 1966.

Samuels, Mike, and Samuels, Nancy. *Seeing with the Mind's Eye.* New York, NY: Random House. 1975, pp. 166–167.

Shertzer, Bruce. *Career Planning Freedom to Choose.* Massachusetts: Houghton Mifflin, 1977, pp. 59–100.

Simon, Sidney B., Howe, Leland W., and Kirschenbaum, Howard. *Values Clarification*. New York: Hart Publishing Company, Inc., 1972.

Stair, Lila B. *Careers in Business*. Illinois: Richard D. Irwin, Inc., 1980.

Sunshine, Leo. *Affirmations: Fundamentals of Prosperity*. Seminars, 1975.

Super, Donald E. *The Psychology of Careers*. New York: Harper, 1957.

Trzyna, Thomas N. *Careers for Humanities and Liberal Arts Majors: A Guide to Programs and Resources*. Ohio: R.M. Weatherford, 1980.

Waitley, Denis. *The Psychology of Winning*. Chicago, Illinois: Nightingale-Conant Corp., 1984.

Waltz, Gary, and Libby, Benjamin. *Life and Career Development System*. Michigan: Human Development Services, Inc., 1975.

Other books to consider for general interest:

Ferguson, Marilyn. *The Aquarian Conspiracy*. Los Angeles, CA: Tarcher. 1980

Harman, Willis W. *An Incomplete Guide to the Future*. San Francisco, CA: San Francisco Book Co. 1980.

Helmstetter, Shad. *The Self-Talk Solution*. Pocket Books. 1987.

Jaffe, Dennis T., and Scott, Cynthia D. *How to Change Your Work Without Changing Your Job*. New York: Simon & Schuster.

————. *Take This Job and Love It*. New York: Simon & Schuster. 1988.

Jeffers, Susan. *Feel the Fear and Do It Anyway*. New York: Fawcett Columbine. 1987.

Kennedy, Marilyn Moats. *Career Knockouts--How to Battle Back*. Chicago: Follett Publishing Company. 1980.

Morin, William J., and Cabrera, James C. *Parting Company--How to Survive the Loss of a Job and Find Another Successfully*. New York: Harcourt Brace Jovanovich. 1982.

Peters, Tom, and Austin, Nancy. *Passion for Excellence*. Random House, 1984.

Petras, Ross, and Petras, Kathryn. *Inside Track--How to Get Into and Succeed in America's Prestige Companies*. New York: Vintage Books, Random House. 1986.

Sheehy, Gail. *Pathfinders*. New York: Morrow. 1981.

Strumpf, Stephen A. *Choosing a Career in Business*. New York: Simon & Schuster. 1984.

Theobald, Robert. *Beyond Despair*. Cabin John, MD: Seven Locks Press. 1981.

Toffler, Alvin. *The Third Wave*. New York: Bantam Press. 1981.

Index